# THE ENTREPRENEUR'S ESSENTIALS

## LESSONS FOR STARTUP & LEADERSHIP EXCELLENCE

### BRETT A. HURT

FOREWORD BY
**JOHN MACKEY**

LUCKY7 PRESS

# CONTENTS

*To two of the strongest women I've ever known and who have invested so much in me.*

*For my mom, Brenda, who sadly passed away 10 years ago. Without her, my love for programming and changing the world through technology wouldn't have blossomed. The love I show in the world is a manifestation of her deep love for me and my sister, Brandi.*

*To my wife, Debra, who has been tirelessly dedicated to our success ever since we began dating 28 years ago. From my first company, Hurt Technology Consulting, to all five of the others, including data.world, Bazaarvoice, and Coremetrics, I've made my most critical business and life decisions with her wise advice and perspective. She's my better half and incredible lifelong partner. And that includes our most important entrepreneurial endeavor, raising Rachel and Levi!*

# TESTIMONIALS

"As a founder and first-time CEO, I'm always searching for helpful strategic and tactical counsel. Brett is best-in-class and has seen it all. Besides his professional expertise, and I can speak from first-hand experience, Brett is a great human being and a model startup leader.

Reading this book is like having Brett on your advisory board. It's a complete startup playbook, it's so helpful, and it's something I continually reference as I learn, build, and grow on my startup journey. Thank you Brett for sharing your lessons with the startup world."

- Noah Zandan
  Founder and CEO, Quantified.ai

"Brett Hurt has proven to be an outstanding investor, mentor, and friend to me and to dozens or hundreds of other local entrepreneurs over the years. His role as a leader and champion in the Austin entrepreneurial ecosystem cannot be overstated. *The Entrepreneur's Essentials* is a valuable and immensely practical guidebook born of years of experience that I and others have used to great benefit. Strongly recommend!"

- Bret Boyd
    Co-founder and CEO, Sustainment

"Whether you're a first-time entrepreneur or a multi-exit founder, there are foundational truths and practical tactics to be learned in Brett's startup bible, *The Entrepreneur's Essentials*. From fundraising to building company culture, Brett draws upon 30 years of operating experience to give founders an indispensable framework to navigate the startup seas."

- Allen Tsai
    Co-founder and CEO, Pani

"I first met Brett cold calling him when I was an analyst at Bessemer Venture Partners in 2005. I stayed in touch with him and eventually he let me invest in him at the start of Lead Edge Capital in the spring of 2008. Brett is an entrepreneur like no other. Hard work, persistent and remarkable at follow-up. I also put him in the less than 1% bucket of entrepreneurs who truly communicate with investors about the progress of their companies....I wish more entrepreneurs would learn this from Brett!"

- Mitchell Green
    Founder and Managing Partner, Lead Edge Capital

"Brett's wisdom comes from a combination of hard work, his own entrepreneurial journeys, helping a vast community of entrepreneurs, and deep reflection of what works and doesn't. For those of us that have been lucky enough to benefit from his advice and sage counsel, it's been a superpower in building our own companies and organizations. Thanks to his writing, it's distilled into a must read for anyone who wants to build or create something new."

- DJ Patil
    Serial entrepreneur and former U.S. Chief Data Scientist

"This book should be required reading for every entrepreneur. The lessons contained herein have positively and substantially impacted my journey as a founder & CEO. Whether you are a multi-exit founder or just getting started, Brett's practical, actionable, and easy-to-understand advice will help you write your own success story."

- Arlo Gilbert
    Founding CEO, Osano

"*The Entrepreneur's Essentials* is a trove of essential wisdom and critical lessons for any aspiring entrepreneur, whether you're contemplating your first start up or working on your 6th. Throughout the book, Brett Hurt shares his own inspiring stories from a life in the trenches as a serial entrepreneur as well as the intimate stories of other entrepreneurs he's known and studied over the years. His approach is vulnerable, practical, and inspiring. The book is well organized and reader-friendly, with chapter titles that allow the reader to easily move around to find the advice they are most interested in."

- Clayton Christopher
    Co-founder, CAVU Venture Partners, Waterloo Sparkling Water, Deep Eddy Vodka, and Sweet Leaf Tea

"I know many entrepreneurs that have had a successful outcome once, and even a rare few who have done it twice. But there is no one I know who racks up win after win like Brett Hurt does. Instead of resting on his laurels, he shares his secrets in *The Entrepreneur's Essentials*. This latest edition is a masterpiece, packed full of thousands of things Brett learned the hard way but freely shares with us."

- Byron Reese
    CEO, Scissortail.AI and Author, *The Fourth Age*

"After helping grow and sell a billion-dollar business as the CFO/COO, I have spent the last 27 years coaching over 12,000 CEO's and their direct reports. I have worked with and built a dear friendship with Brett over the last 14 years and have not only come to admire his unbelievable entrepreneurial instincts but his true passion for sharing what he has learned in the arena.

I have devoured 1000's of business books, articles, podcasts, and trainings. For the most part, it has all been educational entertainment. On occasion, I have felt inspired by what I read or heard but for the most part, it has all been rich with theory and short on practical advice that was relatable and most importantly, actionable. Most of the time implementing the advice felt like wrestling with a ghost and left me feeling frustrated or wondering why the advice did not work for me? This is ABSOLUTELY NOT TRUE of Brett's book, *The Entrepreneur's Essentials*. Brett's book is short on theory and rich with real world, practical, and actionable guidance/examples for anyone who is, who wants to be or dreams of one day becoming an entrepreneur. *The Entrepreneur's Essentials* is like a field guide for any entrepreneur who knows it is lonely but wants an experienced and trusted sherpa by their side. You could read this book from cover to cover and get a tremendous level of insight from it but if you want to have it come alive, keep it close, refer to it often, and when the issues that growth and success show up, turn to *The Entrepreneur's Essentials* as your virtual sherpa to help you not only get to the top but to stay there...which is actually harder than just getting to the top. Thank you Brett for paying it forward with *The Entrepreneur's Essentials!*"

- Kirk Dando
  CEO, Dando Advisors, and Author, *Predictive Leadership: Avoiding the 12 Critical Mistakes That Derail Growth-Hungry Companies*

"Brett Hurt is one of the most insightful serial entrepreneurs whose success has materially helped lay the groundwork for what is today's hottest startup and tech community, Austin, TX. *The Entrepreneur's Essentials* is mandatory for any entrepreneur considering a new venture. I consider Brett to be one of most valuable confidants for both personal and professional life. Through this book, his key fundamentals are available as a roadmap on building a company as well as emotional preparation needed to navigate this journey."

- Bernie Brenner
  CEO, Rollick, and Author, *The Sumo Advantage: Leveraging Business Development to Team with Heavyweights and Grow in Any Economy*

"I have known Brett since my Walmart.com days in 2000 when I was one of his first customers at Coremetrics. I have also been involved with data.world since the beginning and have had the privilege of getting to see Brett lead the company. He is, without question, one of the best CEOs I've ever known, and his wisdom about how to build and scale companies is invaluable to others seeking to build great companies. If you want to get sage advice on team building, product architecture, finding product-market fit, scaling, and great culture, look no further than this extraordinary book."

- Jason Pressman
      Managing Director, Shasta Ventures

"Brett is much more than a serial entrepreneur with multiple wins and a prolific investor. First and foremost, he gives much more than he takes, and the world is truly better off because of him.

Brett has a genuine interest in helping others to be successful. He really is pulling for so many others and he makes his learnings, his time, and his resources available even when it is inconvenient to do so. It would be easy to keep these things to himself (as some business and technology leaders do), but Brett is intentional about supporting others, especially those who are willing to put in the hard work.

As *The Entrepreneur's Essentials* proves, Brett is especially dedicated to connecting with, encouraging, and mentoring the future generations of founders. We have been extremely fortunate to have gotten to know Brett since we moved to Austin more than a decade ago to attend graduate school at Brett's alma mater, The University of Texas. We were constantly surprised by how willing he was to answer our questions (even the most novice ones) and proactively introduce us to other innovators who continue to influence, support, and advise us many years later. His words and endorsement mean a lot because he has cultivated his reputation through doing the hard work, leading and inspiring innovation, and treating others well.

Brett knows that he has a unique perspective as a successful founder and investor as well as a one-of-a-kind network of some of the most accomplished doers and thought leaders. As a B Corp founder who also makes investment bets on early-stage impact startups that serve a greater purpose than shareholder wealth-creation, Brett has put his time and money where his heart is, using his resources and platform as forces for good whose value to society may take many decades or even generations to manifest.

When Brett and his wife Debra invested in the startup we co-founded, Boutiq, it was very special to know they believed in us. But what we still value the most are the words of wisdom Brett shares in his Lucky7 blog, text messages, or coffee chats. And now much of that wisdom is available in this book for so many more entrepreneurs, investors, or "startup curious" people the world over, forever preserved for posterity. Thank you, Brett, it continues to be a great privilege to learn from you and have you in our corner. #HookEm"

- Rena Pacheco-Theard & Dan Driscoll
     Co-founders, Boutiq (boutiq.co || @boutiq)

"Brett is a 'been there, done that' entrepreneur, and this book is generously practical. Jobs and Musk are the most lauded names in our business, but Hurt will be synonymous with actionable value."

- Ari Jacoby
     Founder and CEO, Deduce

"Having popularized some of the most foundational technologies of the internet age (online reviews with Bazaarvoice, data collaboration with data.world, and more), Brett Hurt speaks from experience and authority when advising entrepreneurs like myself. I've shared many coffees, breakfasts, and phone calls with Brett over the years learning from his experience while trying to follow the example he's set both in business and the community. In writing *The Entrepreneur's Essentials* Brett has effectively shared these 'coffee talks' with the world allowing an entire generation of entrepreneurs to take his practical advice and apply it to their own companies. This book has become a regular reference for me and is a must-read recommendation to my fellow founders and entrepreneurs."

- Andrew Eye
    Co-founder and CEO, ClosedLoop.ai

"Brett's approach to entrepreneurship begins with a belief that the best way to create a world-changing business is to Alway Be Learning. Just as the innovations that will change the world can't be predicted, only discovered, the innovators behind those breakthroughs need to go through a process of exploration to even contemplate an 'unreasonable' future. Brett's *The Entrepreneur's Essentials* takes you on that personal journey and encompasses all of life's experiences - management, family, community, and self-education.

Success as an entrepreneur is never as simple or singular as having a great business idea. The road is long and without a complete dedication to the craft of entrepreneurship, the vicissitudes of the journey can easily derail the best laid out plan. *The Entrepreneur's Essentials* provides that life guide, honed over decades as a serial entrepreneur and student of work-life balance. The essentials in Brett's book are not the memoirs of a successful business leader as much as a tribute to the thought leaders, mentors, and executives that have been most influential in helping him become the closest thing to a "renaissance entrepreneur" that I've encountered in my 30 years of investing."

- Scott Booth
    Chairman, Tech Pioneers Fund; Co-founder, Lead Edge Capital; Founder, Eastern Advisors

"Let me tell you a story about Brett Hurt and my interactions with him.... Whenever I ask for help or advice he makes time in his very busy schedule for me. He always has perfect advice and grounds it in real-world experience. Not some theory but rather this is what I have done in the past and here are some options to think about. Aside from all that, Brett is the ultimate positive support needed at the right time and place. He was the first person to help me with my seed round pitch deck that ultimately turned into a unicorn pitch deck. He was that guy that said you have a billion-dollar business in the making. He was the guy that pointed me in the right direction from the very beginning with very genuine and compassionate support backed with his experience and knowledge. I owe a large part of my company's success to Brett and will be forever grateful."

- Ross Buhrdorf
    Founder and CEO, ZenBusiness

"Brett is the epitome of an innovator, a creator, and an entrepreneur. He has done it time and time again. Brett has shared incredibly valuable advice to me over the years, I only wish he had put this all down sooner. I still go back and read these essentials, and think I will regardless of where I am on my journey. These antidotes are fitting for every stage - for investors, builders, or anyone attempting to change the world."

- Adam Lyons
    Founder and CEO, Really; Founder, The Zebra

"Brett has been a great Board Director for us, sharing his hard-earned entrepreneurial insights to enable CoPilot to go further faster. Now everyone can access these gems through his new book."

- Pat Ryan
    Founder and CEO, CoPilot (copilotsearch.com)

"*The Entrepreneur's Essentials* is a must-read for any startup founder, growth stage CEO, as well as their committed employees, investors, and anyone seeking to live a journey of meaning! Brett Hurt does a masterful job of sharing the lessons he has learned as a successful serial tech entrepreneur in a way that will not only resonate with your intellect, but with your humanity. Most importantly, the book offers practical frameworks and tactics to navigate the challenging but exhilarating road of an entrepreneur!"

-Ross Rosenberg
    Chief Strategy Officer at founder-led technology companies and software portfolio company executive (Bain Capital)

"As a serial entrepreneur myself, and someone who has read countless books on entrepreneurship, I can definitively say that Brett Hurt's book is one of the best. Most books are filled with generic advice or simple frameworks, but *The Entrepreneur's Essentials* is chock full of real-life examples and practical case studies. Brett shares what worked for him so that you can distill his learnings and apply them to your own endeavors. If you are an existing or aspiring entrepreneur, this book is for you. You won't regret it!"

- Dave Liu
    CEO, Liucrative Endeavors and Author, *The Way of the Wall Street Warrior: Conquer the Corporate Game Using Tips, Tricks, and Smartcuts*

"Brett Hurt is a brilliant serial entrepreneur who leads with integrity. *The Entrepreneur's Essentials* illustrates not only Brett's extraordinary business acumen but his principled belief in centering diversity, equity, and inclusion in the company workplace. Against the backdrop of a global pandemic that has introduced new challenges and opportunities to entrepreneurs, this book reminds us of the core values that can lead to a successful business, but also a better world. It's a must read for all business and thought leaders."

- Dr. Peniel Joseph

Associate Dean, Justice, Equity, Diversity, Inclusion (JEDI); Founder and Director, Center for the Study of Race and Democracy at the LBJ School at the University of Texas at Austin; Author, *The Third Reconstruction: America's Struggle for Racial Justice in the Twenty-First Century*

"In 1998, I met Brett Hurt when he was starting Coremetrics. He had the crazy notion that 'some day every retailer would have a website.' It seems so obvious today, but it wasn't in 1998. Brett flew across the country to come to my office in New York and although I was at first skeptical of his premise, Brett was the most impressive person I had met in my 16 years on Wall Street. After much thought and discussions about this new business idea and the potential size of the market, 2 days later I wrote Brett a check for $100,000 and within a week, I raised him another $400,000. I like to say I put Coremetrics in business. There were the typical ups and downs of a startup, but Brett had the grit and resilience it took to be successful. That was the beginning of a long journey Brett and I have had together. I was also an early investor in Bazaarvoice and data.world.

Coremetrics and Bazaarvoice were core to my thesis around investing in startups as I introduced Brett to new customers, potential partners, or anyone who might be helpful to his companies. It has always been a great partnership as we learned from each other along the way and Brett's successes gave me more credibility with my venture investing pursuits. Three and a half years ago, I became the CEO of one of my startups, Sightly, which Brett is an investor in. For years, I was giving advice to many entrepreneurs based on my Wall Street business experiences in sales, analytics, and data but I had never run a company. I was going to the dark side and even after investing in 50 plus companies, there was so much that I was clueless about when it came to running a business. I have been turning to Brett for help since I took on this new role as every day is a new challenge. The people part of the business is where I struggle most but even the fundraising piece, where I have helped tons of companies, is not so easy when one is raising money for themselves.

On multiple occasions, Brett has made investor introductions when he sees a fit, which is helpful. It has made me realize how important introductions from stakeholders truly are even though I obsessed over helping hundreds of entrepreneurs. One of my greatest joys was funding and listening to young Wharton entrepreneurs before entrepreneurship was a big focus on the Penn campus. Brett gives back to Penn and Wharton in similar ways today.

Networking drives success. Brett is the consummate networker, and his connections are vast. It helps him with his own businesses as well as with all his investments. We are very aligned with this concept, and it shows with our mutual LinkedIn connections. If you are starting a business, Brett Hurt is one person you want to connect to. If you are the CEO of a startup, Brett can help you. If you are looking for business advice, Brett is your guy. If you just want a great lifetime friend, nobody is better than Brett!"

- Ralph Mack
    CEO, Sightly and Founder, Mack Capital

"*The Entrepreneur's Essentials* is not a textbook; it's a handbook. It's a resource I go back to again and again to seek out the exact advice I need for whatever challenge has come up in my biz. Brett has helped me solve so many problems from which roles to hire when, to negotiating and pricing an investment round, to troubleshooting our lead generation strategies. Brett has the most practical and reliable advice of any mentor in my network. Not only has he scaled multiple software businesses as founder & CEO, but he's also invested in hundreds of other startups and has really seen what works (and doesn't)."

- Suzi Sosa
    Founder and CEO, Verb (goverb.com)

"I met Brett in 2005 through the Bootstrap Austin community. Compared to today the ATX entrepreneurial scene was significantly smaller and everyone pretty much knew each other. He had just started Bazaarvoice and I was just starting Boundless. Since then we have both consistently been 'in the arena' starting and running companies here in Austin. I have always admired Brett and benefited greatly from his advice, both in person, and through *The Entrepreneur's Essentials*. He is a relentless student of business and entrepreneurship, and he is generous with his knowledge and advice, beyond what one could possibly expect from someone as busy as Brett. Last year Brett graciously joined our inaugural company event at Gembah, and we had a great fireside chat about the startup journey in general and about how to build category-defining companies in particular. He recommended the book *Play Bigger* to me, and it is now required reading for all our employees. There are a lot of self-proclaimed gurus out there that provide advice on startups, fundraising, and the entrepreneurial journey. There are few, if any, that have the experience, the thoughtfulness, and genuine desire to help other entrepreneurs become successful as Brett. I highly recommend *The*

*Entrepreneur's Essentials*. Read it, but more importantly, follow the advice. I guarantee it will make a difference in your entrepreneurial journey."

- Henrik Johansson
    Co-founder and CEO, Gembah

"I have known Brett as a successful entrepreneur for almost two decades and have referred several of my founders to him as a sounding board. The Entrepreneur's Essentials is a powerful way to scale his advice and impact on entrepreneurship in Texas. It will save a lot of time and tribulations for any aspiring entrepreneur who reads this as they embark on their journey. I've also been amazed at how he has methodically built data.world as one of his proud Series A investors, and it's been an honor to be involved since the beginning, including their acquisition of Capsenta, which was one of our seed bets."

- Venu Shamapant
    Founding Partner, LiveOak Venture Partners

"*The Entrepreneur's Essentials* is for everyone. Combining wisdom and curiosity, Brett Hurt teaches skill sets that apply to all fields. In my role as rabbi and spiritual leader, I have depended upon the guidance written in Brett's steady hand, especially in times of uncertainty. I have gained courage when pivoting accessibility models that have, in turn, elegantly increased the relevance and outreach of my work. How can spirituality and religious community become must haves for each person? The essential questions of meaning, purpose, and life trajectory are explored here -- sharpening approaches that will assist either in a boardroom or a sanctuary. Bottom line: in my life's work of cultivating and encouraging the best of individuals and communities, buoyed by Brett's wisdom, I know that I am not alone."

- Neil F. Blumofe
    Senior Rabbi, Congregation Agudas Achim

"Brett has been there with critical advice as I navigate the treacherous first-time Founder & CEO waters. Brett's wisdom cuts to the core of any challenge or opportunity, whether in person or prose. His teachings are coated in a depth of experience that only a multi-time rockstar operator knows. We're all lucky to have that same wisdom captured in this new edition of his book."

- Blake Garrett
    Founder and CEO, Aceable

"I had the opportunity to work for Brett Hurt while he was marching Bazaarvoice up the hill towards $100 million in revenue and an IPO. What an exciting and insightful experience it was! I'd run small businesses before working for Brett, but being up close was such an amazing educational experience for me and played a key role in me being able to raise funds and build my own startup, Localeur. Brett invested in Localeur early and has seen us grow from Austin to more than 200 cities around the world today, and he's been a trusted adviser and champion all the way. *The Entrepreneur's Essentials* is like getting the cheat code to all Brett's lessons and so much more from his decades of experience as a successful founder and company builder."

- Joah Spearman
    Co-founder and CEO, Localeur

"Reading this book has been the highest ROI investment I've made in becoming a better CEO. Brett Hurt synthesizes his decades of experience as an operator into tactical and straightforward insights on topics like getting the most out of investors, running quality reference checks on key hires, and everything in-between."

- Gautam Bhargava
  Co-founder and CEO, Ender (joinender.com)

"Building a startup is a daunting process full of innumerable pitfalls. Brett Hurt is committed to helping founders navigate the issues they will face, from raising capital, and managing large teams, to overcoming their own self-doubts. Without Brett's mentorship and insights, I may not have had the courage to get back 'in the arena' to build my latest company. His counsel and experience have helped me in creating hiring processes, go-to-market strategies, and how to get the most out of my advisors and investors. Brett believes in innovation and wants to see entrepreneurs succeed, and he is now codifying his years of learning and experience so all entrepreneurs can access a guiding light when they inevitably reach one of their dark days. As Brett would say, 'Dare Greatly!'"

- Ryan Merket
  Founder and CEO, Momintous

"Starting a company is hard work—scaling one is even harder. In *The Entrepreneur's Essentials,* Brett Hurt distills his experience and lessons learned as a technology and business leader making them accessible for entrepreneurs at any stage, helping founders and companies navigate their journey from irrelevancy to relevancy to must have. Brett's words and stories will challenge, educate, and inspire you. *The Entrepreneur's Essentials* is a must read for every founder."

- Nathan Ryan
  CEO, Blue Sky Partners

"*The Entrepreneur's Essentials* is a must-read for aspiring and experienced builders. The book is an incredibly thoughtful and thorough playbook from a legendary entrepreneur who has been there and done it all. It's absolutely mandated reading for the CEO's we hire through our Venture Studio at Night."

- Ezra Cooperstein
    President, Night (https://night.co/) and General Partner, Night Ventures

"I've known Brett Hurt since 2000, the beginning of Coremetrics, back when I was running Alphablox and we were both backed as young CEOs by Accel Partners. He was a natural entrepreneur back then and he went on to prove it again at Bazaarvoice and now at data.world. Meanwhile, I invited him to become a Core partner to one of my investments - Salsify. He's been a great asset on their journey, which has so far led them to a $2 billion valuation, and contributed on many levels. Overall, Brett's been an invaluable member of the Underscore Core Community, bringing many of his skills to share with our founders and entrepreneurs. It's therefore great that everyone can now benefit from his lessons learned in *The Entrepreneur's Essentials*!"

- Michael Skok
    Co-founder and Partner, Underscore VC

"Brett is a rare breed of founder. He operates with complete transparency, the utmost integrity, remarkable grit, and a childlike curiosity. He is energized by lifting up his teammates and partners.

When speaking to our founders, I often reference Brett as an example of what entrepreneurial success looks like.

Even more importantly, while Brett is a world-class founder who loves to win, he cares even more deeply about helping others win. I strongly recommend reading *The Entrepreneur's Essentials* to learn from this true master of his trade."

- Adam Zeplain
  Co-founder and Managing Partner, mark vc

"Brett has put down on paper everything I've ever thought of while mentoring CEOs of tech startups over the past 20 years, and then some. I was lucky enough to have Brett as a 'mentee', and in the end, he has done what all mentors hope for, which is to pay it forward – particularly by writing *The Entrepreneur's Essentials*. Rather than learning the hard way or trying to find that perfect mentor, Brett has instead taken all his learnings from a career of building successful companies and assembled them together into a step-by-step guide through the different stages of building a successful company. Brett's guidance is practical, empathic, and spot-on, and takes out much of the mystery of successful entrepreneurship."

- Bong Suh
  Serial entrepreneur and CFO, Grabango

"Brett is deeply and holistically interested in both the process of entrepreneurship and the people who choose an entrepreneurial path. As a trade association and think-tank founder who sought to repurpose those skills to start and lead an early-stage B2B SaaS venture, I've benefited immensely from his personal mentorship, leadership, and hospitality over the better part of a decade. It is rare for a leader's published work to provide the same value and transmit the same shared passion for building as a personal relationship. Having experienced both, I can say Brett's does."

- Hudson Hollister
    Founder and CEO, HData

"As is demonstrated in his own words - "For an enterprise to be maximally profitable, it must have a purpose beyond profit." – Brett Hurt fully understands the invaluable role entrepreneurs play in building a beloved community. This second edition of *The Entrepreneur's Essentials* is a gift to us all. Brett's deep knowledge, passion, vast wisdom, boundless expertise, personal experiences, and heart for what's right and good make this book so much more than a 'how-to' manual. I have seen Brett inspire college students to find meaning in their lives regardless of their career paths. I can't think of anyone who wouldn't benefit from reading this book – including this university president."

- Colette Pierce Burnette, Ed.D.
    President and CEO, Huston-Tillotson University

"When I think of which entrepreneurs are the most inspiring, I think of Brett Hurt. I've had the pleasure of watching Brett build business after business after business. I've also had the pleasure of becoming friends with him. For those who don't get to spend time with Brett, *The Entrepreneur's Essentials* is the next best thing. Smart, insightful, and filled to the brim with real tactics and strategies... if you're starting a business, you need to read this book. If you're growing your business, you need to read this book. In short: READ THIS BOOK."

- Mitch Joel
    Founder, Six Pixels Group and Author, *Six Pixels of Separation* and *CTRL ALT Delete*

"When founding in building a company, you're figuring a lot of it out as you go. There is no playbook.

There's a lot of content out there on the initial founding of a company, and the successful exit, but not a lot about the in-between.

One of the most helpful resources I've found on my entrepreneurial journey that zeros in on the lessons of the building and scaling years is Brett Hurt's blog, Lucky7. In it, he shares wisdom and experiences around lessons he's learned (including the hard ones). You get to walk in his shoes of building multiple successful companies, and really bridge the gap on how to get from founding to exit. I wish more entrepreneurs chronicled their journey this way, so we can learn from each other.

Brett has been such an inspiration to so many founders here in Austin, and I look forward to his insights and wisdom reaching more entrepreneurs who are also figuring it out as they go!"

- Adelle Archer
    Co-founder and CEO, Eterneva

"Brett has been a game-changer and accelerant for my career as well as me personally as an Advisor and a friend. Having been through the rollercoaster of trenches himself with several entrepreneurial endeavors, Brett is able to cut through the noise and provide sound, practical, and actionable advice that's grounded in reality vs. academia. His direct and to the point approach to business and life has been instrumental in helping me scale Ordergroove while helping our company avoid paying the 'dumb tax' on many issues we've faced. On the personal level, Brett has made me a better person and parent as a leader, always providing an authentic and relatable perspective."

- Greg Alvo
    Founder and CEO, Ordergroove

"Brett's teachings get me the most valuable thing of all: clarity. The clarity to act in the right direction. In this way, he has helped me stay on the yellow brick road as an entrepreneur, without getting distracted by the scarecrow, lion, tinman, and monkeys in the trees."

- Jesse Stein
    Founder and CEO, Audience.co

"Coming from one of the most successful entrepreneurs, most active angel investors, and most inspiring leaders in Austin, we're all lucky to have access to Brett Hurt's newest book. Embracing his framework of meaning & the creative process of entrepreneurship unlocks the startup in all of us. It is a must-read no matter what stage your company is at."

- Josh Baer
    Co-founder and CEO, Capital Factory

# FOREWORD

## BY JOHN MACKEY, CO-FOUNDER AND CEO OF WHOLE FOODS MARKET

It has been a privilege to become friends with Brett Hurt over the past several years. Not only is Brett extraordinarily intelligent, with exceptional entrepreneurial talents and leadership skills, but he has also created six excellent companies that have all created tremendous value for millions of other people. His new book, *The Entrepreneur's Essentials,* is also going to create even more value in the world by helping entrepreneurs launch and build better and more successful organizations. When I think back on my own journey as an entrepreneur and as a leader, I only wish Brett's book had been available to me when I was starting out. It would have become my Bible and I would have hungrily lapped up its wisdom. It would have saved me from dozens of mistakes and provided me with the invaluable wisdom and guidance I needed to grow Whole Foods Market quicker and more skillfully.

One great example of this wisdom is Brett's insight that the highly successful entrepreneurial journey goes through three distinct stages — "irrelevance to relevance to the must-have". This certainly was true of my own entrepreneurial journey with Whole Foods. Back in 1978, Renee Hardy and I started up a small natural and organic food store in Austin, Texas that we named "Safer

Way" — which was a deliberate spoof on Safeway's name. At the time of Safer Way's birth, there were no more than about 10 small natural and organic food stores in Austin. There was nothing unique or special about Safer Way, except for one thing — we were 100% vegetarian and a lot more purist than our competitors — minimal to zero refined sugars, refined grains, alcohol, or coffee.

While our youthful idealism did successfully appeal to a very narrow niche of health-oriented vegetarians, I think it is safe to say that Safer Way was at the stage of "market irrelevance". We managed to lose $23,000 of our initial $45,000 in capital in the first year of business and only made a whopping $5,000 in year two. Renee and I were only paying ourselves $200 a month and we moved into the store, which was an old Victorian home, and lived on the third floor to save money. We knew that we needed to do something radically different if we were going to have a successful business and become relevant in the marketplace. We made four major changes that brought us to "market relevancy":

1. We relocated Safer Way ½ mile away to a different location that quadrupled the size of our store. This much larger space allowed us to open one of the very first natural food supermarkets in the United States. We were then more than twice as large as any of our other Austin natural foods competitors.

2. We expanded our product mix to include everything a dedicated natural and organic foods shopper might want including meat, seafood, coffee, beer, and wine. Although we didn't sell most conventional brands of food such as Coke, Pop-Tarts, Kraft Macaroni, and Cheese, or factory-farmed meats, we were a "one-stop shop" for all-natural and organic foods.

3. We merged with one of our strongest Austin competitors, Clarksville Natural Grocery. This not only eliminated a tough competitor, but it also doubled our intellectual capital and our team members — both of which proved to be crucial to our success.

4. We changed our name from Safer Way to Whole Foods

Market. This was a necessary change to make the Clarksville Natural Grocery entrepreneurs happy since they didn't want to be called Safer Way. That may have been the main reason to change our brand name, but in retrospect, it is very clear that Whole Foods is a far superior brand name than Safer Way ever could have been.

The first Whole Foods Market was a tremendous success from the start, despite no advertising or any other marketing except for the viral word of mouth (there were no social media back in 1980)! Whole Foods had higher sales on our first day of business than Safer Way and Clarksville combined would do in a week. And Whole Foods just grew and grew and grew from that point. Within less than six months we had the highest sales of any natural/organic foods store anywhere in the United States. We had definitely achieved "market relevancy" — at least in Austin Texas.

It is impossible (and quite inappropriate) to try to tell the entire 41 years of history of Safer Way and Whole Foods Market in the Foreword of Brett's book on entrepreneurship, so that tale will need to wait for a different context. What is important to say here is that over the next 40 years Whole Foods transitioned to the third stage of the successful entrepreneurial journey to the "must-have" that Brett writes about in this book. We had become the "category king" of dedicated natural and organic supermarkets. Today we have over 500 stores in three countries with annual sales of over $19 billion. While Whole Foods did not invent the idea of natural and organic foods, and we did not actually open the very first natural foods supermarket, we did define and build the category itself. In building this category we have had a major impact on the way Americans eat today and have impacted the entire food retailing industry. Natural and organic foods are now "must-have" foods found everywhere.

Although I have now known Brett for ten years now, I think I really got to know him better when he joined our *Conscious*

*Capitalism* movement and eventually served on our Board of Directors. Conscious Capitalism has four major tenets:

1. Every business has the potential for a higher purpose besides only making money.

2. All of the major stakeholders in a business are interdependent and all are important — customers, employees, suppliers, investors, and communities. The business should be consciously managed to create value simultaneously for all of these stakeholders.

3. Organizations today need more Conscious Leaders — leaders who embody the higher purpose of the organization and are servant leaders to all of the major stakeholders.

4. Every organization should create Conscious Cultures that allow everyone working there to learn, grow, and flourish.

It was a natural fit for Brett to participate in and serve the Conscious Capitalism movement because that is exactly what he has been doing as an entrepreneur since his first business startup. When he first began to be involved, I would have called him an "unconscious conscious capitalist" because he was instinctively already doing all the things that conscious leaders do, but he didn't yet know the tenets or speak the language. Once he began to participate regularly in our CEO Summits and serve on our Board, he began upgrading our "source code" and our Board processes. Brett brought high self-confidence, good listening skills, creative ideas, and the same quality of wisdom to the Conscious Capitalism Board that he is now sharing with all of us in this book.

I was definitely sad when Brett decided to leave our Conscious Capitalism Board, but he had really good reasons for doing so, including starting up his sixth business — data.world. I have been so impressed with Brett as an entrepreneur, and with his intelligence and his integrity, that I jumped at the opportunity to invest in his new business. data.world is growing very well, and I'm sure it will end up moving from "irrelevancy, to relevancy, to must-have" and will create great value in the world for all of its major stakeholders. One thing I'm completely certain about: the investors in this company will be some of the best-informed investors of any startup company that has ever been created. As I type these words, I recently received the 188th investor update that Brett and his team have put out. Just about every week, these investor updates go out to all the investors and advisers of the company and it enables all of us to see the steady progress, triumphs, as well as some of the challenges data.world faces.

*The Entrepreneur's Essentials* discusses the importance of organizational culture. One of the first things that impressed me about Brett as a leader is how much he truly cares about culture. Soon after I had first met him, I remember him talking about the culture at Bazaarvoice and I told him, "I can tell you'll always have a great culture there because of how much you personally care about it as CEO." I've always believed that one of the CEO's most important jobs is to focus on creating and growing healthy organizational cultures. The CEO needs to also be the CCO — the Chief Culture Officer — and Brett shares that belief. Bazaarvoice was named the #1 company in Austin to work for when it was small, then medium, then large. They won in all three size categories as they grew over time and no other company has ever done this in Austin. His most recent company, data.world, just won its fourth annual Best Place to Work Award in Austin and I have no doubt that they will eventually duplicate Bazaarvoice's "Triple Crown" of cultural success.

One of Brett's best qualities, as well as one of my favorite chapters in this book, is his intense curiosity and determination to continuously learn and grow. Besides his MBA at The Wharton School, Brett had the great honor to be selected to participate in the Henry Crown Fellowship Program where he studied with several other highly skilled, intelligent, and entrepreneurial leaders for two years. I know that Brett rates that as important to his growth as his MBA was. In addition, Brett is a very dedicated reader. As President Harry Truman said, "Not all readers are leaders, but all leaders are readers," and Brett is both. He reads widely in business, technology, history, and philosophy, as well as keeps up with current events. Brett also learns directly from some of the smartest people in the world today, which he meets at various conferences such as TED.

Brett also understands the vital importance of mentors and coaches to help us avoid making foolish mistakes, as well as challenging us to break out of our ruts and our comfort zones. As entrepreneurs, we have an ethical obligation to our companies and to ourselves to continually learn and grow. One of the things I learned at Whole Foods was that whenever I got stuck, the company would also get stuck. Whenever I broke out of any dysfunctional patterns then it freed the company to do the same. As entrepreneurs, we have a much larger impact on our companies than we realize — both our strengths and our weaknesses are magnified and reflected throughout our organizations. Brett understands this and is constantly working to become a better leader, entrepreneur, person, husband, father, and friend. From my perspective, he is continually learning and growing and is setting a wonderful example for all of us. *The Entrepreneur's Essentials* is one of Brett's gifts to his fellow entrepreneurs as he shares the many lessons he has learned over the years. I believe you will find great value in this book and I hope you really enjoy it.

— John Mackey

# PREFACE TO THE SECOND EDITION

As I write this, I'm on the way back from the main TED conference in Vancouver, sitting next to my good friend Dr. Peniel Joseph on a United Airlines flight. Peniel is a terrific leader and founded the Center for the Study of Race and Democracy at the LBJ School at the University of Texas at Austin. He also serves as an Advisory Board member at data.world. It was an incredible TED, with all of the goodness of being back together in person as the pandemic becomes more endemic. I believe this was my 12th TED, and it did not disappoint, with one of my favorite entrepreneurs, Elon Musk, closing it out today. I named Elon the entrepreneur of the decade in a 2013 *Lucky7* blog post, and that's still true for this decade with his and his team's amazing achievements at SpaceX, Neuralink, The Boring Company, and, yes, Tesla. I'm not saying I love everything about Elon, but no one touches him and his team in terms of raw output in getting truly "impossible" things done. Once his TED talks go live, I'll share them with you on the Digital Companion - you'll want to watch them.

It was Peniel's first TED, and it was special to share it with such a good friend. It is appropriate that I'm sitting next to him too as I write this. Peniel helped me more than any other friend with the open letter I wrote on the importance of diversity in tech companies, which I originally shared on Medium.com at the end of 2020. It was the most important piece I wrote that year, and it has now been adapted into Chapter 23 of this book to give it a proper conclusion. Thank you, Peniel - you are a real mensch.

This pandemic has had a very long arc, and I sometimes chuckle to myself at my naivety at the beginning of it. I sent a message to our team that we would be going home for two weeks to protect ourselves, our families, and our hospital systems. I had no idea at the time that it would be nearly two years until we started to get comfortable enough to get back into the office on a regular basis. The pandemic was a time of transformation for our nation and ourselves. It has also proven to be a time of extraordinary suffering and loss for so many, with over a million Americans dead and many businesses shuttered. We are in the midst of the Great Resignation, or the Great Realization, as my good friend Chris Hyams, the CEO of Indeed and also an Advisory Board member of data.world, put it at the Culturati conference on April 4, 2022.

I had my own realizations during the pandemic. Some of the practices that I believed so strongly in, like working together in an office every weekday to get stuff done together, faded away as I saw the level of productivity we could have working from home, with modern tools like Slack, Zoom, Google Docs, and our own data.world. I believed that everyone needed to be based in Austin while I was the CEO of Bazaarvoice. We only hired someone outside of Austin when we absolutely had to, and that was once we grew internationally to the point where Bazaarvoice needed a London office. I felt like I had made the right call in doing so - our culture was incredibly strong and Bazaarvoice was named the #1 place to work in Austin when it was small, medium, and then large. But I have to be honest that the culture at my current company, data.world, is just as strong, and as of this writing, we have around 30 percent of our 123 people located outside of Austin, across 21 states. And we've won a Best Place to Work award in Austin every year since our inception! Sure, we had no choice — we were doing our part to protect ourselves and society by bending the curve and all. But, as they say, necessity is the mother of invention.

I remember when my good friend Josh Baer, CEO of Capital Factory and investor in data.world, tweeted: "Be a butterfly, not a turtle. Use this reset as an opportunity for growth and transformation — don't just retreat into your shell and come out looking exactly the same" (@JoshuaBaer, April 18, 2020). I realize as I write this it may come off as privileged, and indeed it is. The reality is that the pandemic has been good for the knowledge economy workforce. The level of flexibility that we have now is unprecedented. Now that the vaccines are here and so well proven, you can easily blend the best of working in-person with working at-home, while being able to enjoy a guilt-free workout during the day or drop off or pick up your kids from school. I'm not saying it's all been easy for people in the knowledge economy during this time — mental health has been a real challenge and people have worked to nearly the point of burnout in some cases. And I also worry about young people just starting out in their careers and may really need that high-fidelity, in-person learning that occurs at the office. But I believe that we are learning to take the forced-by-necessity lessons of the pandemic to build back better than we did before. And it is clear that tech was the biggest winner during the pandemic, from the incredible impact of tech during this critical period to valuations that tech companies, including data.world, have enjoyed.

Another realization I had during the pandemic is that my online book, *The Entrepreneur's Essentials*, should also be transformed. It became so natural to see speakers over videoconferencing, so why not make my book more accessible instead of only offering it in text on Medium? And then, serendipitously, Technion, the oldest university in Israel, came along and asked me to do just that. They wanted to leverage my book as the foundation for their entrepreneurial leadership course. As a proud Jewish American, I felt honored and humbled by the opportunity. Challenge accepted! To reach students most effectively, I recorded myself reading each chapter, so that they could either watch it on YouTube or listen to it on SoundCloud. Technion loved it and it was a success with their students. Now there is a long waiting list for the course. Tikkun olam!

The first edition of *The Entrepreneur's Essentials* evolved from my blog, Lucky7.io, named in honor of my mom. I had helped many entrepreneurs (still do, and always will) and had codified the lessons I was teaching them in Lucky7 blog post after post. Then I compiled the best of those into the book in a very organic way, publishing as I went and finally finishing it in August of 2019. It was good, but not *great*. I worked with David Judson, the Co-founder and Editor of Urbānitūs on a series about leadership during the pandemic. He wanted to feature data.world and how I was leading during this trying time (dare I say, "unprecedented time," for the last time). I collaborated with him on it, and the series turned into a product that I was more proud of than anything I had written to date. That led to the idea that David and I could work on the second edition of my book together. I knew that if I wrote for another ten years, I wouldn't write as well as him. David enthusiastically agreed and it became a real partnership, with us regularly working on it every weekend with the goal to turn the second edition into my first print book. And that is what you are holding in your hand right now, and I really hope you enjoy it as much as we enjoyed working on it together. It's a product that I'm proud to have in print *and* also give away for free online at TheEntrepreneursEssentials.com, to honor the spirit of the first edition.

— Brett A. Hurt, written on Thursday, April 14, 2022, the day
before Passover

# INTRODUCTION
## A JOURNEY OF MEANING

As with any entrepreneurial endeavor, *The Entrepreneur's Essentials* is a book of many dimensions. Readers, I hope, will find inspiration in my struggles and successes, along with those of others shared here. I have sought to be as practical and prescriptive as possible; in a sense, this is in part a "how-to" manual. You will find tactical advice on everything from naming, to fundraising, to hiring, to communicating with your customers and team. This is balanced with strategic counsel, from how to choose early on whether you want to be rich or "king," to how you should align with the dynamics of natural networks, to the true nature of risk and how to cope with it. I've also tried to be historical, placing the 60-odd-year-old model of venture-backed innovation both in the context of the two-century-old story of modern capitalism, as well as in the emerging future of commerce. This is a future of "Conscious Capitalism" and the "public benefit corporation" that places social and public good as responsibilities alongside profitability.

But more broadly, all of this, while critical, is mere background.

The real goal of entrepreneurship is, and must be, to live a journey of meaning. No matter what religion you follow, what meditative practice you engage in, and which philosopher or role model you admire, success is borne on the realization that the secret to life is to live one of meaning. That meaning is defined by you, and it is often very elusive to find your core truth. So when I boil it all down, this is not a book about business and commerce. Rather, *The Entrepreneur's Essentials* is a book about meaning, through the prism of business and commerce. And just as Sir Isaac Newton discovered the prism in 1672, breaking light into its component colors and learning how to recombine the Sun's rays, the entrepreneur is the *discoverer* of this prism of meaning. Entrepreneurialism is about innovation. A journey where you're combining not the rays of the Sun but instead new ideas, concepts, and technologies into products and services that you then refract into the marketplace in ways before unseen. And just as Sir Isaac is remembered for his remark about "standing on the shoulders of giants," this quest for meaning is not one you can take alone.

Sure, with boosts from the media and Hollywood we often celebrate the "hero entrepreneur"... Steve Jobs, Elon Musk, Jeff Bezos, or Bill Gates. But entrepreneurship isn't an individual journey — you absolutely need great people to join the journey with you. Entrepreneurship is a team sport. And those who answer your call will need to identify with the meaning that you pursue for you to have a very meaningful journey *together*.

In this book, we'll discuss the "sages" of business and business literature, from Clayton Christiansen, who wrote *The Innovator's Dilemma,* to John Doerr who authored *Measure What Matters,* to Scott Galloway, who wrote *The Four*, and many more. To do that, and as entrepreneurialism is about innovation, this book carries a bit of innovation of its own, which is what I've dubbed the "Digital Companion." This is at www.TheEntrpreneurs-Essentials.com, where some will choose to read the book free online, while others will use it to support the new conventional, paper-bound edition. In a sense, it is a digital bibliography and there you will find — to bolster the learning from this book — further work of these and other giants, to read, to listen to, and to watch.

But the foundation of them all, the broad-shouldered "giant" to carry my Newtonian metaphor, is Viktor Frankl.

Frankl was a physician and psychiatrist in World War II Vienna. As he was a Jew during that fateful time, he and his family were swept up by the Nazis and he lost his parents and wife to the horrors of the Holocaust. Frankl was to survive three years in four concentration camps, including Auschwitz, a miracle he attributed to his deep commitment to finish a manuscript, an irrelevancy in the desperate hopelessness of Auschwitz. But this was the beginning of his search for meaning.

We all strive for meaning in our lives as Frankl eloquently described in his most important book, *Man's Search for Meaning*. We will discuss Frankl further in this book, and I will include him and many others who have informed my own search for meaning. But Frankl's basic message is that there are three ways to discover meaning. The first is by launching an endeavor, however, remote its success may seem at the outset. The second is by experiencing something or someone larger than yourself, by experiencing love in the sense of striving for true understanding. And the third stage is triumph, overcoming the once-seemingly impossible, which in his case was to simply survive. These three lessons, learned amid indescribable horror, were to yield the fruit of Frankl's later life and successful career as a therapist, author, speaker, founder of logotherapy, and inspiration to millions.

Drawing on this, I have discovered my own morphology of meaning that applies to the creative process of entrepreneurship. It is a quest summarized in three stages: the first, *irrelevancy*; the second, *relevance*; and the third, *must-have*.

In my career, I have founded six firms, three of which became large companies, one of which, Bazaarvoice, went on to a public offering with a unicorn valuation, and another, my current company data.world, which is still quite successfully evolving through this conceptualization of commercial meaning and relevancy.

The irrelevancy stage is the hardest. At the outset, you have an idea that is a kind of free atom, not affected by others nor significantly affecting others in the marketplace. Your family and friends may think you are nuts to put your ego out there in a way that you could fail. Entrepreneurship is celebrated, yes, but most cheering know deep down that they will never be brave enough to take the journey. When founding Coremetrics in 1999, we embraced what came to be known as "Software as a Service," or "SaaS," before the concept really existed. The phrase, "the end of software" had yet to be coined, and we struggled to explain to customers just what our model of web analytics was and how it worked. Luck plays a big role in entrepreneurship and we were at the right place at the right time with our pioneering business model. The towering success of Salesforce.com, founded about the same time and as of this writing with a market cap of $187 billion, really validated that model. And soon we won Walmart.com, the world's largest retailer as a customer. And, with that monumental milestone, we became relevant.

This made us appealing to the many retailers newly online who were flying blind as the existing solutions to provide the *core metrics* to run their business were not keeping up. Our delivery model was superior to our competitors and eventually, we disrupted them and became one of the global market leaders. We moved to the third stage, becoming a must-have in the industry. Even though the dot-com bust almost killed us, putting 97 of our 100 customers at the time out of business, we recovered well and were eventually bought by IBM for almost $300 million.

The journey for Bazaarvoice was similar. It was completely irrelevant at the beginning as Brant Barton, my co-founder, and I left Coremetrics in 2005 to together build the "voice of the marketplace." Most everyone thought we were crazy with the then nearly-unknown idea of enabling customer reviews at retail sites. In particular, our insistence that negative reviews would not be censored struck many as suicidal. But we quickly proved that this made the reviews credible, and customers reading credible online reviews were found to convert at rates 90 percent higher than those who did not. As we became the hot new movement in online retailing, we became relevant with a vengeance. After Facebook opened to the public, Twitter, Snapchat, and Instagram were founded. The tsunami of social media, along with the 2007 advent of the iPhone, hit the marketplace. And we became a must-have as Facebook partnered with us and keynoted one of our Client Summits and Google invited us in to do an early integration for product reviews embedded in Google Search, to help launch a new form of advertising. Ultimately we went to an IPO with an over $1 billion market cap, and we were named one of the top five IPOs of 2012 by the *Wall Street Journal*.

And now, since 2016 after a brief attempt at "retirement," I am working on data.world as my sixth startup. Just the same as before, data.world started out as irrelevant. Many of my longest-time friends, even successful entrepreneurs, were skeptical about the idea. Our initial idea at data.world was to be kind of a "GitHub for data", and early press captured that as we worked hard to become relevant. With a lot of hard work building functionality and attracting hundreds of thousands and then eventually millions of community members, data.world began to grow. We became the world's largest collaborative data community. Universities started to use us to help teach their data science and analytics courses. Governments began to sign up. Over 90 percent of the Fortune 500 made their way to data.world and joined to access the world's largest collaborative public data catalog. We grew as fast as GitHub did during its early years. Attention from the media helped, including an essay by Industry Standard founder John Battelle, which I also share on the Digital Companion mentioned above. We became relevant for public data work. And then the big challenge — we needed to commercialize to become relevant for private data work.

At data.world, we have actively moved through the struggle from irrelevancy to relevancy and are working our way toward the must-have stage right now. You'll learn more about how we are doing that in the coming pages. But it's certainly led by the fact that just weeks before the publication of this book's second edition, we concluded a $50 million growth fundraising round led by Goldman Sachs.

As you embark on reading *The Entrepreneur's Essentials*, I've done my best to help you on your journey from the identification of your big idea to the movement from irrelevancy to relevancy to the must-have. As you read ahead, I hope that you will learn that all businesses ever created, no matter how small or great, followed this same path. Many entrepreneurs never make it beyond the irrelevancy stage but for those who do, the challenging endeavor will be the most psychically rewarding journey you can take. And don't discount that when it does, luck and *a lot* of help from others will have helped you, and your team, make it so.

It is all about the pursuit of meaning. It is perhaps counter-intuitive that for an enterprise to be maximally profitable, it must have a purpose beyond profit. For some, this is an uncomfortable duality, even a conundrum. Quite the contrary, the embrace of this duality, of meaning, is the essential point of *The Entrepreneur's Essentials*.

Yours in the entrepreneurial arena,
Brett A. Hurt

# PART ONE
# **FOUNDING**

# CHAPTER 1
# THE SOUL OF THE ENTREPRENEUR

*"The reasonable man adapts himself to the world: the unreasonable one persists in trying to adapt the world to himself. Therefore all progress depends on the unreasonable man."*

## — GEORGE BERNARD SHAW

Beyond that familiar quote, there is a great deal of wisdom for entrepreneurs in playwright Shaw's 1903 book from which it comes, *Maxims for Revolutionists.* The book is easy to find online and I recommend it, as he could well have been describing Mahatma Gandhi, Galileo, or Rosa Parks. But I begin with that maxim here as I really believe he is describing you. Shaw's insight captures the overarching focus of my book, *The Entrepreneur's Essentials.*

This insight about adapting to the world speaks to me, as it should speak to all entrepreneurs. Because at no time in history has the world faced the challenge to adapt that it does today. And entrepreneurs, broadly defined, are the people to lead this adaptation.

I do need to update Shaw's point slightly. The "world" to

which he refers is not just the physical world, but it is society as well — of which we are a part. So in this broader sense, we do have to adapt ourselves to new realities, planetary and local. I am, for example, a vegetarian (mostly a vegan) and I believe we have to adapt our diets to a more environmentally conscious system of food production and consumption. We need to adapt our lifestyles to reduce our carbon footprint. The pandemic, still with us as I write in the spring of 2022, taught us a great deal about adapting for the good of us all, as we masked up, distanced ourselves from one another, and learned through a time of great pain about the importance of adapting the world to its interdependence. But none of this changes the fundamental insight of Shaw. Quite the opposite.

Because in the century or so since Shaw made that argument, the world has entered what scientists call the "Anthropocene," a term that dates to no earlier than the 1960s. It refers to this new age in which we bear witness as the Earth is fundamentally impacted and shaped by human activity. We have adapted the world to us in ways that Shaw probably never envisioned, adding both complexity and urgency to his maxim. Climate change is the best example. About this, we know a great deal in Texas where I live, with hotter summers, colder winters, more hurricanes along the coast in the south, and more tornadoes in the north. On the Digital Companion, which I referenced in the Introduction, you'll find some more detail on this. A deadly freeze in February of 2021 taught us many things, including the need for thoughtful entrepreneurs to get deeper into the energy space.

The reality is that we cannot return to the world before the Anthropocene. We must proceed along the contours of the world we've created, following the wisdom of Shaw, adapting it and its institutions to the new realities of climate change, urbanization, growing water scarcity, a transforming economy, and so much more.

This is the call to entrepreneurs, a call to your soul. Only unreasonable entrepreneurs, like you, willing to persist against the current, can adapt the world to the transfor our economy and society so urgently needed. In the next decade, we need to create between 30-40 million new jobs in our rapidly transforming economy. We need to create new models of transportation, energy production as I mentioned, as well as learning and housing. In the realm with which I'm currently most familiar (at data.world), we need to adapt our institutions to the explosion of data that is now at the operational heart of every business and institution — another subject into which you can do a deep dive on the Digital Companion.

There are many tools and means to think about and strategize business success. We've reduced these tools to the familiar acronyms of ROI, or EBITDA, or the KPIs of our age: clicks, page views, time on site, conversion, net bookings, retention/churn, Net Promoter scores, etc. These are important tools; as a CEO I have KPIs I check every day the way a doctor checks pulse, temperature, or oxygenation. And then there are "OKRs," about which you'll learn more in the chapters ahead.

But the success of these commercial metrics is increasingly dependent on something hard to concretely measure but essential. This is the soul of the business, of the innovation ecosystem, and of the entrepreneur who brings both together. Hence my need to start my book here. Soul is *THE* essential.

Building on that, there are two essential concepts to which you, as an entrepreneur, will adapt the world; both subjects are near to my heart. These are the ubiquitous *access* wrought by digitalized knowledge and the *hybridization* of institutions. And to both, I will return.

As our economy is transformed through global markets, changing demographics, and truly revolutionary technologies, Shaw's *Maxims for Revolutionists* is more valid today than ever. And we need entrepreneurs who think not only about the bottom line, but about better outcomes for those who have been excluded from large parts of the economy, and whose prosperity and talents are critical to our success. Again: Soul. This is why you'll read much more in this book about another set of concepts I hold dear, the Public Benefit Corporation and Conscious Capitalism, about which I'll also share much more later.

This is the moment that the world needs people like you. People with your soul founded the greatest country in the history of the world. The world benefits from your ambition, your dreams, your daringness, and your willingness to walk into what former president Teddy Roosevelt called "the arena."

You create the jobs. There is no company that anyone goes to work for that didn't have a brave creator at the beginning of it all. Your company can grow beyond you, but no one at your company today would be there if it were not for your giving it birth.

You define this soul, this essential, of the company. It was your unreasonableness, your "craziness," your dream, and, perhaps most importantly, your values that seeded its birth. Others can lead and tap into that soul, but if it weren't for you there would have been no soul in the first place.

There's much that Mark Zuckerberg and I disagree on, but also a great deal where I think he's spot-on: "The company shouldn't be run to try to build something that is cool, it should be run to build something that is useful and enduring," Zuckerberg said in an interview with Kara Swisher, on the Digital Companion. "And I still believe that."

So do I.

Another source of wisdom is John Chambers, the legendary founder and former CEO of Cisco Systems. Again, I include ways to read and hear more from Chambers on the Digital Companion. But a few thoughts he shared in another of Swisher's interviews are helpful here.

Chambers is worried that we've lost our edge as a startup nation of entrepreneurs and he argues that we need to get it back. His new investment firm is, as he puts it: "Really focused on where

the world is going, not where it's been." He points ou
decades ago, America had 90 percent of the world's venti
Ten years ago it was down to 80 percent. And today. He said in
2018, it's probably 50 percent.

"Basically you try to bring the country back together," Chambers said, speaking to the role of entrepreneurs that I am advocating for here. "And you have the courage to lead."

Since Chambers made those remarks in 2018, there are indications that a rebound is well underway. I dwell on venture capital and urge heed to Chambers' thoughts not only because I'm an angel investor myself. But because venture capitalism is the driver of our future economy, even society. Shortly before I began revisions for the second edition of this book at the beginning of 2021, the flow of VC investment totaled $156.2 billion in the United States, according to *PitchBook*. That U.S. figure was amid a doubling of venture investment globally. The numbers don't mean everything, and much remains opaque. But the money of this particular, soul-backed color, and its flow, are the best metrics we have for the health of the broader ecosystems of innovation, which include social entrepreneurialism and the creative sectors such as music, film, and art.

As I say, we can't measure soul the way we measure market share or productivity growth. But we can get better insight into the entrepreneur-invigorated ecosystem, animated by soul, with an eye to VC investment than with anything else I can think of. After all, as an investor, what I'm really investing in is soul, and after listening to more than 3,000 startup pitches (and backing more than 124 of them as of this writing), this is what I look for above all else when betting on an entrepreneur. And where those bets are going — mine and those of countless other VCs — is an ever-evolving portrait of the feedback loops between all elements of innovation that in turn nurture the best entrepreneurs. This is why we are seeing an explosion of entrepreneurial activity in cities like my hometown of Austin and other emerging hubs of the so-called "knowledge economy."

The trend that Chambers notes is not necessarily a zero-sum game and it is entrepreneurs in new regions who are fueling the rebound that data suggest is occurring. If we follow VC investment as a marker of the innovative spirit of entrepreneurs, we see it diffusing and spreading. As I started writing this second edition of *The Entrepreneurs Essentials* in early 2021, Silicon Valley's share of total U.S. VC investment — which has been falling since 2006 — was forecast to fall below 20 percent for the first time in history. But it's not disappearing. It's going to places like Austin, Miami, or Denver. As I conclude this book in mid-2022, the past year has seen not just a record amount of capital raised, but also a record for venture capitalists investing in new regions: "We're betting that the future of America is going to be built in the middle of the country, in places with good government at a reasonable cost of living," wrote Palantir Co-founder Joe Lonsdale, in the *Wall Street Journal* about his decision to move his firm 8VC from San Francisco to Austin.

My good friend Josh Baer has talked about the incredible opportunity we have in front of us if we just seize it in his *Texas Startup Manifesto*, which I also reference on the Digital Companion. Josh argues that if we work hard at it, together, then Austin can become a beacon for our nation — both in creating the new economy as well as bringing the old economy and those that have been disenfranchised for decades, along for the ride. I agree with him, and others do too. Just look at the Austin region, in fact now No. 9 nationally and No. 21 internationally, ahead of both Tokyo and Toronto, as the destination for VC investment in the entrepreneurial soul.

Many, of course, attribute Austin's growing appeal to the pandemic, the flight from the old "Gateway Cities" of San Francisco or New York, and the dynamics of housing costs and lower taxes. I certainly concede these are factors. But focusing too narrowly on these headlines obscures the broader dynamics of deeper trends that were underway well before our lives were upended by COVID-19, but that are trends nonetheless accelerating because of the pandemic.

I certainly don't diminish the devastation wrought by the pandemic, the pain, and the irretrievable loss of almost a million lives in America as I write, more than six million worldwide. We need to recognize and confront the failures that the pandemic unveiled, such as the racial, educational, and health disparities in America. But we can do that more effectively, without disrespecting the suffering and loss of so many, when we as entrepreneurs embrace the opportunities and responsibilities within the trends illuminated by this global scourge.

This deeper set of trends, now so clearly revealed, is the entrepreneur-led renewal that will determine the future of the next stages in education, healthcare, social equity, and certainly a new era of business defined by Conscious Capitalism. Animating all of this will be the concept of *access*, the huge shift that binds so many trends together.

At the outset of the pandemic, Zoom (or Google Meet or Microsoft Teams), telemedicine, streaming, online classes, document sharing tools like Google Docs, collaboration tools like Slack or data.world, digital signatures, online or curbside shopping, and instant message apps were useful, even critical sometimes. But not yet essential. Some of us were more familiar with them than others — those of us in the tech sector had a head start to be sure. So did the digital natives, who don't remember a world without the internet and who certainly have never used a rotary phone. But quickly, as all of us grasped and mastered these relatively new tools and apps, often to literally keep lives and families together and companies afloat, they've become an informational ecosystem of their own, one encompassing so many more than the tech-savvy or digitally native.

As we emerge from more than two years of cocooning,

masking, and working and learning from home, these are no longer just useful tools, fortuitously at hand. They are the building blocks of the new knowledge economy and knowledge society that the seers have been predicting for decades. In a word, universal and ubiquitous *access* is the attribute of hope I see towering on the near horizon.

Coupled with this idea of *access* is the second point I want to make, and this is the emerging concept of *hybridization*. We don't know exactly how our court systems will work now that even the U.S. Supreme Court has "worked from home." But we do know that the tools of virtual communication will continue to shape the criminal justice system. We don't know how temporary regulations allowing online medicine to bend around privacy compliance laws will evolve. But we do know that, according to the CDC, telehealth visits increased by 50 percent in the first quarter of 2020 when compared with the same period in 2019. And all the data now says telemedicine is here to stay: "Commercial interest in telehealth has boomed, with both startups and established companies, such as Amazon, providing virtual care services," wrote *NatureMedicine* magazine in 2021. "An area of particular activity has been behavioral and mental health, where multiple companies are vying to provide remote counseling."

Imagine what our new familiarity with these tools will mean over the long term to those living in remote areas who can't easily travel for medical care, or for those with disabilities whose mobility is limited. We don't know precisely how schools, businesses, and local governments will organize themselves when virtual *access* and connection are no longer emergency workarounds but rather exciting options to improve everything.

This fusion of the digital and analog worlds is hard to imagine, but it is more than just frictionless video communication — as central to our lives as that has become. Think of the way the mingling of cultures through immigration and innovation has created the kosher vegan tamales that are easy to find in Austin.

"What," you ask? Well, just supercharge that melding process of immigration, innovation, and new knowledge and soon you have, as just one example, the first COVID-19 vaccine itself, history's first mRNA vaccine licensed for use in humans.

This work began with a Hungarian immigrant researcher at the University of Pennsylvania. Her decades of pioneering work, and that of those who followed her, were incorporated into a trans-Atlantic consortium. This became the science-in-the-fast lane, distributed collaboration between U.S.-based Pfizer, which is headed by an immigrant CEO from Greece, and Germany-based BioNTech, headed by an immigrant CEO from Turkey. The other vaccine miracle worker, Moderna, is a venture-backed startup that was not even a decade old at the beginning of the pandemic.

"There could hardly be a stronger proof of venture capital's utility," wrote Sebastian Mallaby, in *The Power Law — Venture Capital and the Making of the New Future*, a great book published just as we were going to press.

I marvel at the pace with which scientists, the private and public sectors, and global institutions, all mobilized to get shots in the arm *in less than a year* from the first sequencing of the virus' DNA. But let's not forget that this stunning entrepreneurial tale, enabled by access to multiple minds, labs, and research, was in many ways a mere dress rehearsal for our future. So much to be done.

Let's take education. Before the pandemic, my son, for example, was already attending the innovative K-12 school Alpha. Like some other schools, including Austin's public Liberal Arts and Science Academy, or LASA, Alpha has been pushing beyond the show-up-and-be-counted model for some time. But still, my son's learning accelerated during the pandemic. Gone was the commute and the wasted time. He attended school via Zoom, made the grades he needed to (and excelled), and then spent the other seven hours per day programming and playing complex games online with friends, constantly chatting via Discord (a

Slack-meets-WhatsApp type of tool). He had more time to live his passion, not less.

Not long ago, I was on a call with a fellow CEO to learn more about "Massive Open Online Courses," or MOOCs, where nearly 400,000 students are enrolled in more than 2,900 classes offered by 160 different universities — all free. Yes, we need to close the so-called "digital divide" ASAP. And the suffering of students without bandwidth in East Austin in the early days of the pandemic is shameful in a city like Austin — one of the wealthiest and most educated large cities in the United States.

The aperture is opening on *access* to our primary knowledge need: education. And it's not just learning for those of traditional school age. There are incredible opportunities for those eager to learn to plug into the best minds and organizations.

Or we can take the example of arts, culture, and entertainment. Of course, we're going back to live music here in the Capital of Live Music. Just as Broadway exploded with theater in 1919 after a year of closure during the flu pandemic the year before, we had a great SXSW festival in 2022. But it was hybrid, and certainly will continue to be. At the same time, the new streaming services of the Alamo Drafthouse, the Austin Film Society, and others will continue to bring access to new films and filmmakers to audiences around the world. For the first time ever, a movie produced for a streaming service, Apple TV+'s *Coda,* won three Oscars — including for Best Picture — in 2022.

This trend of ubiquitous access was already apparent in the music scene before the pandemic. With the rise of social media platforms like Spotify, songs now compete more vigorously for attention and this is changing the nature of the music itself, with artists seeking to get to "the hook" of music faster. As the genre is changed by technology, it also is changing such institutions as the Grammy Awards, which is rethinking the categories of music.

Needless to say, this is important for music and culture industry entrepreneurs. But it's also a critical moment for social entrepreneurs, as the opportunities to advance the critical and long-delayed reckoning between Americans of all races are now being moved ahead at digital speed. Here in Austin, my friend Dr. Peniel Joseph, founder of the *Center for the Study of Race and Democracy* at the University of Texas at Austin, and author of a seminal book on civil rights history, *The Sword and the Shield*, spoke in honor of the late Rev. Martin Luther King during the pandemic at my synagogue — by Zoom of course. But he will continue to speak at countless engagements around the country in the future, as well as in person, in ways that would have not happened before we all became accustomed to the technology.

As I was writing this chapter, we at my company data.world hosted a free and open *Data Resource Hub* for the study of policing in America, enabling widespread access for researchers, policymakers, and the public. The hub combines information collected by the Policing in America Survey with existing data assets produced by federal, state, and local agencies and other non-profit initiatives. Microsoft, members of Congress, and many others have been eager to partner with us on this.

While this would have been technically possible before the pandemic, it would have been practically awkward if not impossible. Countless other examples abound of new ways to work, new ways to reskill our workforce for the well-paid tech jobs of tomorrow, and new ways to produce power from green energy sources that are being thought through and acted upon because of this new reality of *access*. It is into these areas in which you, the entrepreneurs, are taking us, and will take us, going forward.

These twin concepts of *access* and *hybridization* are key to where I want to close this chapter on *"The Soul"* of any company, and the culture that is informed by that soul. These two concepts are now foundational to the soul and culture of any new entrepreneurial venture going forward.

Most new startups don't spend a lot of time thinking about culture. But in my experience and that of others, including Cisco's

John Chamber who I referenced earlier, this is critical. What is your vision and how is it different? Who are your customers and how will you treat them? Who will be your employees and how will you treat them, and how will you expect them to treat others? How will you build your leadership team?

Or said differently, how will you make the world adapt? What is your unreasonable soul?

Whether you are an entrepreneur now or whether you will become one, you will peer deeply into your own soul as you ask these questions. And the answers never stop coming. You have many opportunities and great responsibility, but you also must be mindful that the road is long, often lonely, and filled with ups and downs.

As an entrepreneur, you will know the triumphs and the defeats like no one else. You have ridden the emotional highs and lows in ways that no one but other creators can understand. The company means more to you than it can mean to anyone else — because you were there at its inception. You were in the hospital room for its birth, along with perhaps a few other proud parents (your co-creators). The parent has the most history with the child, even when the child grows into an adult. It is easier to be the grandparent, cousin, or just the friend, acquaintance, or bystander.

There are many operators, but there are very few creators. Many benefit from the few courageous souls who dare to begin in the first place. Your being results in their doing.

You will always be a creator at your core. That is who you are. You were born to change the world. From the nurture of your sweat, many flowers will bloom. When you die, the world will remember the garden you seeded. You will be remembered more for creating than those who were just a part of it. Because without you, none of it would have existed — the world would have merely stayed static and the future wouldn't have progressed.

Your soul is our future.

This future is the "arena" I mentioned at the outset. Not long ago, I met an up-and-coming entrepreneur with a fantastic idea that I'm sure will be very successful. I asked if he had ever read *Man in the Arena,* by Theodore 'Teddy' Roosevelt. He had not. So I shared it with him, as I've shared it with so many others. Interestingly, it's from a speech Roosevelt gave in 1910, just a few years after Shaw penned *Maxims for Revolutionists.*

Both Shaw and Roosevelt may have written more than a century ago, but they were speaking to you today:

> *"It is not the critic who counts; not the man who points out how the strong man stumbles, or where the doer of deeds could have done them better. The credit belongs to the man who is actually in the arena, whose face is marred by dust and sweat and blood; who strives valiantly; who errs, who comes short again and again, because there is no effort without error and shortcoming; but who does actually strive to do the deeds; who knows great enthusiasms, the great devotions; who spends himself in a worthy cause; who at the best knows in the end the triumph of high achievement, and who at the worst, if he fails, at least fails while daring greatly, so that his place shall never be with those cold and timid souls who neither know victory nor defeat."*

**— THEODORE ROOSEVELT, IN HIS SPEECH "CITIZENSHIP IN A REPUBLIC," 1910**

# CHAPTER 2
# THE PARALYZING FEAR OF GETTING STARTED

It is said that before entering the sea
a river trembles with fear.

She looks back at the path she has traveled,
from the peaks of the mountains,
the long winding road crossing forests and villages.

And in front of her,
she sees an ocean so vast,
that to enter
there seems nothing more than to disappear
  forever.

But there is no other way.
The river can not go back.

Nobody can go back.
To go back is impossible in existence.

The river needs to take the risk
of entering the ocean
because only then will fear disappear,
because that's where the river will know
it's not about disappearing into the ocean,
but of becoming the ocean.

## — KHALIL GIBRAN, "THE RIVER CANNOT GO BACK"

It's only human nature to want to share the good parts of a story first: The liberation of becoming an entrepreneur, the sheer thrill, the exhaustion transforming to euphoria, the discovery of that essential among the essentials of this book — the 'soul' of the endeavor. So full disclosure now that you've completed Chapter 1, *The Soul of the Entrepreneur:* I haven't been straight with you. Like most storytellers, and for that matter like most entrepreneurs, I haven't told you everything right away.

What you also need to know is that the handmaid of the unleashing soul — both your own and that of your creation — is fear. Fear that will stalk you outright. Fear that will sneak up silently. Fear that can contort itself into depression. Fear that will seep slowly and destructively into the very same soul we talked about in Chapter 1.

Often the fear is rational. Will my money run out? While I'm still at the drawing board, will my competitors get to the market first? Will I fail and be a failure before friends and family? Oftentimes, the fear is irrational. Am I deserving of success? Is it my time to do this? Do I have the energy and do I have the skills to deliver on my vision? Is my idea as good as I think it is?

Ironically, self-doubt disproportionately affects high-performing individuals, a group that includes you, the entrepreneurs for whom this book is written. As the late Robert Hughes, the author and social critic once wrote in *Time Magazine*: "The greater the artist, the greater the doubt. Perfect confidence is granted to the less talented as a consolation prize."

I really share Hughes' stance on this. But fear and its derivatives of self-doubt, angst, and even depression, I must tell you, are among the occupational hazards for the entrepreneur. I want to talk about my own experience of this through the six companies I've founded or co-founded, from the very first company, a consultancy — which I started while working on my MBA at the Wharton School of the University of Pennsylvania in 1997 — to the most recent, data.world, birthed in 2015. In particular, the point I want to elaborate upon is that even though the space between Hurt Technology Consulting LLC and today's data.world is light years in terms of both scope and scale, the formative angst of both is very similar. And I also will share some solid ways to cope with fear. But before getting into my own specific experience, you need to understand just how universal this reality is for every entrepreneur.

As I emphasized in Chapter 1, *The Soul of the Entrepreneur,* there is nothing more rewarding in a career than being a creator — an entrepreneur. You get to build something from scratch and, if amazing people decide to join you and the world embraces your creation, it is *truly* euphoric. There is nothing like it: You made your small contribution to society. Or maybe a large contribution. You created something new, alongside a great team. But... if it fails... it is truly gut-wrenching. Again, the questions: What if the world *rejects* your creation? What if your market timing was really off? What if a competitor kicks your ass? Your name is all over this, sometimes quite literally in the name of the company itself (as is the case with the $70 billion-plus creation of Michael Dell). Whatever your fear is, however, that paralyzing fear when you are getting started is *normal*. People have this perception that we entrepreneurs are totally comfortable in jumping off the figurative cliff and building our company's wings on the way down. But that is bullshit, and I'll get into that further in Chapter 6, *The Fallacy of Risk in Entrepreneurship*. And we sometimes perpetuate that myth by glamorizing each other. The truth is that great entrepreneurs are usually risk-averse, a topic we will explore later.

That said, entrepreneurship is *really* scary. A good example is Elon Musk, as of this writing the world's richest person — and, I have to mention, a recent transplant to my hometown of Austin, Texas. As you can see in Musk's interview with *The New York Times*, on the Digital Companion, even this titan is not immune. "There were times when I didn't leave the factory for three or four days — days when I didn't go outside," Musk said in a 2018 interview that alternated between laughter and tears as he described the panic and the anxiety as he raced to meet production deadlines for the Tesla Model 3 amid insecure funding and a threatened probe by the Securities and Exchange Commission.

Another good description of this comes from Vidhya Ravi, the founder of Travelsheets, a web portal that helped travelers develop unique itineraries. Of all the fears Vidhya wrote on Medium in 2020, the one that hit her hardest was the fear that she simply wasn't up to the task.

"Over the last twelve years, I've quickly started, abandoned, or dismissed five or six viable startup ideas by simply telling myself that I didn't have the experience to do those startups — essentially, I didn't know what I was doing," she wrote, in a *Medium* essay linked on the Digital Companion. "I finally caught on to the biggest secret in the corporate world. Everyone feels like they don't know what they are doing, at least some of the time."

And then there is that offshoot of fear, a dimension of the entrepreneur's journey that frankly should be discussed more openly. This is depression. Some VCs, such as Homebrew, one of our investors at data.world, have incorporated the subject of founder depression into their model of support for entrepreneurs. And it's something I encounter and endeavor to help with among the entrepreneurs whom I mentor.

One of the best explorations of this, linked on the Digital Companion,  was produced by Catherine Shu of the online technology magazine *TechCrunch*. She found depression surprisingly widespread among founders and her article describes the battles of a number of them, anonymously of course.

"If I'm feeling really depressed I won't come into the office around others, I won't answer the phone, and will reschedule calls/meetings," one founder told Catherine. "The reason is I basically cannot function properly, speak well, or make sound decisions."

Another founder told Catherine: "If anything, I think the tech community is conducive to depression because it applauds excess and the lack of life balance."

As if that was not enough on the somber side of entrepreneurialism, there is one more harsh reality that compounds the dynamics of fear. As Microsoft CEO Satya Nadella remarked once at a gathering of CEOs I joined: "You can't have a bad day as a CEO." What he meant was that if you are in a bad mood, if you are feeling fearful, you can't project that mood within your company. And part of what Satya said is right, of course. Senior leaders, and especially CEOs, are typically seen as stoic, fearless personalities. Fear is not something people believe leaders experience, much less something that plagues them. Yet, the senior leader knows fear all too well.

I actually think this is a very common state of being for entrepreneurs starting out, regardless of their experience or success. But it isn't something we talk about, especially if you are a founder *and* CEO. Of course, we are supposed to project confidence, right? What Satya meant was that if you are in a bad mood, if you are feeling fearful, you can't project that mood within your company. Company employees will model their CEO's behavior, and his point is that you need to strive to be the ultimate model of performance, confidence, and positivity.

Fair enough. But Satya left something out. I'm quite sure he would agree with me that, along with the virtues of a commander's boldface amid any storm, leadership is equally about authenticity. Projecting confidence is paramount, for sure. And many are the self-help business books that draw on the hard-as-nails examples of military leadership, of Ulysses Grant, George Patton, or, more recently, Stanley McChrystal, whose swagger resonates in his three books on leadership. But today's entrepreneurial leadership, particularly in the fast-emerging economy of data and digital innovation, is about building creative teams, about co-creation of new knowledge, of flat hierarchies. This demands that you, the entrepreneur and leader, be human and show your humanity too. I believe it's a critical factor of success. I'm not suggesting you freak out your team if you yourself are feeling freaked out inside. I am saying that you should never fake a "good day," when the reality is otherwise, but rather demonstrate authentic resoluteness and sincere resolve when the clouds gather and the headwinds pick up. In other words, show your humanity.

You know that old expression, "It's lonely at the top?" It's true. But it's less lonely when you have the means to cope with the inevitable fear and its threats of paralysis. So let me turn to my personal experience, which I believe is instructive, both on my early lessons on fear as well as those that came later, when one might have thought that my success would have extinguished my fears.

I founded my first business in the early stages of my time at Wharton. Hurt Technology Consulting started out as a one-man consultancy. Interestingly enough, I had written all my application essays when applying to Wharton around my passion to ultimately start my own business. I certainly never would have guessed that I would do so in my first semester. But I had arrived at Wharton from Deloitte Consulting where I'd been an analyst and in fact, I was technically on a leave of absence from Deloitte. But life is what happens when you are making other plans, as John Lennon famously sang, and a senior manager from Deloitte called me in a panic in November of 1997, right before the winter break after my first grueling semester. He had sold a client - the Louisiana Department of Labor - on a project where he would build a system to replace the tracking of their adult education system with a client-server design to replace the state's current paper-based filing systems. This would allow for more efficiency and better reporting and analytics. The problem was that he had a very small budget and no idea how to build it. So he turned to me. And I was in.

Talk about fear. I had two weeks over that winter break to create the entire system. From scratch. While proficient from the age of 7 in programming, I also had to learn a new programming language. I did so with the help of a very smart friend who happened to be visiting the Wharton campus to consider whether he would also earn his MBA. And I worked my butt off. I was determined to prove that I could do it. I literally worked every day and night until around 3 a.m. over that two-week period, including during the Times Square ball drop on New Year's Eve, where I paused to watch the ball drop on TV for five minutes and then returned to work.

My fears were massive. What would happen if I failed to deliver on time? Would the system work? My wife Debra played a big role, believing in me through my moments of deep doubt while standing clear so that I might prove myself to myself. And I did! My system worked, was fully documented, and got deployed successfully all over the State of Louisiana. The former senior manager, now an entrepreneur himself, was a hero. And I kept Hurt Technology Consulting LLC up and running, contracting with brilliant undergrads in Wharton's Jerome Fisher Program in

Management & Technology, and they shared in the financial success.

In 1999 I took the next step, founding MBA ZoNe with two classmates, Brenda and Marc Mizgorski. It was an online community for MBA students, conceptually much like the early version of Facebook and also based on advertising. I learned a great deal, including the fact that I didn't like selling advertising, and worked my way through many fears and anxieties. This was my first business with co-founders, another source of fear. Will we get along? Will we clash? As with many fears, these were unfounded. As Mark Twain put it, "I've had a lot of worries in my life, most of which didn't happen." These fears were in that category. The only conflict we ran into was that I just wasn't passionate about it (be true to one's self) and ultimately I sold my equity to Brenda and Marc and they continue to run the company today.

Next, and again while still a student, Debra and I launched BodyMatrix, in some ways inspired by my parents who were always retail and direct marketing entrepreneurs. We successfully sold sports nutrition products all over the world, managing the global enterprise from a brownstone in downtown Philadelphia. One of the early frustrations, and frankly a source of the fear that the enterprise might even fail, was that we were effectively blind to our customers' needs, habits, and behaviors online, which were masked by a web browser. In my parents' stores, you could at least ask a customer, "Are you finding everything you need?" and "How did you hear about us?" But not here. So, I built the technology to "see." Having written the original code for the e-commerce platform we constructed, I knew all of the code inside and out. I did what I thought was most logical. I wrote the customers' actions as they occurred directly into the Microsoft Access database that powered the site. Where did they visit us from - recorded. What products did they look at - recorded. What products did they buy - recorded. What products did they search for - recorded. What products did they abandon from their shopping cart - recorded. How did they find us - recorded.

These innovations, meanwhile, drew attention around campus, both from professors and classmates, a couple of whom became co-founders in the creation of my fourth business, Coremetrics. This was my first foray into enterprise software, as we sold the analytics tools we'd developed to "fix" the customer visibility problem at BodyMatrix to other firms. Somehow, and perhaps insanely in retrospect, I kept all four businesses going while concluding my MBA. When I graduated in 1999, I sold the first three businesses as fast as I could and doubled down on Coremetrics with a singular passion that was to carry me along an often rocky and scary road, straight into and through the 2001 dot.com crash.

For readers who may not remember, the Nasdaq Composite peaked at 5132 in March 2000. A year later, the index was in the 1900s. The Dow Jones Internet Composite Index fell to a fifth of what it had been just 12 months earlier. It's hard to imagine now, but Amazon's value fell from the sky by 94 percent, its shares reaching $6 in September of that year. For comparison, Amazon was hovering around at $3,400 a share when I was wrapping up this book in the spring of 2022.

"The market had gone cold, investors were holding their money close, and the last thing you wanted to be was a young company with dot-com at the end of your name," wrote historian Margaret O'Mara in her seminal book on the technology business, *The Code - Silicon Valley and the Remaking of America.* You can read all about that period in her book, a review of which you'll find on the Digital Companion along with an interview of her. But I was there with Coremetrics, serving the dot-coms, along with so many others. It was bad.

Not to revisit that terrible time, except to say that fear of the very sector in which you've staked your life and future as it collapses is a raw, intense elixir combining everything we've been exploring in this chapter. But managing that, along with managing our business, is what carried us to the other side. And arriving at the other side, having conquered that fear, really was a kind of revenge of the nerds in California's Silicon Valley, Austin's Silicon Hills, Boston's Technology Corridor, and elsewhere. After we survivors tended our wounds and moved on, the first two decades of the 21st Century were to become the Golden Age of technology in my view, one that continues to accelerate and further reason that I am writing this book.

Which takes me to 2005, and the founding of my fifth company, Bazaarvoice, an online engine that powers and enables customer reviews — both positive and negative — for some of the largest retailers and brands that sell through retailers worldwide. After weathering the dot.com bust successfully at Coremetrics, we soon found ourselves at Bazaarvoice in the Great Recession, which began in 2007 and deepened in 2008. I was giving speeches reminding entrepreneurs and others that this was something we hadn't seen as a nation since the Great Depression. And we hadn't. There was plenty to fear as a CEO. I put on as brave a face as possible, but was also candid with my team. Even though our sales and revenue remained strong, beating all of our goals, I imposed a six-month hiring freeze as a precaution against things getting worse. Everyone took on more work and we got through it as a team.

Amidst that storm, however, one of the biggest name brand retailers in the United States moved to remove negative reviews from its site. This was a "stand your ground" moment that we had to fight with every tool we could muster. I certainly didn't want to lose the customer, but the credibility of our entire company — and theirs too — was on the line. A global engine with a mission of enabling transparency to customers and potential customers simply couldn't survive if it was seen to be mere cherry-picking propaganda. Our mission statement was, "Changing the world, one *authentic* conversation at a time." Again, we prevailed, but not without many an anxious moment and many a sleepless night. We took Bazaarvoice public in 2012 and I exited as CEO, earning enough for my labors to never work again should I so choose. Debra and I soon became investors in startups ourselves, co-founding Hurt Family Investments. I took three years off in any operational capacity. I read. I traveled. Debra and I spent time in India studying and learning Vedanta, a 5,000-year-old Indian philosophy on how to achieve happiness in life. I took on short, part-time stints at the University of Texas at Austin as the Entrepreneur-in-Residence and also at Austin Ventures as a partner. And then I took the leap that was hardly forced upon me, plunging again into, among other things, that river of fear — but this time from the shore of a financially secure, "proven" entrepreneur.

But why? As just described, I had started successful companies before. data.world was my sixth. I had a bigger network than ever before. I had more know-how then at any other point in my entrepreneurial career, including the lessons that hardened me in writing my blog *Lucky7* over the years to help other entrepreneurs. I had spent three years in deep reflection. I had seen over 2,000 startup pitches, which really do have the effect of making new mental connections, what VCs call "pattern recognition." I had worked behind the scenes at the once-powerhouse Austin Ventures, seeing how the VC industry *really* works. I had served as an Entrepreneur-in-Residence at both The Wharton School and my undergraduate alma mater, the University of Texas at Austin. I knew company culture like the back of my hand — Bazaarvoice had been rated the best place to work in Austin when it was a small, medium, and then large-size company, winning #1 in all three categories as we rapidly grew. Alongside my excellent co-founders, I had spent months researching the viability of data.world. In short, I was, rationally speaking, more prepared than I had ever been before. So why was I afraid?

One of the most famous entrepreneurs in Austin once told

me, after Bazaarvoice, "Be careful what you do next. Everyone is watching. You are near the top of the entrepreneurial heap in Austin, so choose wisely." This message was coming to me from an entrepreneur who had experienced a lot of financial success but had never stepped back into the entrepreneurial arena directly. Why? Because they had made enough money? I had, too. Or was it because they were afraid of failing if they did it again? Fear in the arena is eternal. So must be the effort to confront it.

*We are the creators.* Don't we have an *obligation* to overcome that fear and continue to create? To *live* our meaning? I want you to realize that feeling is *normal.* As you feel that fear beginning to paralyze you, I have some advice. *Keep moving.* That is the only way through it. Find that state of execution *flow.* Remember that ancient bit of wisdom, "This, too, shall pass." Or, as my CEO coach, Kirk Dando, says, "The road to heaven goes through hell." Be strong. Get that momentum going. No one is going to do it for you. As Dr. Seuss wrote, "Unless someone like you cares a whole awful lot, nothing is going to get better. It's not."

There are many ways to talk yourself out onto the ledge of fear, but only a small number to talk your way down. So among them, when you find yourself in the grip of fear, I recommend:

First, talk to someone about it. This could be your co-founders. It could be your spouse or best friend. Don't just carry that burden alone. Everyone sometimes needs a friend to help them overcome their fears. You are human. I'll never forget a class I took at Wharton where we all laid out our fears. That class helped me commit to continuing as  an entrepreneur after graduation. While most of my classmates took high paying jobs my salary was the grand total of $0 for the first six months post graduation and then $60k for the next six months after that, a far cry from the $150k+ that most of my classmates were making two decades ago right after graduation.

Second, do something that centers you again. For some, this is meditation. For others, like me, this is exercising. Or it may just be going on a long walk or a beautiful hike alone. Or going to a conference or reading a book that helps you overcome your fear and keep moving. Whatever you do, take care of yourself.

Third, if you find yourself sitting there, paralyzed, remember that momentum begets momentum. Pick up the phone and call a potential Advisory Board member, which could be some guru in your industry who may help give you confidence, or tell you what to change. Call a potential client. Call a potential partner. Let the market speak to you. *Get moving* and your fear will start to dissipate.

Fourth, once you have overcome your fear, talk about it like I'm doing in this chapter. Let's normalize this for other entrepreneurs instead of just talking about the "glory" or our "successes". Entrepreneurship is *hard* — it is the ultimate journey of self-discovery.

For me, that feeling dissipated about three or four months into data.world. I found my state of flow, bolstered by my amazing co-founders, and today we are the largest collaborative data community in the world, with feature-rich enterprise offerings for our clients and many integrated partners, such as Microsoft Power BI, Tableau, and Google Data Studio. Momentum is building every day. But... we still have *plenty* of execution challenges ahead. And there will still be periods of fear. And I will work through it, keeping in mind that placing one foot in front of the other is the only way to get to the other side.

Again, fear is normal, even for the most experienced entrepreneurs. Maybe even more so because they have more face to lose. Because we know how hard the journey is. Because we aren't as naive as we used to be. No matter our level of experience, let's talk about this more and not hide behind our "success stories." Founder depression — and fear — are real issues to deal with.

So always, keep walking. No one said it would be easy to be an entrepreneur, but the journey is the reward. Fear will come, and it will abate. Learn from your mistakes and don't marinate in them. Just keep walking.

Take it from one of the ancients, one of history's greatest philosophers:

*"We can easily forgive a child who is afraid of the dark; the real tragedy of life is when men are afraid of the light."*

**— PLATO**

# CHAPTER 3
## ADVICE FOR THE MIDDLE-AGED ENTREPRENEUR

*"Don't aim at success. The more you aim at it and make it a target, the more you are going to miss it. For success, like happiness, cannot be pursued; it must ensue, and it only does so as the unintended side effect of one's personal dedication to a cause greater than oneself or as the by-product of one's surrender to a person other than oneself...*

*"Happiness must happen, and the same holds for success: you have to let it happen by not caring about it. I want you to listen to what your conscience commands you to do and go on to carry it out to the best of your knowledge. Then you will live to see that in the long-run — in the long-run, I say! — success will follow you precisely because you had forgotten to think about it."*

### — VIKTOR FRANKL, PHILOSOPHER, AUTHOR, HOLOCAUST SURVIVOR

While throughout this book I argue that we're living in technology's "Golden Age," it is equally true that the entrepreneur's journey gets tougher the closer you are to the "Golden Years." Or if not tougher, it is certainly a different journey. It demands a different set of skills— and the leverage of those skills — on the part of the midlife entrepreneur who wants to be successful.

To be clear, I certainly want to encourage would-be entrepreneurs in their forties, fifties, and even sixties. Sure, Bill Gates and Mark Zuckerberg both founded their famous companies at the age of 19. The late-blooming Steves, Jobs and Wozniak, were 21 and 26 respectively when they founded Apple. But the Silicon Valley myth that a would-be founder older than 35 is "over the hill" is just that, a myth. It's a myth that gets reinforced in popular culture in many ways, which sadly include such initiatives as that of PayPal Co-founder Peter Thiel's fellowship program that provides $100,000 grants to would-be entrepreneurs so long as they are below age 23 and drop out of school. In fact, there is even some evidence made in a study, linked on the Digital Companion, by the National Bureau of Economic Research that companies founded by late-bloomers co-relate to faster growth. And after all, if you're successful as a manager/executive of a big company, the easiest way to earn that CEO title to which you aspire probably is to start your own company and "promote yourself," doing pretty much what you were for them but on your own.

The examples are both inside and outside of technology abound. David Duffield founded PeopleSoft in 1987 when he was 46, then as CEO led it to become the world's second-largest application software company before selling it to Oracle in 2005 for almost $11 billion in cash. Then, at age 63, he founded Workday, which became even bigger (and ultimately competed against Oracle and his prior company). Workday is worth over $57 billion as of this writing. Henry Ford founded his eponymous carmaker when he was 40 and didn't introduce the Model T until he was 45. Robert Noyce founded Intel with Gordon Moore at 41 and two decades later became the first CEO of Austin's SEMATECH. Julia Child wrote her first cookbook at 50 before rocketing to worldwide fame. Steve Jobs may have been 21 when he founded Apple, but he was 52 when he and his team invented the world-changing iPhone. Or there's the remarkable example of Jack Weil, the son of a Jewish refugee exiled from Prussia, who founded Denver-based clothing manufacturer Rockmount Ranch Wear when he was 45; he remained active as CEO until he died at the age of 107. (He is also credited with inventing that Texas icon, the bolo tie.)

That said, young people are generally cognitively sharper, or so it's argued. They often have a huge advantage in the lack of distractions of family, mortgages, and other obligations. But in my view, the exorbitant advantage that the younger entrepreneur enjoys — which is yet one that the midlife founder can overcome —boils down to what is known as the "Planck Principle," named for the famous German physicist and Nobel laureate Max Planck. He argued a half-century ago that innovation comes not from converts won over to a new idea, but from the fact that a new generation comes along to look at the world from a fresh perspective.

"It rarely happens that Saul becomes Paul," Planck wrote in his autobiography, making a Biblical reference to the conversion of the ancient apostle. "What does happen is that (innovation's) opponents gradually die out and that the growing generation is familiarized with the ideas from the beginning."

I would put this idea somewhat differently: the younger entrepreneur enjoys the advantage of *not knowing what is impossible* and also *not knowing how hard the journey will be*. Those meanwhile pondering a startup after years as an employee — even as an executive star— can be burdened by the blinders of established ways that often limit their ultimate success. So in my view, if you're older than 40 there's still plenty of time to get "into the arena." It's just that for a variety of reasons, often the less experience you have in an industry, the better. This is counterintuitive, I know. And don't discard your copy of Malcolm

Gladwell's book *Outliers*, which famously argued that you need 10,000-plus hours to master anything from computer code to the cello. Experience does count. I'm sure Elon Musk has put in his 10,000 hours and then some on everything from engineering cars to rockets to public transit tunnels.

But in an age when business paradigms shift around faster than whiteboards in an open office plan, the successful midlife entrepreneur will be the one who embraces this imperative.

A slightly wonky example helps to frame my thinking on this. It comes from a study I encountered while writing this book, and it's adjacent to my views shaped as a data entrepreneur. In perhaps the most comprehensive experiment ever to study cyber-security decision-making, the MIT Sloan School of Management in 2018 paired a group of seasoned data security executives with a control group of inexperienced graduate students to test who might fare best in a simulated threat environment.

The exercise, linked on the Digital Companion, was complex, akin to the flight simulators to train and test pilots. It modeled various investment decisions, fixed cyber attacks on data with fixed impacts, as well as random attacks and random impacts. And it collapsed five years of decision-making into an interactive online game in which participants conducted 1,479 simulation runs. Ultimately, 38 professional cybersecurity executives with an average of 15 years of experience each "competed" with 29 graduate students who were in a general course on information technology and had no cybersecurity expertise. While the two groups performed differently on different aspects of the simulation, overall there was no significant difference in the success rates of the two groups. In other words, 570 years of collective experience among the "seasoned" executives were of virtually no utility when it came to anticipating and managing threats to data in a rapidly changing and evolving sector. Of the two groups, which do you think is the most likely to produce the entrepreneur who will found the company that ultimately slays the dragon of cyber threats? I'm sure you know what my guess would be.

The study concluded with the insight I would make more generally. This is that decades of experience indeed have great value, but the hubris of the experienced can hide important paradigm shifts in plain sight. My point here is that you just need to be aware of your blind spots and compensate accordingly.

One who has really excelled at seeing around vulnerabilities is my good friend Cotter Cunningham, who bucks the flavor-of-the-day entrepreneurial stereotype in many ways and who is somewhat of a legend in Austin technology circles.

After college, Cotter followed a standard career path, working his way through several jobs and ultimately rising to the post of COO of publicly traded BankRate, a personal finance company based in Florida. After eight years as COO, Cotter's entrepreneurial journey began at age 46 with the euphoria of being his own CEO followed by a gut-wrenching pivot. Cotter's first company was called Divorce360.com. After more than a year, it was a miserable failure. And the funny (and fortunate) thing is that Cotter has never been divorced! But instead of crying in their beers about it, Cotter and Tom Ball (who was at Austin Ventures at that time) decided what to do next: they founded the interactive, online retail coupon company ultimately named RetailMeNot in 2006. In 2017 it sold for $630 million after a successful IPO.

Some years ago, I interviewed Cotter when I was the Entrepreneur-in-Residence at the McCombs School of Business at the University of Texas at Austin. You can watch that discussion on the Digital Companion.

"If I had started a business at 20, I wouldn't have known what *not* to do, I wouldn't have known what *to* do. I would have just kind of had to find my way," Cotter said back in that conversation. "When you start a business at 45, you know what doesn't work. You know how your boss has treated you, you know how you don't want to be treated... a lot of our culture is based on my wanting to do things differently than the way things were done at the companies where I had been previously."

It was ultimately a conversation with his wife that pushed him to make the leap, he recalled. "I was bitching about the way things were going, and she said, 'Well if you're so smart, why don't you do better?'," he recalled. "That was it, I said, 'What the heck'."

And what was his secret for a midlife jump into the entrepreneurial stream? "It's all about persistence. Persistence, at least in my case, is not something I was born with. It is something I've developed as a skill," he said. "I've always persisted. Don't give up."

Another friend who I mentored as a midlife entrepreneur is Suneet Paul, Co-founder and former CEO of the fintech firm NewComLink (now Vyze, which was acquired by Mastercard). In addition to thoughts similar to Cotter's, he underscores his use of a Board of Advisors with diverse competencies as key to seeing around those paradigmatic corners I've described.

"I've lived the real business world, had the chance to do different things and take risks while working for more established companies, learn from mistakes, and try something new the next time," Suneet wrote me not long ago. "It is not like starting a company and learning business acumen at the same time."

So if you're ready for the journey despite a streak or two of gray in your hair, forget about age and get to work. Everything I wrote in Chapters 1 and 2 about both the euphoria and pain of the entrepreneur's ride is just as valid for you as for any other would-be founder. But I do have a few additional words of advice.

First, you need to shrug off the big-company attitude and get centered. And fast. When you are a big company executive/manager, people pay attention to you most of the time but it isn't very genuine and you start to believe their bullshit. For example, you get on the phone with a business partner and they kiss up to you. That is because you have the resources of a big company — possibly even billions of budget and thousands of people under your purview. You are in for a rude awakening if you expect that type of treatment toward anyone at a startup. You'll get on the phone and you'll have to really hustle. They will think, "Why am I wasting my time speaking with this small-company person?" Ironically, they'll especially think this if they are working in a big company because they are more cautious about taking risks on a "no-name." You don't have the legitimacy that comes with decades of building a stable brand. You are an ant again. Actually, you always were an ant, you just lost perspective, and now is the time to realize that. It's just like you were when you were a child and everything was a blank slate. Get rid of the executive swagger, get ready to fetch your own coffee, and when done put your cup in the dishwasher yourself. It's a new day. Don't skip ahead, but Chapter 17, *Action-Oriented Communication*, will also help you on this front. Meanwhile, at the outset of this chapter, I quoted the author Viktor Frankl. His book *Man's Search for Meaning* is a good book for everyone, but for the midlife entrepreneur, it's the critical guide with which to begin. Frankl will help you find your inner passion.

The interviews on finding meaning in times of hardship on the Digital Companion, recorded with his grandson Alexander Vesely, will move and inspire you.

Second,  you need to learn how you've been conditioned, even manipulated, your whole life. This is a big topic, but you need to master the automatic reflexes that we develop as humans, which people in turn exploit to steer our decision-making. An expansive look at ways to gain mastery over your interaction with the world is in one of my favorite books *Influence: Science and Practice* by Robert Cialdini. This is important because it will put you very much in tune with human behavior. In short, Cialdini explores the counter-intuitive ways that influence works. Much of his focus is on the human need to reciprocate gestures and our unconscious desire to be part of a consensus before making a decision. This is why he insists on the critical responsibility to focus on personal commonalities to win the trust of your counterparts in any negotiation. Most importantly, Cialdini offers not just a primer on how to influence customers, partners, and employees but also the means to do so ethically. As a good person, you can leverage his insights for the greater good in your business instead of evil. And you can always ward off the evil by being informed on how it can manifest due to our collective, hardwired vulnerabilities. The book is also full of very practical early-stage marketing advice so you can break through the noise. You'll really need that starting out, and the big companies you worked for figured this out at their beginning. In addition to linking to his books, I also include a video in which Cialdini explains the six "short cuts," which are behavioral concepts, to break through noise: reciprocity, scarcity, authority, consistency, liking, and consensus.

Third, you need to think big or you will quickly fall into the pattern of being a "first-stage entrepreneur." By this I mean your bootstrapped firm will stay small, limited to consulting or services, and will never have more than 20 or so employees. This compares with what I call "second-stage entrepreneurs," whose companies are product-based, can bring in investment, and are ready to "swing for the fences." And of course, it also compares even more dramatically with "third-stage entrepreneurs," those who are all grown, have returned investor capital, and are well on their way to long-term growth — like hometown Austin heroes Whole Foods or Dell. Indeed, you do have more to lose than the younger folks but reflexively playing for safety will serve as a weight and you will be unlikely to achieve financial freedom. The best book on how to get the courage to think big and take on the slumbering giants is *The Innovator's Dilemma* by Clayton Christensen. Much more on him when we get to Chapter 6, *The Fallacy of Risk in Entrepreneurship.*

Fourth, you must constantly work on self-improvement, take time to reflect, and embrace vulnerability. I'll have much more to say on this in Chapter 14, *Seven Lessons Learned on the Journey from Founder to CEO.* But these insights come from my own lessons in midlife and they are critical to the success of the mature founder and CEO. Reflection also includes the reality that you must own the long-term vision of the company to keep the fires lit and carry the torch. By embracing vulnerability, I'm suggesting here that you need to build on the concepts I outlined in the previous chapter on overcoming fear. Remember that everyone is watching you and will, to a large extent, mimic your behavior. If you close your mind to learning because of your prior success or try to fake what you don't know, others will do so too, with dire consequences.

Fifth and finally, you must have the humility and self-awareness to surround yourself with great mentors, from your angel investors, to your VC investors, to your Advisory Board, to your Board of Directors, and to your CEO or executive coach, which in my case is Kirk Dando who has also become a very good friend. You are going to need them. You have a much harder pivot than younger people because of your material and family encumbrances and your big-company attitude.

The big idea here is that the fundamental difference between the twenty-something entrepreneur and the forty-, fifty-, or even sixty-something, is that those of you in the latter group must be willing to discard old ideas and ways of doing things and learn new ones. As humans, our brains are not programmed for this, our temperaments are not suited for this, and our social standings are often a sheer dead weight on our ability to look anew and afresh. In a phrase, you've got to embrace change internally if you are going to effect change externally.

In conclusion, let me leave you with a thought from journalist

Barbara Bradley Hagerty, a reporter at *National Public Radio* and a writer for *The Atlantic:*

> *"Our brains resist change, they rail against it, our amygdala will always want the safe bet. But are the obstacles truly insurmountable? Is it a brick wall? Or is it a sliding door, which, once you decide to approach it, begins to swish open? Because even though our brains prefer safety in the short run, in the long run, they crave meaning, challenge, and novelty."*

— **BARBARA BRADLEY HAGERTY,
*LIFE REIMAGINED: THE SCIENCE,
ART, AND OPPORTUNITY OF
MIDLIFE***

# CHAPTER 4
# THE IMPORTANCE OF AN ALWAYS BE LEARNING LIFE

*"The illiterate of the 21st Century will not be those who cannot read and write, but those who cannot learn, unlearn, and relearn."*

## — ALVIN TOFFLER, AUTHOR, AND FUTURIST

It's hard to exaggerate just how important the credo "Always Be Learning" is to the life of the entrepreneur. It's also easy to invite confusion on this topic, in an age in which we bathe in information. After all, aren't we learning more and learning it faster than ever before?

Not quite.

I know it may feel like we are learning more. We are certainly exposed to more information. And this explosion of knowledge enriches our lives. Today, the entirety of human knowledge doubles roughly every 13 months, according to a calculation first created by the futurist Buckminster Fuller. Stir that with the theory of "Singularity," pushed by Google's artificial intelligence czar Ray Kurzweil, and all that's behind it, and soon the entire store of human knowledge will be doubling every 12 hours.

In my world — and I suspect in the world of the entrepreneurs and aspiring entrepreneurs reading this book as well — we scramble in the face of this reality. New channels, new apps, new markets. You have 15 blogs and 20 newsletters you like to get through, in addition to the more regular news feeds. Your iPhone pings relentlessly with the bold and the bonkers. That podcast ran longer than your morning jog, so you need to catch up later along with the other three you've promised yourself to get to. But first, check your email, texts, your Twitter feed, Slack, LinkedIn, Facebook messenger, WhatsApp, and your voicemail (if you still have it, which I don't). How do the Q3 KPIs stack up against those from Q2? What about those changes in tax law? Just exactly how does a "SPAC" work and how did it become so popular overnight? No wonder you feel guilty about your secret desire to read a novel.

I get it. We live at the intersection of two imperatives. On the one hand, there's never been so much that you need to learn in a world and business environment that is as fast-changing as the Texas sky. On the other hand, we're being deluged with data, information, and knowledge in such volumes that it's all but impossible to keep those three categories apart — a continuum in fact at the heart of what we do at my company data.world. I often tell aspiring entrepreneurs and veterans alike that this is what I call "Red Queen Syndrome."

You probably recall her from high school when you read Lewis Carroll's *Through the Looking Glass*. There's the part when Alice is schooled by the Red Queen in that important life lesson that today's entrepreneurs fail to heed at their peril. It's where Alice finds herself running faster and faster with the Red Queen — but staying in the same place.

"Alice looked round her in great surprise" reads the story, describing her dash to nowhere. " 'Why, I do believe we've been under this tree the whole time! Everything's just as it was!'

" 'Of course it is,' said the Queen, 'what would you have it?'

" 'Well, in our country,' said Alice, still panting a little, 'you'd generally get to somewhere else — if you ran very fast for a long time, as we've been doing'."

So I'm here to deliver the bad news. Running faster and harder, becoming more "efficient," creating another "metric" to surpass, and doubling the speed in your podcast listening, will not do much to curtail the fire hoses of words and numbers. Sure, you could use a digital detox. You need to get your phone under control and check your email less frequently. Do those things, as smart leaders everywhere now advocate. But that alone won't keep the Red Queen and her syndrome away. What I'm talking about here is moving your focus to the far end of that data-information-knowledge continuum. To be clear, the CEO of data.world is not telling you that you need to ignore data and information. Far from it. What I am saying is that managing both requires you to actively seek *knowledge*, even *wisdom*. You need to embrace an "Always Be Learning" mindset and practice.

Another way to think about this Red Queen dilemma might be with the insight of a more recent author, one whom I admire greatly and discuss below. This is Yuval Noah Hariri and the insight, or at least my interpretation of it, comes from his book *Homo Deus - A Brief History of Tomorrow,* and more on him awaits you on the Digital Companion.

In the course of our evolution into the literate, high-tech species that we are today, the explosion of information that we have invented and rely upon is essentially a huge algorithm. It's an ever-expanding, data-driven methodology that organizes modern life.

"In literate societies, people are organized into networks, so that each person is only a small step in a huge algorithm," Harari argues, "and it is the algorithm as a whole that makes the important decisions."

Don't misunderstand. This growing "algorithm" is not the enemy. I'm not advocating some back-to-the-land, off-the-grid lifestyle where we turn our back on technology. Harari's algorithm is the architecture of the 21st economy and the best hope for civilization in the face of so many challenges. Aviation is six times safer than it was 30 years ago and 22 times safer than it was 50 years ago. The next time you board a plane, consider that the technology around you is monitoring everything happening inside the plane, everything that's happening outside the plane, and everything else happening in some 50 time and space dimensions. Hundreds of thousands of cancer patients have been successfully treated without physical intervention thanks to the "CyberKnife" that incises tumors with so-called "radiosurgery."

Just think of the COVID-19 pandemic, how successfully we migrated to Zoom, and the medical miracles that are now creating, however slowly, the exit. Marc Andreessen, the Netscape founder, and famous venture capitalist recently wrote a great essay on this in his publication *Future*.

"Moderna, a product of the American venture capital system, created the first mRNA COVID vaccine within two days of receiving the genetic code for COVID by email," Andreessen wrote in the essay, which is on the Digital Companion.

But while the global algorithm is the source of virtually all progress and prosperity, mastery of it — which is the job of the entrepreneur — requires us to step outside of it, to gain a holistic perspective, to see it from the outside. In short, to practice an *Always Be Learning* life. Steve Jobs' inspiration for the I-phone didn't come from his Twitter feed. No, it came from the many books he read. These include *Zen Mind, Beginner's Mind*, by Shunryu Suzuki, *Diet for a Small Planet* by Frances Moore Lapee, and *The Autobiography of a Yogi* by Paramahansa Yogananda. Bill

Gates reads a book a week and claims his all-time favorite is *Business Adventures*, a collection of anecdotes from business more than 50 years ago. Warren Buffett somehow finds the time to read at least 500 pages a day. "Go to bed a little smarter each day," Buffett has advised. "That's how knowledge builds up. Like compound interest."

But so many don't. I'm sure you've met more than a few of the arrogant jerks who've memorized the jargon of your specific field or sector but have nothing new to add. These are among the many people who have stopped learning, and never realize it. They are stranded in the realm of the Red Queen but don't realize that they are simply running in place. Unfortunately, I've worked with a few of them in my career and it is *crushing* to a person like me who has an *Always Be Learning* mindset. Frankly, I fear the number of those who have stopped learning — those ruled *by* the algorithm rather than choosing to rule *it* — is growing. The arrogant, wealthier ones among this bunch believe that they got to that point because of their "genius" and completely discount luck, circumstance, or more importantly the giants on whose shoulders they stand and who made their successful journey possible.

I have certainly enjoyed great success in life, and I frankly have worked very hard for it. But I owe everything that got me to the point that I could attain that success to a very long list of people. I reflect on those who comprise that list often, and I credit them at every opportunity. It includes my computer teacher back in middle school, my wife, my mother to whom my *Lucky7* blog and this book is a tribute, my CEO coach, my co-founders, some of my investors and advisors, and many, many others.

As far as practicing an *Always Be Learning* life, well that is a little harder to cover. And it's about far more than just books, as essential as they are. Let me tell you how I do it:

First, as suggested, I read obsessively — and I cast a very wide net in doing so. I regularly consume *Wired* magazine and have since the first issues. It does an amazing job of covering how technology is evolving and also changing society. I read the *Wall Street Journal*. I regularly read so many articles shared by friends on Facebook from *credible* sources, like *The Washington Post* and *The Atlantic*.

I regularly read books — lots of them. As I mentioned above, one of the books that stirred me most was Harari's *Homo Deus: A Brief History of Tomorrow*. I think it was written to scare you in many ways, and in fact, he suggests as much, caveating his dire predictions in one passage as, "less of a prophecy and more a way of discussing present choices." But he makes great and original points and his book makes you think.

As an aside, I should also mention that Harari is an inspirational entrepreneur as well. In Chapter 18, *Forming Your Company's Values,* I'll get more deeply into the values and social responsibilities of entrepreneurs and the concept of Conscious Capitalism. But Harari is a living example of this. His company Sapienship is making investments in the development of animal-free food products, including cultured meat and lab-grown milk, areas where Debra and I are investing as well. And I'm also impressed that in the early months of the COVID-19 pandemic, in response to then-President Donald Trump's elimination of U.S. funding to the World Health Organization, Hariri personally donated $1 million to the agency at a critical time.

A couple of years ago, I held two incredible discussions on *Homo Deus* with a diverse group of readers, including Steve Adler, the mayor of Austin where I live, and author and serial entrepreneur Byron Reese, whose books include *Wasted, How We Squander Time, Money and Resources and What We Can Do About It.* Reese is one of the most brilliant people I know in Austin and we are proud investors in his past company, Gigaom, and his new company, JJ Kent. John Mackey, the co-founder, and CEO of Whole Foods Market called Byron's most recent book, *The Fourth Age*, the best book he's ever read on artificial intelligence. I would agree. It is incredibly practical and places AI in a thorough historical context.

Both of these books relate strongly to the work of author Simon Sinek, whose books include *Start With Why.* Among the resources I include on this chapter's Digital Companion section are links to a number of Sinek's TED talks that go to the heart of the argument I am making here. "Very few people or organizations know why they do what they do," Sinek argued at TED, framing the dilemma I describe here about those who have abandoned the *Always Be Learning* mindset and yet don't realize it.

Another book that is attuned to the concept I'm sharing here is *Mindset: The New Psychology of Success,* by Carol Dweck. Her term for continuous learning is "growth mindset," a reference to the power of simply believing that you can improve, grow and master new skills. Dweck refers to people who view talent as a quality that they either possess or lack as having a "fixed mindset." By contrast, people with a growth mindset enjoy challenges, strive to learn, and consistently see potential to develop new skills. Take a few minutes to check out her TED talk, which I link to on the Digital Companion.

Along with books, I read a lot of blogs, such as the essays *on First Round Review,* the magazine produced by the VC firm First Round Capital, and almost anything written by Benedict Evans. Evans is a brilliant market strategist and helps you think more sharply about industry evolutions. He is clearly a superpower for the VC firm of Andressen Horowitz as one of their general partners. His weekly newsletter is a must-read, in my opinion.

I listen to a lot of podcasts while exercising, and on the way to and from work as we resume doing so. I used to think that the single best podcast for entrepreneurs was Reid Hoffman's *Masters of Scale.* Not long ago on *Masters of Scale,* Reid interviewed Barry Diller in a two-part series on Infinite Learners, which is an awesome listen and, of course, something you can find on the Digital Companion.

Today, I think the crown for best podcast for entrepreneurs goes to Mike Maples, Jr. for *Starting Greatness*. It is even more practical and actionable than Reid's. Also, there are links on my Digital Companion to a lot of great content on Kara Swisher's *Recode Decode*, such as an *amazing* interview with Scott Galloway, serial entrepreneur and author of the book *The Four: The Hidden DNA of Amazon, Apple, Facebook, and Google*. Galloway is a brilliant market strategist who predicted that Amazon would buy Whole Foods given the overlap between Amazon Prime customers and Whole Foods shoppers. That catapulted him to tech-Nostradamus-like fame, and then Swisher tapped him to start a podcast together named *Pivot*, which is also terrific. Another podcast that I love, which is not tech, is Malcolm Gladwell's *Revisionist History*. All six seasons are just exceptional, and I look forward to listening to them each summer.

Earlier in this book, I mentioned my good fortune to be chosen for a year-long Henry Crown Fellowship for mid-career entrepreneurs run by the Aspen Institute. This is a two-year program of periodic seminars and projects designed to develop community-spirited leaders. Along with the other twenty-plus fellows, I read a lot of material curated for us by the Institute. This included Aristotle, Mahatma Gandhi, Rev. Martin Luther King Jr, Plato, Leo Tolstoy, and many others. The Henry Crown Fellowship for me was like a second MBA — but in a more profound way. I don't say that lightly because my MBA from the Wharton School deeply shaped my growth. But the fellowship gave me new and broader insight and understanding. The ancient philosophers Aristotle and Plato ground you in the essentials of human behavior, which have not changed very much — though we've made progress in our cultural values on such issues as equal rights for women and people of color. Gandhi and Rev. King give you the confidence and know-how from their creation of movements, and entrepreneurship is in many ways about creating movements, changing the world as I wrote in the opening chapter. They certainly imbue you with awareness of how easy you have it compared to their circumstances. This is not to minimize how difficult it is to create a movement of any kind, whether it changes a nation or an industry. Their historical examples, and those of so many other truly great leaders who changed the course of history, like author and abolitionist Frederick Douglass, are important sources of wisdom and inspiration to help build your confidence as you face the natural resistance you will to any kind of change.

Second, I engage myself in select conferences, such as TED, which I call the world's best classroom with the world's best students, and the Aspen Action Forum, where fellows from the Aspen Institute, including Henry Crown Fellows, gather every year. Both of these ignite and further my continued learning. I've gotten value as well from Techonomy, the annual thought leadership conference in New York. In 2016 the founder David Kirkpatrick, who authored *The Facebook Effect* with Mark Zuckerberg, interviewed his co-author right after the presidential election, an experience I'll never forget. Zuckerberg has come a long way since then on his understanding of the issues of misinformation and I hope he progresses further. I go to a few off-the-record events every year, which is frustrating because I can't talk about them here but those are the rules. I've attended Goldman Sachs' annual Technology and Internet Conference in San Francisco. I also usually attend the annual policy conference of the American Israel Public Affairs Committee. I learn a lot about America, Israel, and Washington at AIPAC and we are proud supporters of the organization at Hurt Family Investments.

Third, I seek out mentors. Lots of them. We have over 30 Advisory Board members at data.world, and I had a similar number of advisors at Bazaarvoice. I have an incredible mentor in Jason Pressman from Shasta Ventures, who led our first round of funding and serves on our Board of Directors (I've known Jason for 18 years and he is just exceptional). Jason sparks and stirs my thinking. Gary Hoover, the founder of what became the business information service D&B Hoovers, is a great mentor. His long email threads, with lots of business-focused analysis, provoke my thinking. He is a very independently-minded libertarian thinker. If you haven't read Gary's book *The Lifetime Learner's Guide to Reading and Learning* you are missing out. A C-Span interview with Gary is on the Digital Companion. Gary's book will systematically take you through this process so you too become a lifelong learner. Whole Foods Co-founder John Mackey is a guide too. I've been very fortunate to be mentored by him over the years. His commitment to veganism has impacted my diet and several other things and it was an honor to serve alongside him on the Conscious Capitalism Board. But my number one mentor is my wife, Debra. I'm serious. When we got married I had $1,000 to my name and she had $2,000. Twenty-six amazing years of marriage later, I can't count how many times my best friend has helped me.

Fourth, I do a lot of reflecting. Over the years, I've evolved from my introverted youth to become much more extroverted and I ruminate on things a lot. This helps reinforce my learning. I've learned over the years not to beat myself up — just to reflect and realize I'm human and constantly evolving. Going to India to study the Hindu philosophy of Vedanta under Swamiji Parthasarathy was an *incredible* experience that helped me. The philosophy of Vedanta enabled me to gain control of my mind, which is where the secret to happiness resides. And another book I will recommend is Parthasarathy's *Governing Business and Relationships*. Another friend and mentor who has helped me with this is Kirk Dando, my CEO coach. We do a trip together every year to reflect together on our hikes. More resources on Vedanta, Parthasarathy, and Dando are, again, on the Digital Companion site.

Fifth, I actively try to shake myself up and question what I think I know. That's why I went to India to study Vedanta in the first place. That's why I've had a few dinners with Bruce Sterling, the former Austinite, and absolutely brilliant science fiction author. I follow his very edgy *State of the World* interview on the

*WELL* every year with our local, brilliant Jon Lebkowsky. The WELL, an acronym for the "Whole Earth 'Lectronic Link," is the world's oldest continuously operating virtual community and it was founded by the thinker Stewart Brand whom I write about in *Chapter 6, The Fallacy of Risk.* I also spend a lot of time reading on *Quora* about topics that you would probably never guess that I'm interested in.

And back to podcasts for a moment, I occasionally listen to *Waking Up* by Sam Harris, which was recommended to me by Rabbi David Wolpe of Los Angeles, named the most influential rabbi in America by *Newsweek* magazine. It is different. Harris is a brilliant, independent thinker. I find that listening to him stokes my individualistic gene further. Thinking independently, and rationally, is incredibly important as an entrepreneur. You have to actively work on not riding the inevitable emotional highs and lows of entrepreneurship, and Harris is about as emotionally grounded as one can get, a trait honed by years of meditation. I personally do not meditate but I do other things to stay grounded, such as going on long walks/hikes and vacations to think or read a great book, which captures the wisdom of the ages, in a very slow and deliberate manner.

These are just some of I escape the realm of Lewis Caroll's "Red Queen" and step outside the dynamics of Hariri's global "algorithm" to look back upon and reflect upon it. I realize, of course, that I have the good fortune and opportunity to attend invitation-only conferences, drop in on TED conferences and have lunch with well-known authors, thinkers, business leaders, and academics. So it's important to underscore here a point I sought to make in my opening chapter. These are resources that everyone can access. The entry that I'm privileged to enjoy is great, of course, but its relevance is diminishing by the day as everyone increasingly has access to the finest of minds and ideas. You might say that the tools wrought by the "algorithm" are exactly what allows us to understand it at a higher level of awareness. There is no innovation you cannot explore online, no author or thinker you cannot follow or even interact with on Zoom. Virtually all the knowledge in the world's universities is now as close as your laptop or even your phone.

Yes, this new world of exploding knowledge can be bewildering at times, even exhausting. If we let it. Or, we can use this new reality as history's greatest opportunity and we can truly live the *Always Be Learning* life. My parting thought here is a plea that you actively seek knowledge and wisdom.

> *"The saddest aspect of life right now is that science gathers knowledge faster than society gathers wisdom."*
>
> **— ISAAC ASIMOV**

# CHAPTER 5
## BOOTSTRAP OR VC?

Two roads diverged in a yellow wood,
And sorry I could not travel both
And be one traveler, long I stood
And looked down one as far as I could
To where it bent in the undergrowth;

Then took the other, as just as fair,
And having perhaps the better claim,
Because it was grassy and wanted wear;
Though as for that the passing there
Had worn them really about the same,

And both that morning equally lay
In leaves no step had trodden black.
Oh, I kept the first for another day!
Yet knowing how way leads on to way,
I doubted if I should ever come back.

I shall be telling this with a sigh
Somewhere ages and ages hence:

Two roads diverged in a wood, and I—
I took the one less traveled by,
And that has made all the difference.

## — ROBERT FROST, "THE ROAD LESS TRAVELED"

Any conversation on the virtues of bootstrapping your way to success as an entrepreneur versus growing to scale with the investment of venture capital dollars usually boils down to one question: "Do you want to be rich, or do you want to be king?", as business scholar Noam Wasserman once framed it so well.

It's a very good question. It's also the frame for the central paradox of entrepreneurial decision-making.

It's a paradox because in my experience of mentoring entrepreneurs at the start of their journey, the answer is usually, "Well, both!" At which point, I'm always tempted to invoke another paradox, that of "Buridan's mule," posed by the 14th-century philosopher Jean Buridan. In his hypothetical paradox, Buridan imagined a hungry mule placed at an equal distance between an appealing stack of oats and an equally desirable stack of hay.

You've probably heard a version of the story and already beat me to the punch line: Buridan's indecisive mule starved to death trying to make up his mind. This, I'm sad to say, is the fate of many a would-be entrepreneur who have not decisively come down on one side of the question or the other.

Not that it's impossible for an entrepreneur to have both their oats *and* hay. Mark Zuckerberg did. Elon Musk enjoys the two. Peter Thiel and Jeff Bezos are further examples of the extraordinarily rich who are also "kings" of their realm... but they are also major outliers. Their storied success should not distort your vision. One example of the role of fate's capricious hand is Zuckerberg's 2006 rejection of a $1 billion offer from Yahoo's then-CEO Terry Semel. There are several versions of the story, but the prevailing one is that Semel's team wanted him to return to the bargaining table with a sweetened offer of $1.1 billion. But Semel, in a fit of pique, refused. Later, it was revealed that Facebook's investors and board were prepared to force Zuckerberg to sell if Semel had returned with that price. How different history might have been if that'd happened? Semel resigned from Yahoo! a year later and now serves on the board of the Los Angeles County Museum of Art. Facebook's valuation, meanwhile, hit $1 trillion in May of 2021, and Zuckerberg retains full control of his company.

I'm dwelling on this because I want you to keep in mind that in the constellation of entrepreneurs, the odds of superstardom as defined by these tech titans are akin to those in Hollywood where 20,000 aspiring actors arrive each year, with only two or three making the proverbial breakthrough. In fact, at any given moment there are only perhaps 10 to 15 "A-list" actors living the dream of Tinseltown; if you think about it, you can probably name them. The rest are waiting on the proverbial tables or selling the proverbial cars. To build on this analogy, the dichotomy in the VC realm breaks down into two empirical views to think about it as an entrepreneur.

Before I get to those two things, I have to flag some resources here. Because the data and research on this numerically-friendly topic can be overwhelming. Those of you with scuba gear handy, however, will find three portals ready for you to dive deep off of the Digital Companion. One is *Pitchbook*, the most user-friendly source for commercial and financial data in the United States. A full subscription with three seats will set you back $25,000. But there's a great deal for free at the site. Second is the Global Entrepreneur Monitor, (GEM) which is an academic consortium run since 1999 by Babson College in Wellesley College in Massachusetts and the London Business School. If your geek bonafides include a passion for math, you'll swim in their reports.

Three is the training portal, known as VC Lab, that's focused on ethical and transparent investing. It's a cool project created by Founder Institute's Adeo Ressi. So back to the two views of the proper arc of startup life and I'll boil the basic math down.

In the first view, the grand narrative is from above, the venture-backed economy is *the* source of dynamism in America and the global economy. In 2021, American venture capitalists, or VCs, almost doubled their investment over the prior year, according to Pitchbook. The headline-grabbing numbers reveal that venture-backed companies raised $329.9 billion in 2021, nearly double the previous record of $166.6 billion raised in 2020. A gem from GEM, among countless more penetrating insights, is the finding that optimism is bounding back globally after the first difficult year of the pandemic. Many new starters see new business opportunities improving as a result of the waning pandemic, according to GEM. Supporting this view, the entrepreneurial economy was set to soar in 2022 concludes the annual report of Intuit. Its latest New Business Insights report predicted 17 million new small businesses will be formed in 2022, a third consecutive record year for entrepreneurship.

One chief exponent of this view that times are better than ever for the VC ecosystem is the brilliant Sebastian Mallaby, author of the marvelous new book *The Power Law — Venture Capital and the Making of the New Future.* Venture capital is fast becoming "an enduring pillar of national power" in America, argues Mallaby in the riveting 2022 book, and I share his enthusiasm. At data.world, for example, we finished 2021 with $82.3 million of funding and began 2022 with our largest fundraising to date in Goldman Sachs leading our $50 million growth round.

The second view, the parable of caution that is backed by a different dataset, is that behind those alluring numbers are some Hollywood-like figures that bear attention — particularly if you are pining for oats *and* hay. In the work the GEM research consortium produced in 2021, a key finding was that 137,000 startups are launched worldwide every day. It's an impressive number, but sobering when you consider that about 120,000 are shut down every day. In the smaller universe of true startups in the United States, not just a spinoff or a new business license, the estimate is that 250,000 are created annually.

And of those, just 4,000 will be technology startups, the sector where most — but by no means all — VC activity takes place, reports *TechCrunch*. The five-year survival rate for all new businesses in the U.S. is just 20 percent; for tech startups, it is half that. So, each year 20,000 would-be stars arrive in Hollywood; the output is three megastars. Each year 4,000 would-be Tech Titans launch themselves into the national venture ecosystem. You do the co-relational math.

But that's where my analogy with Hollywood ends.

The good news is that despite the daunting odds, your options are far richer, and the entrepreneur's prospects are hardly a gamble on rock stardom versus presentation of the evening specials. But to truly understand your odds and options, you must look into your soul and answer this question — rich or king? — honestly, forthrightly, and most importantly, early.

While theories, opinions, academic papers, and books abound on the reasons for these dynamics of success or failure, my own view is that the most important factor of all is the founders who do not confront this fundamental question. I'm not alone in this perspective.

"Four out of five entrepreneurs, my research shows, are forced to step down from the CEO's post. Most are shocked when investors insist that they relinquish control, and they're pushed out of office in ways they don't like and well before they want to abdicate," wrote Wasserman in his seminal essay, *The Founders' Dilemma*, which is linked in a package of his work on the Digital Companion. "In fact, how founders tackle their first leadership transition often makes or breaks young enterprises."

Since I've already brought up Hollywood, I'll expand on

Wasserman's insight, and liken this actual reality to the famous "red pill" in the 1999 film, *The Matrix*. If you recall the scene, the rebel leader, Morpheus, offers the main character, Neo, the choice of a red pill or a blue pill. The blue bill represents comfort, without want, and without fear. In short, a comfortable if machine-generated dream world where all can stay in their artificial reality, the only one they've ever known, generated by the Matrix. The red pill, on the other hand, offers entry into the "truth of reality." As Morpheus describes it: "You take the blue pill...the story ends, you wake up in your bed and believe whatever you want to believe. You take the red pill...you stay in Wonderland, and I show you how deep the rabbit hole goes."

I'm coming to the choice of the pill. But first, a quick review of the decision points that you're probably familiar with. The "classic" journey begins with a bootstrap. The entrepreneur launches in their garage on the back of savings, a credit card, or a gift from parents, other family members, or friends. You're "king" with 100 percent ownership of your business. If you want to take off that day, there is no one watching over you. You are 100 percent empowered to do whatever you want with your life and business. Perhaps there's an angel investor involved, or there's a group of investors in a so-called "seed round," in which case you're out a 5-20 percent share depending on terms and valuations. With that help, you can build out your initial team and maybe get your product moving into the marketplace, depending on how complex it will be to build and market. And you're still very much in charge. A year or so later, you realize you can't expand without more capital. Enter the first VC and the "Series Seed" or "Series A" round, depending on how far along you are. Many entrepreneurs can hang on to 50 percent or more through this round, particularly if there's the beginning of a track record as defined by annually recurring revenue, or ARR, and happy, highly referenced customers. Maybe.

But the heat is on in many ways, and you're expected to grow faster than ever before. And, with a bit of luck, let's say you do. Soon you've got a valuation of $10 million or more, and you could even be profitable, even if still modestly so if you really wanted to. But you're ready to take your baby to the next level. Enter the negotiation called "Series B," and, by conventional logic, this is where we move our prototypical entrepreneur on to the stage where they must confront the "founder's dilemma" and ponder surrender of the crown, and fealty to a new demanding board of directors with clout. You may still get to drive a Tesla. In fact, odds are you will if you keep on growing fast from stage to stage. But you're about to trade it for your throne. Because sooner rather than later, your investors will be demanding the proverbial "exit" via IPO, merger, or acquisition with, in VC-speak, a 10X or higher ROI on their investment. And you're driving the even better, more expensive Tesla (how about the Plaid) on to your next gig. With the company you birthed and nurtured fading in your rearview mirror. Agonizing.

That's the decision tree you face. Right? Wrong! Stop. Cut. Roll back the tape to the safe house where Trinity took Neo to meet Morpheus.

In fact, you made the decision back far closer to that early scene in my anecdote. You chose the red pill when you took that *first* outside investment. You just weren't really aware you were doing so. And the purpose of this chapter is really to implore you to nurture that awareness of what the question in the title, *Bootstrap or VC?* is all about. Said differently, you need to make that choice between Buridan's oats and hay at the outset of your journey. And there are plenty of good reasons to choose one color pill over the other.

Let me make this personal. My father was a great husband, father, grandfather, brother, inventor, entrepreneur, patent-holder, and natural-born comedian. He had a huge influence on my life, especially on my drive as an entrepreneur. And he chose to be king, over being rich.

My father was an entrepreneur in Austin, where I was born and live now after long stints on both coasts. He blended his passion with his business. He loved to go fishing off the Texas coast, mainly around Port O'Connor on the Gulf of Mexico, and he would spend two or three days almost every week doing that. But he wouldn't just fish — he would innovate. He developed the world's first halogen fishing light. Fish are like insects in that they are attracted to the light. He patented this invention and shipped the product all over the world. Dad became successful as a result. Among some of his other innovations:

- The first synthetic food for monarch butterfly breeding. This earned him accolades in a worldwide monarch fan club.
- The largest hand-made, hand-ground telescope. The mirror has to be accurate to one-millionth of an inch. Dad hand-ground the mirror for eight hours per day, using lasers to measure precision, for more than a year. It was tremendously better than any telescope that most people could afford to buy.
- A fiberglass, street-legal race car. At over 500 horsepower and weighing 2,000 pounds with an almost perfect 50/50 distribution of weight between the front and rear axles — an innovation first pioneered by BMW — that made dad's car a breathtaking driving experience.
- The first robotic fishing boat. This was an ongoing project when he passed in his sleep from a heart attack, and he had been working on it for over three years. You controlled it using a color digital interface from the shoreline. Because of its silence, this helped him catch the older fish, those smart enough to avoid the sound of a motorboat. As a result, Dad caught fish that he would weigh and record so that they would go down

in the Texas record books. But then he would unhook them and return them to the lake, letting them continue to live.  He wasn't looking for glory.

I could of course go on about my father's innovation: his hand-made aquariums, huge kites, remote-controlled miniature race cars, koi ponds, and so much more. But the point here is that he was someone who chose my metaphorical blue pill — though his outcome was hardly a machine-generated reality. But it was predictable. He knew what he valued in life, which he lived as a king, even if he never got rich. When I was 10, Walmart approached my father, asking to carry his products in all of their stores nationwide. Dad turned them down. I remember intensely pushing my father to do the deal. Dad declined. He did not want to ramp up his operation to that level. Potentially, it would have made him extremely wealthy. It also would have complicated his life. And he knew he was happy already. I remember him looking me in the eye and saying, "Son, one day you may realize the value of keeping life simple... or you may not."

Of course, I do realize the value of the choices he made. And one could not find a more exemplary and honorable entrepreneur's journey, designed within the context of the life that he chose to live. There's nothing wrong with this choice, to become and remain what I've called a "stage one" entrepreneur. This is the route of many small retailers, consultants, service providers, and all manner of sole proprietorships. What binds them all, however, is an iron law of growth. Stage one entrepreneurs, by definition, fund growth and expansion from ongoing profits. Consequently, by definition, stage one entrepreneurs can never move faster than emerging competitors to dominate a sector, swing for the proverbial fences, or dent the universe with cutting-edge innovation. If you believe small is beautiful, take the blue pill.

My choice has been vastly different from that of my father. I took the red pill. I use that vivid metaphor because it expresses the one-way nature of the decision. I've made this case many times before, over coffee with students, in lectures to university and trade groups, and fairly recently before Bootstrap Austin, an organization founded by my good friend Bijoy Goswami, a philosopher of entrepreneurship who has brought together and inspired so many leaders throughout Austin. It was through Bijoy's organization that I met so many future colleagues, including Eric Simone and Josh Baer, who became early investors in Bazaarvoice. Not only is the red pill choice one-way, a true crossing of the Rubicon, it usually leads to a finite journey that means no matter how much you love and cherish the firm to which you give birth, you're ultimately just a surrogate parent to your "baby." It's a deeply personal choice and I dwell on it so because all too often it's made casually, even inadvertently.

In my case, it was not until my fourth business, founded while I was still at Wharton as discussed in Chapter 1, *The Soul of the Entrepreneur,* that I took the red pill. This was when I created Coremetrics in 1999, initially funded with $2 million in angel backing. Once I made that decision, I realized I would likely never be king like my father but I've certainly gained financial freedom and the different kind of joy that comes from being at the center of the business-wrought innovation that is changing the world.

- With Coremetrics, I was able to raise $64 million, navigate the dom.com bust of 2001, become the No. 1 ranked web analytics firm according to Forrester Research, and ultimately exit with an almost $300 million sale to IBM in 2007.
- With Bazaarvoice, we built a company from inception to IPO on around $12 million of capital use (out of the $24 million we raised) in seven years, creating over a thousand jobs and impacting clients all over the

world. We really started the global social commerce movement and changed the face of commerce forever.

- The Bazaarvoice experience also illustrates other tools at your disposal once you've taken the red pill, including selling equity in smaller tranches before the IPO stage. I did so on four occasions at Bazaarvoice. Enlightened investors understand and appreciate that this is in their interest and it can strengthen your hand in the market when you reach that IPO moment. In fact, doing so enabled me in 2008 to turn down a $250 million bid from a brand name tech titan and then exit with a $1 billion IPO four years later.

- And now with data.world, I'm on my most ambitious and exciting journey yet, having raised over $132.3 million to date to build the world's most meaningful, collaborative, and abundant data resource in the world. So far we've created around 110 jobs but we are just getting started and having a big impact all over the world. We are a proud Certified B Corporation, and public benefit corporation, and every commercial customer we win allows us to live our global mission of providing the most meaningful, collaborative, and abundant data resource in the world - for free if you are working in the open and benefiting humanity in the process. You can reach our annual public benefit corporation report on the Digital Companion.

For me, this is truly the "arena" about which I wrote in the very first chapter. In this arena, it almost always requires capital to build a complex, difficult-to-copy solution. It isn't the early days of technology and venture capital anymore.

The story of venture capital really begins with Georges Doriot, who immigrated to the United States in 1920 and whose many achievements included becoming a professor and assistant dean at the Harvard Business School. In 1957, he put a new ball into play in the capitalist game, inventing the VC model with what is now regarded as the first VC vehicle: his company American Research & Development, or ARD. Through ARD, Doriot invested $70,000 (for a 70 percent stake) that enabled the launch of mini-computer maker Digital Equipment Corp (DEC). Some 11 years later he was to net around a 571,400 percent return on that $70K, earning as much as $400 million from DEC's IPO. I also must mention that Doriot backed the launch here in Texas of future President George H.W. Bush's first company, Zapata Offshore, a maker of oil rigs.

But in the broader sense, VCs didn't meaningfully exist prior to the 1970s, and throughout the 1970s and 1980s, it was almost all corporate VC money — by definition largely focused on strategic investment as the first priority and financial return as the second. Now VC capital — by contrast seeking financial return as the first priority — is available in the tens of billions. And if you have a business that is going to be of any significant size, you will almost always need to raise money at some point. If you don't, someone else who is more aggressive will likely launch into your industry with massive amounts of capital and almost always overtake you. You will be left with a niche business, which may be your goal — there is certainly nothing wrong with that. You may be king in your own castle, but you won't be #1 in your realm.

In my view, the hat trick as an entrepreneur is to swing for the fences by launching a huge business idea, get it profitable early, and then get funding to accelerate your growth (if needed, which it almost always will be). Dell (Michael), Facebook (Zuckerberg), Microsoft (Gates and Allen), and a rare few others are examples of this. I personally failed to do that with Coremetrics and I paid dearly for it with dilution, complicated even more with the timing of the dot-com crash. But I don't look at VCs or angel investors as evil — and of course, I now am one at Hurt Family Investments, alongside my wife Debra, having invested in 124 startups directly and 40 VC funds, which allow us to have multiples of that in indirect investments. I'll cover my lessons learned on investing in the *Helping* section of this book.

VCs are the capital enablers for big business ideas. And if your interests are aligned with them, you can both make a ton of money. It is prevalent all over the Valley. Most of the entrepreneurs driving the nice Teslas grew their businesses fast with VC capital, got them public, and sold a vast amount of stock (as I mentioned often even before they went public). As a model, this has taken time to really become broadly accepted here in Austin and in other places outside the Valley. I used to frequently lament Austin's aversion to VCs, and argue that our city's entrepreneurial ecosystem would be better off, economically, with more people swinging for the fences in ways you can only do with help. There's growing evidence this is occurring, and in fact as of mid-2021, the Austin region was No. 9 nationally and No. 21 internationally, ahead of both Tokyo and Toronto, as the destination for VC investment. More recently, startup funding flowed in Austin last year, delivering 387 deals valued at a record-setting $4.9 billion — or 211% growth compared to the previous year — per data from PitchBook.

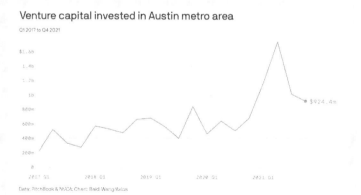

**Venture capital invested in Austin metro area**

Q1 2017 to Q4 2021

Data: PitchBook & NVCA; Chart: Baidi Wang/Axios

One good way to think about this was posed by my friend, VC Neeraj Agrawal of Boston-based Battery Ventures, a firm with a $9 billion portfolio and an early investor in and Board Member of Bazaarvoice. He has described the partnerships between entrepreneurs and VCs as less a "venture" than an "adventure," akin to the relationship between the Sherpas and climbers who scale the heights of Mt. Everest.

"... perhaps my role as a VC is that of an adventure travel guide," Agrawal wrote in an essay linked on the Digital Companion, "someone who's climbed the mountain many times before, who knows both the terrain and the phases of the climb intimately, and can serve as a guide for others brave enough to take up the challenge."

I can't think of a better way to describe the VC/entrepreneur partnership than that. This is how the world is being remade and I believe the solutions to so many of the world's problems will emerge from this still-emerging ecosystem of capitalism for the 21st century. Consider the remarkable example of the German startup BioNTech, founded with venture backing only in 2008. That young David partnered with the 172-year-old Goliath of Pfizer at the outset of the pandemic and this David-Goliath team created in less than a year the first, and by far most widely deployed, COVID-19 vaccine that has certainly saved millions of lives.

At the end of the day, you have to balance what is best for you personally with what is best for the business. Depending on how competitive and capital intensive your market is, the best thing you can do is be open to all options to fuel growth. Whether to take the blue or red pill, again, all depends on your personal ambition. I hope I've convinced you here that between this stark choice of "rich vs. king" the role of the VC-backed CEO is more nuanced, and might be characterized as a "viceroy." A viceroy may not be king, but they are still a ruling sovereign with vast responsibilities and a lot of authority. To frown on others that raise money and think they are idiots for doing so is a religious argument, not a rational business argument. And the world needs rational, focused, and innovative business pioneers as never before.

So back again to the metaphor of that film, *The Matrix*, with this exchange:

*TRINITY: (to NEO) No one has ever done anything like this.*
*NEO: That's why it's going to work.*

# CHAPTER 6
## THE FALLACY OF RISK IN ENTREPRENEURSHIP

*"Take calculated risks. This is quite different than being rash."*

## — GEN. GEORGE PATTON

To understand the dynamics and reality of the entrepreneur's risk, a good place to start is the ultimate study of success and failure. This is Charles Darwin's theory of evolution first published in 1859. You've certainly heard some version of this a million times: the virtue of competition is that it weeds out the laggards. The "survival of the fittest" is what business is all about; the iron laws of nature reward the strong over the weak.

Sound familiar? From boardrooms to locker rooms, we've all heard some version of this classic argument analogizing Darwin's insight to the dynamics of software markets, political campaigns, or the upcoming final game of the World Series. There's just one problem. This pervasive understanding of Darwin is wrong. Much like our understanding of the entrepreneur as a risk-taker, jumping off cliffs and building wings on the way down to fly.

So, let me try and explain this perhaps odd connection between the fallacies in the popular understanding of what

Darwin learned from his trip that produced his treatise, *The Voyage of The Beagle,* and the deeply rooted myths about risk and entrepreneurship.

In recent years, many scientists have lamented the pervasiveness of "bad Darwinism." But the best argument I've heard of why this is wrong came from Stewart Brand, the famous counter-culture thinker who founded the *Whole Earth Catalog* in the late 1960s, the Global Business Network scenario planning group in the 1980s, and most recently published his sixth book: *Whole Earth Discipline: An Ecopragmatist Manifesto.*

Brand, who I had the chance to meet once at a TED conference, has eloquently argued that we've radically misunderstood and misconstrued Darwin. It's not the best competitor who wins out in the evolutionary sweepstakes. Rather, it's the species most adept at *avoiding* competition, the one who masters *specialization*, who finds a *niche* with the fewest rivals within a given ecosystem. Sure, when all else fails, competition in nature is inevitable. Just as it is in business. But a better way to think about evolution is that it is about *the survival of the best specialist.* After all, the world's some 5,000 species of lizard didn't evolve from the earliest reptiles by seeking out snakes and hawks to challenge, but by adapting to habitats not easily accessible to their predators. And drop in on a conversation with Brand and economist and cultural critic Tyler Cowen that you'll find on the Digital Companion.

Given the more entrepreneurs that we back as angel investors, and the more I practice entrepreneurship myself, the more Brand's re-reading of Darwin appeals to me. It's a pretty good way to think about risk in the business ecosystem as well. For the myth of the intrepid, risk-taking entrepreneur placing all his or her bets on a spin of the wheel is an idea that just needs to be excised from the world. Yes, of course, entrepreneurs *are* brave as I wrote about in Chapter 1, *The Soul of the Entrepreneur.* But that doesn't mean they don't work *really* hard to mitigate risk, including before they even start their new business.

In other words, successful entrepreneurship is not about risk-taking but risk mitigation. Or, to paraphrase a famous general, about risk calculation. Risks are what you take after you have examined the hazards and uncertainties through the eyes of potential customers, studied them with industry experts, explored them with potential partners, and validated your startup idea with your own judgment and analysis of market timing.

A related bit of heresy comes from entrepreneur Peter Thiel, the founder of both PayPal and Palantir and an initial investor in Facebook, who frames the argument as, "Competition is for losers." Culturally, socially, and even psychologically, he argues in his book *Zero to One*, many if not most new entrepreneurs see competition as validation — if others are doing it, it must be right. And fierce competition, he readily concedes, will make you better in a narrow slice of endeavor. But it certainly will not make you financially successful. Instead, he counsels in a great lecture included on the Digital Companion, "You always want to aim for monopoly and you always want to avoid competition."

And equally important, as business scholar Clayton M. Christensen so magnificently describes in his seminal book *The Innovator's Dilemma,* is an understanding of the distinctions between "sustaining innovation," practiced by established companies, vs. the "disruptive innovation" of new startups. The varying stages of innovation involve different elements of risk and mastery of the nuance is critical, as I explain below. A detailed review is linked on the Digital Companion, which yields a full understanding of innovation as the essential value that entrepreneurs create. Christensen makes the case that it is by innovation that entrepreneurs change the world and carry humanity forward. So let's truly understand just what innovation is and how risk-taking is just one of many elements.

Lastly, I encourage attention to the book I've mentioned

earlier, *The Power Law — Venture Capital and the Making of the New Future,* by Sebastian Mallaby. You'll find a review on the Digital Companion but he describes a key metric of risk — the so-called "Perkins Law," named for Tom Perkins co-founder of the VC firm, Kleiner-Perkins: "Market risk is inversely proportional to technical risk." In other words, if you solve a truly difficult technical problem you will face minimal competition.

So against that backdrop, I want to get to how I've applied some of these principles to my businesses (and frankly sometimes failed to apply them). But first, I need to summarize these foundational concepts because in my view Christensen — without specifically saying so — really builds on Brand's framework of understanding with his book. I encourage you to pick it up next after you've finished this one. In fact, Steve Jobs famously described *The Innovator's Dilemma* as the only business book worth reading.

For if Brand focuses on our misunderstanding of how species operate within a specific ecosystem, Christensen's refinement of this is how entrepreneurs misunderstand what he calls the "value network," the system of inputs, suppliers, production cycles, and, of course, customers. In my analogy here, innovation in the "value network" is the equivalent of evolution in the ecosystem. And value networks differ in the three stages of entrepreneurship we discussed in Chapter 3, *Advice For The Middle-Aged Entrepreneur.* This pernicious myth of the swashbuckling risk-taker feeds in part on the lack of understanding that there are two very different kinds of broad innovation.

"Sustaining innovation" is that which enables an existing, successful, well-run company to iterate improvements that keep its margins high and investors happy. This would be like a "Stage 3" business in my typology. Think Gillette and the last razor you bought among the 4,000 iterations since the company's founding in 1901. "Disruptive innovations," however, are those that break the cycle of incrementalism and introduce something brand new, displacing incumbents and bringing new value and creativity. This is the innovation in my "Stage 2" description of businesses, or even in some cases, "Stage 1." My favorite example in this latter category is Netflix, which at Stage 2 upended the $6 billion, 8,000 store Blockbuster Video that was well into Stage 3. Now in mid-2022, Netflix is itself a Stage 3 company, and the new headwinds the company faces reflect the entry of newer and more nimble streaming rivals. I include some much more detailed analysis on this dimension of risk from Vox's *Recode* podcast and my blog on the Digital Companion.

The "innovator's dilemma" is the insight that an organization may — and in fact, must — excel at sustaining innovation as it matures. But maturity, the demands of customers, the challenge of continued revenue growth, and the resulting imperatives and corporate culture in the now-mature firm, *lock* the organization into one value network. This success, in turn, all but eliminates its ability to break into the new value network demanding the products created by disruptive innovation. It would have been easy in theory for Blockbuster to break into streaming with the advent of the Internet, but its value network, and all the corporate systems contoured around it, made this impossible. And, as we know, Netflix founders Reed Hastings and Marc Randolph ate the lunch of Blockbuster CEO John Antioco. But as noted above, Christensen's cycle continues.

I realize I'm belaboring risk in the abstract here. But I need to emphasize Brand's and Christensen's insights because they frame the concrete elements of risks and threats that I'm coming to, and they help explain my own bias on the subject. I'm a very risk-averse entrepreneur. This comes as a result of bootstrapping my first three businesses and almost failing on my fourth, Coremetrics.

Abstractly, my brush with disaster at Coremetrics was in part because I had not really internalized these distinctions about the intricacies of risk and innovation. But more concretely, almost failing at Coremetrics was due to market timing; I was too early, I had failed to foresee the dot-com bust, and I was frankly overcapitalized. We were just trying to do too much, too fast. There is a natural digestion period and capability zone for any company at any point in time. Your job as an entrepreneur is to push the limits of that, but I simply pushed way too far. I pushed to the point where I jeopardized the *core* of Coremetrics. Our foundational offering was a Web analytics product called "eLuminate" that gave online businesses deep insights into their customers' behavior while shopping within their digital storefronts. But eLuminate was melting down and therefore making our customers very unhappy. Which meant we were perilously close to failing before Coremetrics had a chance to take off, with a strong, customer-loved core product.

In addition to this experience, my risk aversion I alluded to above also comes from the fact I'm a product of bootstrapped entrepreneurs — my parents, who took minimal risk. As I wrote about my father in my tribute to him, which is online on this book's Digital Companion, he turned down Walmart when I was 10 years old and the retail giant wanted to sell his product in all of its stores nationwide. He was already happy with his life and he didn't want to take on the complexity and risk. But even though my parents took little risk, I witnessed them go through the inevitable ups and downs in business. And their support was critical when I was going through my own humbling experience of earning my living through entrepreneurship.

Living this harsh lesson at Coremetrics, with six projects going at once in our first year of business, was overly ambitious, to say the least. This drove nearly everyone in the company crazy and, as mentioned, our foundational product — the retail-focused Web analytics that we eventually became well known for — was failing. I realized that nothing would matter if we didn't get Coremetrics fixed. And fixed fast. I had co-located Coremetrics in San Francisco and Austin, where we had the 60-member R&D team based. I was working out of our San Francisco office but dropped everything to fly to Austin to spend the month with our team there, where I launched the "Stand & Deliver" project. We would stand and deliver for our customers, investors, families, and ourselves. We immediately killed all extraneous projects, which in retrospect were essentially the kind of "sustaining innovations" that Christensen describes. They might have been fine at a later stage, but I had allowed them to overshadow the "disruptive innovation" of eLuminate.

Ultimately, we did deliver for our customers, investors, families, and ourselves by shoring up the core of Coremetrics. Most of the extraneous projects never again saw the light of day, which in hindsight I've regretted when we reached the later stages of our business. For example, I wish that we had gone back into building a personalization engine to deliver individually targeted merchandising discounts based on the data Coremetrics was collecting. Indeed, personalization became a big opportunity for the industry overall. But I digress - the point is I'm convinced that, at that early stage of our business, if I hadn't decided to "Stand & Deliver" and focus, Coremetrics would have failed in 2001 and almost no one reading this chapter would have ever heard of the company.

Andy Dunn, the Co-founder, and CEO of Bonobos wrote a great piece in Pando Daily (featured on the Digital Companion) that describes the nature of the overcapitalization that can erode the focus of a business, which is what happened to us. He writes in part:

> "Prior to a lobotomy I just underwent which removed shiny new object syndrome (SNOS) from my brain, I was both an asset and a threat to my own company. The company is trying to do one thing, and I would come up with another. I can't tell you how dangerous this is. If the founder doesn't know what the company is doing, the company won't either.

"In some cases the shiny new object you come up with saves the company. In other cases, it sinks it. If it's the former, they will call it a pivot and hail you as brilliant. If it ends up being a distraction or taking the company off-course, they will call you delusional and un-focussed."

Needless to say, by the time I got to my fifth business, Bazaarvoice, I had learned a great deal from this do-or-die moment. The organization has gone on to become a global success story as a mostly customer-funded and very capital-efficient business, especially leading up to our IPO.

Another deep thinker on these topics who I recommend is the author Malcolm Gladwell. He is one of my favorite writers, and his famous book, *The Tipping Point,* was a source of early inspiration for us at Bazaarvoice. His book, *Outliers,* is a critical study of the ingredients of success, and his essay in the New Yorker, entitled *The Sure Thing,* further illuminates this fallacy of risk. Again, there's a link to it on the Digital Companion and I highly recommend it.

Gladwell notes a long list of the reasons entrepreneurs fail: from trying to sell to customers already well served by competitors, to misunderstanding financial controls, to underemphasis on marketing. Summarizing the work of other experts, he makes the point that taking over an existing business is often a better bet than starting from scratch. This is an important consideration, though I started both Bazaarvoice and Coremetrics from scratch, and Debra and I have also angel-backed companies over the past ten years that have started from scratch. In my view, the key is knowing the market. In the world with which I'm most familiar, SaaS (Software as a Service) businesses, if you know the market — and you make sure that clients will pay for your solution (ideally selling it before actually building it) — you are not taking much risk. SaaS businesses are like an annuity that you earn through both great products and services. In SaaS, you should be able to both pre-sell and collect a good portion of cash up-front from your clients.

"The failures violate all kinds of established principles of new-business formation," Gladwell writes.... "But a good many of these risks reflect a lack of preparation or foresight."

Or as Christensen puts it: "Managers who don't bet the farm on their first idea, who leave room to try, fail, learn quickly, and try again, can succeed at developing the understanding of customers, markets, and technology needed to commercialize disruptive innovations."

Which is the essence of risk mitigation. No one has articulated this better than Alex Honnold, who is not an entrepreneur but a rock climber. Honnold is best known for his free solo ascents of big walls, in particular his free-soloing of El Capitan, in Yosemite National Park in 2017. On the Digital Companion, you'll find a brief talk he gave at TED in which he describes his years of getting ready, a practice run on less challenging Half Dome, his study of the 3,000-foot face of El Capitan, rehearsal climbs with ropes to map the terrain and his rigorous mental preparation before execution.

He describes the point just beyond the riskiest stage of the climb:

> "I knew that I had done it. With 600 feet to go, I felt like the mountain was offering me a victory lap," he said. "I climbed with smooth precision and enjoyed the sounds of the birds swooping around the cliff... I reached the summit after three hours and 56 minutes of glorious climbing. It was the climb that I wanted, and it felt like mastery."

As you scale the face of your own El Capitan, here are some questions to ask yourself every day as you journey toward your mastery:

First, do customers truly love what you do?

If you don't know, ask them — directly. And if you don't have customers yet, ask those who you hope will be. There is no substitute for face-to-face market research. If customers love you, and the market is big enough, you'll be just fine as long as you always remember to serve them well. Just keep in mind that it's not a laundry list. Working from their priorities and trying to build *everything* they ask for is a fool's errand. Practice the Pareto principle, sometimes called the 80/20 rule. Build the 20 percent that you and your team believe will solve 80 percent of your customers' problems, or at least deliver 80 percent of the real value.

Second, are you positioned well competitively?

Do you have some technological insight that your competitors don't? Is there something truly novel that will be loved by your industry? As Netflix has proven, it often takes less than you would think — look at how long it took Blockbuster to get religion about the threat that Netflix became with incredible speed and excellence.

Third, how many people have you talked to who are experts/veterans of the industry you are seeking to serve?

Make the list long and keep it growing. I suggest being as transparent as possible about your plans. It is so hard to start a business in the first place, as I discussed at the outset in Chapter 1, *The Soul of the Entrepreneur*. Given this, there is almost no risk in being this transparent. I'm not suggesting that you go to Google and ask someone there to assess your plans for building a better search engine. I am suggesting that you go to people who pay Google and tell them, very transparently, about your plans for a better search engine. See if they would be interested or if it is already game-over due to Google's size. One caution here, though. As with your queries about what to build for customers, don't make the mistake of listening to these experts blindly. Many of them will never take the risk of starting a business of their own. So be careful as they may tell you things that are inaccurate to dissuade you from starting something new. But you'll form a pattern after speaking with enough of them, especially if they are the "cool kids" of their industry. In Chapter 16, *Selling to the "Cool Kids,"* we'll discuss how to understand who the cool kids are and how to reach them.

Fourth and lastly, what are you doing right?

Ask yourself this question every day. This is related to what we discussed in Chapter 2, *The Paralyzing Fear of Getting Started.* Fear happens when you don't have confidence in your actions. A great way to build confidence is to assess that you are doing it right.

Fast forward to today, now six years into my sixth business, and it's fair to ask: Have we gotten it all right at data.world? Of course not. We've made many mistakes along the way, and the heartbeat of what we are doing — with a mission to "build the world's most abundant, collaborative, and meaningful data asset" — is very difficult and uber ambitious. But we are having a blast and doing our best to mitigate our risk and maximize our opportunity. And, most importantly, customers love our enterprise data catalog product and the COVID-19 pandemic only accelerated their adoption of it.

Let me leave you with one more bit of insight from one of my favorite entrepreneurs:

> *"If you're prepared and you know what it takes, it's not a risk. You just have to figure out how to get there. There is always a way to get there."*

> **— MARK CUBAN, ENTREPRENEUR**

# CHAPTER 7
# WHAT'S IN A NAME?

*"The beginning of wisdom is to call things by their proper name."*

## — CONFUCIUS, CHINESE PHILOSOPHER

A company name can be symbolic, like Xerox. It was crafted in a 1958 corporate rebrand from the underlying technology of the firm's product itself, invented two decades earlier. This was "xerography," which fused the Greek words for "dry" and "writing" and the company name was spun from that. Or, it can be fun and spirited, like Steve Jobs' Apple, which he claimed came to him when he was on an all-fruit diet. And the bite out of the logo is a nice touch — a clever nod to Eve's bite out of the apple in the Garden of Eden. A choice of name can be inspirational and aspirational, such as Tesla, honoring the pioneering electrical engineer Nikola Tesla who invented the technology enabling today's remarkable cars. Or, a name can be personal and pragmatic. Think Dell, Ford, Chrysler, or McDonald's, as just a few among the many named for their founders. A name can be serendipitous, such as what happened as Richard Branson was wondering what to call his small record shop in London and an office staffer in the room remarked, "Hey, we're all virgins in business."

What it should never be, however, is hastily considered and casually chosen.

A company name should have longevity and it shouldn't be limiting. Eventually — and hopefully — you'll grow into international markets, other industry verticals, and many product lines. Imagine if Jeff Bezos had named his company to reflect book sales, like one of his early rivals did with CDNow.com. It was pretty clear what they sold but they never expanded beyond that or stayed in business. Bezos may have started with books but they now represent less than 10 percent of Amazon's revenue. A name should explain your mission but also be memorable, with a great story behind it. Tesla qualifies in this category. A name should have resonance. Intel's founders conceived the name as a portmanteau of the words "integrated" and "electronics." But it also evokes business intelligence and insight. Can you imagine how impressive a logo on your laptop would be if it said, "Microchip Inside?" Brevity is overrated as a virtue in naming, but concision is helpful. Imagine if we were still calling Yahoo! by its original name — "Yet Another Hierarchical Officious Oracle."

A stanza in the song, "No New Tale to Tell" by Love and the Rockets, really captures the spirit of naming:

> "My world is your world
> People like to hear their names
> I'm no exception
> Please call my name
> Call my name"

For the full song, visit the Digital Companion.

I put much thought and consideration into naming a new startup. It isn't an easy exercise when done right and it requires a lot of reflection and a healthy dose of inspiration. This was certainly the story with data.world.

As we were conceiving the radically new concept behind the startup we were planning, my co-founders and I wanted a name that would reflect the incredible ambition of our mission. This was, and remains seven years later, "to build the most meaningful, collaborative, and abundant data resource in the world." And we have, with tools that help companies and institutions make sense of the oceans of data that are growing exponentially, comparable in a sense to what Sir Tim Berners-Lee did when we created the World Wide Web to organize the chaos that was the internet in 1990. On the Digital Companion, you can watch Berners-Lee's TED talk on linked data (or, in our nomenclature at data.world, knowledge graphs, which make linked data possible) that helped inspire us.

The naming happened spontaneously while we were brainstorming our foundational idea, which initially was the brainchild of our brilliant Co-founder and Chief Technology Officer, Bryon Jacob. In the midst of the brainstorming, I blurted out, "It's like data.world!" We quickly searched and found out that the ".world" top-level domain had come into existence a few months before. We slept on the name and it eventually stuck with us — data.world was a perfect name. We would not be limited by geography, industry verticals, or expanding into new product lines (data is a truly huge industry with unlimited total available market, or TAM). We lowercased the name because we wanted to reflect the utility nature of our platform — kind of like you "plug into" data.world, which our customers and community members can do as we back the product suite with a full set of interfaces, or APIs, in tech jargon. We also thought lowercasing data.world would "understate" the amazing power of our platform, a bit of humility to frame our boundless ambition. Plus, it is a shout-out to the original protocols of the Internet, like FTP, gopher, and telnet, that all of us as data.world used heavily "back in the day."

The case of how I came up with the name of Bazaarvoice is a very different story and I remember the naming epiphany as if it were yesterday.

Our first-born Rachel was just six months old. We were in Cabo San Lucas in April 2005 using our last few weeks of vacation at Coremetrics before I left to take the plunge to start Bazaarvoice with my Co-founder, Brant Barton. I was reading Chapter 4 of *The Cluetrain Manifesto* and it hit me — big time. That chapter, *Markets Are Conversations,* moved me more than almost anything I had ever read (it *is* a manifesto after all!). Its central thesis builds on the idea that the original form of marketing was the conversations taking place in the ancient bazaar.

"The first markets were filled with people, not abstractions or statistical aggregates," the four authors who collaborated on the book wrote. "They were the places where supply met demand with a firm handshake. Buyers and sellers looked each other in the eye, met, and connected. The first markets were places for exchange, where people came to buy what others had to sell — and to talk."

The ultimate point is that nothing has changed, it's just that conversation — or marketing — now takes place through massive intermediation, at a planetary scale, and at the speed of light. It's a powerful book, all online for free, and of course linked on the Digital Companion. And it was the book's insight that hit me like a thunderbolt: The "voice of the marketplace" — it was perfect!

Bazaarvoice, of course, is an engine that powers and enables unfiltered customer reviews, engagement, and feedback for literally thousands of corporate retailers and brands around the world, in more than 40 international languages. Its user-generated content — including reviews, Q&As, and video — is literally the means for the 21st-century version of that conversation that enabled the trade of a knife or a cotton blanket in the ancient bazaar.

While the book is not specifically about naming conventions, implicitly it is so. For conversations open with introductions, and the name introduces the introduction. Think of the way the waiter begins at a nice restaurant. "Hi, my name is Chad, and I'll be your server today. We have a few specials I'd like to recommend..." The name of your startup is the opener of every transactional "conversation" you will ever have.

So "Bazaarvoice" was it. Just as the name Coremetrics six years earlier had described exactly what the company did, providing the foundation for your most important metrics to run your online business, Bazaarvoice described exactly what we were setting out to do. It was a bit of an irreverent name intentionally, as we realized immediately that it was likely to be confused with *Bizarre*voice. But that was actually a good thing in this case. There was meaning in that — the voice of customers would indeed sound "bizarre" to all of the corporate people that had been locked away in their corporate towers instead of walking their store aisles like Sam Walton, the founder of Walmart, used to do to "keep it real" and then taught his children how to do that in his book , *Made In America*.

Hence Chapter 4 of that irreverent book, that *Manifesto,* gave us a great story behind the name. We were out to change the face of commerce forever, which was growing increasingly digital and mobile, and we needed a radical calling card to do so. The fear of negative reviews had held the industry back from embracing the voices of their most important stakeholders — *their customers.* "You mean that customers can write negative things about the products *we've curated?!*", our earliest customers often said. *Yes,* just like they can *talk* to each other about your products over dinner. Or in the bazaar. Early on, we had some serious battles with household name companies that wanted to censor negative reviews and comments, which of course would have destroyed the credibility and trust of the product. But the name, or the story behind the name, was our primary tool to make the case for unfettered commentary, even when it was critical, or even hyper-critical (i.e., the dreaded one-star review). It seems so obvious now but back then it wasn't — only around three retailers had customer reviews on their websites in 2005. Everything is clear in hindsight.

The name Bazaarvoice, like Coremetrics, also has a practical dimension. It is near the top of the alphabet, which matters if your primary marketing expense will be tradeshows. Why? Because everyone alphabetizes the list. Yep, just like the days with the Yellow Pages where plumbers would name themselves ABC123 Plumbing to be at the top of the Yellow Pages. I picked up this little tidbit out of Guy Kawasaki's brilliant book, *The Art of the Start*.

So I phoned Brant and told him the name and the backstory. He was *in*. We were locked. But not without plenty of sometimes difficult deliberation ahead. We were just hiring our initial Chief Marketing Officer, Sam Decker, and we were still a few months out before our launch. He hated the name. The VC firm Austin Ventures hated the name. The famous angel investor and celebrated marketer, John Hime, who never invested in Bazaarvoice, hated the name. "Just call it Bvoice," John said, "long names are horrible." Sam asked Guy Kawasaki what he thought. I thought, "Wow, this is going to be good - I love Guy." But, sadly, he hated it too. Guy suggested "Pheedbax" as his top pick. He also passed on investing even though he had invested in Coremetrics. Whatever happened to the top of the alphabet, Guy? As CEO, I stuck to my guns and, as my co-founder, Brant did too. And now I just smile when everyone says they love the name.

This is all easy to say now, after establishing a global brand name, a *Wall Street Journal* top-five IPO of 2012, and thousands of clients in over 40 international languages. It is much harder to say when you are two guys, a dog, and a PowerPoint. Sam and I have good laughs about this every now and then. But I've yet to have that laugh with John or Guy. Perhaps this chapter will stoke that fire.

There's a caveat in all of this, of course. Which is that you shouldn't let yourself or your team get so far caught up in the weeds of naming that it distracts you from so much else that is critical to startup success. There's a cottage industry out there of naming consultants, online name generating tools, and endless sources of advice. All of these are fine for brainstorming, and for inspiration perhaps. But it truly comes down to your own search for a name that aligns with your vision and goals. And there are plenty of companies that have done just fine with what I think are graceless names. The Canadian courier, that country's equivalent of UPS, is called "Purolator," for its origins in making oil filters, a business it abandoned decades ago. Purolator had $2.2 billion in revenue in 2020. Or there's IKEA, an acronym contrived out of the initials of the founder, Ingvar Kamprad, and the first letter in the names of the town and province where he was born in Sweden. It seems to me that IKEA might have been better used as part of a login password. But IKEA has been the world's largest furniture retailer since 2008, operates in 30 countries, and has revenues of over $40 billion a year. And as for where you are in the alphabet, just think of YouTube.

But I still believe that these are the exceptions that prove the rule. In all seriousness, my point here is to urge you to think deeply about your company name. As with Coremetrics, it took me weeks to come up with the name Bazaarvoice. And it has served the company well. As compared to PowerReviews, which was one of our primary competitors, the name Bazaarvoice was superior for several reasons. First, it was not just limited to a reviews product. Second, it had a better story behind the name. Third, it was descriptive of what we did. Fourth, it had global appeal. Bazaar is an ancient word, traveling from Persian, through Turkish, and into Italian as "bazarra" in the 16th century. Today it's a globally relevant term. Fifth, as mentioned, it was at the top of the alphabet (at least the English alphabet).

Later on, it led to the b: moniker in our rebranding prior to IPO, so it was also playful. b: bold. b: authentic. b: changing the world. Which is what every entrepreneurial endeavor should be about. I proudly displayed a "b: authentic" sign outside my office, and I hope that is shining through here.

> *"There is all the poetry in the world in a name. It is a poem which the mass of men hear and read. What is poetry in the common sense, but a hearing of such jingling names? I want nothing better than a good word. The name of a thing may easily be more than the thing itself to me."*
>
> **— HENRY DAVID THOREAU, AMERICAN NATURALIST**

# CHAPTER 8
## TO BE STEALTHY OR NOT?

*"If intelligence is our only edge, we must learn to use it better, to shape it, to understand its limitations and deficiencies — to use it as cats use stealth, as katydids use camouflage — to make it the tool of our survival."*

## — CARL SAGAN, COSMOLOGIST AND COMMUNICATOR

During mid-2015, just shy of three years since we had taken Bazaarvoice public, I was on an extended break to catch my breath. To spend more time with my young family. To read broadly. To travel to India to study Vedic wisdom. To see what my parents' life had been like as entrepreneurs focused on lifestyle, in contrast to the very intense work pace that I'd been living since before I even finished grad school. Sadly, both of them had already passed away, and this was a time to honor them. I had also taken time to mentor students as the Entrepreneur-in-Residence at the University of Texas at Austin's McCombs School of Business.

But after this long intellectual and emotional deep breath, and having had the time to reflect on both the state of the world and the technology so rapidly transforming it, I was itching to "get back in the arena." As a bundle of new ideas was surging through my mind, and having recently given a commencement address at University of Texas at Austin on how we are in a new Golden Age for technology, I was very deliberate in my first round of discussions. I texted two good friends who I had worked with at Bazaarvoice and was amazed by Jon Loyens and Matt Laessig. I asked them if they would like to privately brainstorm new business concepts with me — but only if we could think of something even more ambitious and better for the world than Bazaarvoice or Coremetrics. Ultimately, they were to become my co-founders of the radical new data catalog platform and community of open datasets that is data.world.

But the extraordinary technical complexity of what we were setting out to do (to date we've banked 60 patents and counting), the unique logic we were carrying into the venture, and its groundbreaking nature in a global space dictated we enter a kind of wormhole of secrecy until reaching our public launch destination. We wanted some buzz, of course, as we wanted the marketplace to be curious and know that we were "up to something." But we wanted to reveal that "something" on our own terms. So much so, that for much of the first year of building and beta testing our URL was stealthco.world.

This is one way to go about a launch. But it's certainly not the only approach I've used, and it may not be yours. Just how fast and with whom you share your ideas and plans is a tricky set of decisions that many new entrepreneurs make — or don't make — for the wrong reasons.

When you put your idea into the wild too early, there is much that can go wrong, from simply the distractions of the gawkers to the erosion of your intellectual property or worse. When you emerge from behind the curtain too late, rival actors may well have stolen the stage. Which is why the word "stealth" is tricky. With its mystique hinting at a John LeCarre novel or a space-based video game, it invites the notion that it's all or nothing: a sound-deadening "cone of silence" out of the novel *Dune* vs. a jubilant block party for everyone you've ever known.

It is neither.

As I've endeavored to emphasize throughout this book, the language and jargon of the entrepreneurial and startup realms often frame decision-making as a set of binary choices. In fact, at most of the milestones on your journey as an entrepreneur, you'll find few "on-off" buttons. Instead, there are many dimmer switch-like "rheostats" that demand constant attention, judgment, and frequent adjustment. This question of stealth is just one of the decisions you will face. And so I pose the question that is the title of this chapter as repeated and ongoing food for thought throughout the many stages of launching your new enterprise.

As with much of my entrepreneurial advice, the right answer very much depends on the unique nature of your startup and your co-founders. Again on that term, "stealth," I sometimes think we should ban this word from our vocabulary because of the binary thinking it invites. Not only does it promote on-off/yes-no thinking, but also the danger that what you end up cloaking is not your idea, but your self-confidence. It can cloak your belief in what you're building, even the "soul" animating your endeavor about which I wrote at the outset of this book. At the moment you ultimately move to launch and hit the market, you, your co-founders, and everyone else involved need to be completely aligned on the "true north" of your mission. A reluctance to talk about that mission is often a pretty good sign that the founder hasn't figured out the true north. When I meet entrepreneurs who won't share their business idea, I'm very skeptical of them as entrepreneurs. Contrary to popular belief, exposure is not an idea killer as you get to crowdsource advice on how to evolve your idea and see current and historical parallels to it. Fear, however, will suffocate innovation and creativity while it's still in the crib.

This doesn't mean that I don't believe in being in stealth mode

— of course I do. But you should share your business idea with the "right" audience, especially those that can really mentor you or to whom you can ultimately sell your solution or product. I've never seen an overly protective entrepreneur build a very large company.

In place of a stealth strategy, consider this your "reveal strategy," which would be the staged sharing to your concentric circles of co-founders, investors, formal, and informal advisors. This also includes your allies in related sectors such as the suppliers you intend to use, the news media, and of course the representative slices of the base clientele you hope to ultimately capture as your market. As legendary VC Marc Andreessen once argued in a blog you'll find on the Digital Companion, figuring out the product-market fit is the most important criteria for the success of any startup. You do this in the "arena" I describe in Chapter 1, *The Soul of the Entrepreneur,* not in stealth mode.

As the serial entrepreneur and VC, Peter Thiel phrased in the notes for a Stanford lecture series that formed the basis of his popular book, *Zero to One*: "The bigger the secret and the likelier it is that you alone have it, the more time you have to execute." You'll find those notes on the Digital Companion as well and I encourage you to look them over.

Making Thiel's point differently, I'd say it's all about context. Every startup is unique. Osano, a company that we've invested in, is a data privacy platform offering a one-stop solution enabling firms to comply with data compliance rules and regulations around the world. Its talented founder Arlo Gilbert kept it under tight wraps until the moment of launch in 2019. In contrast, another entrepreneur we've backed, the energetic Eddie Madongorere, was totally transparent about his plans for MOON UltraLIGHT, a best-of-its-kind smartphone light accessory, long before he launched in 2017. Both approaches have been successful. As I was writing this chapter, Osana raised another $11 million to double its workforce. MOON UltraLight, meanwhile, was named one of the best inventions of 2020 by *Time* magazine.

Personally, the approaches I have taken pretty much cover the waterfront of stealth — or better yet, reveal — strategy.

My first company, a consultancy, didn't need secrecy. It was quite the opposite as I was actively recruiting fellow students at Wharton as subcontractors. My second, an online community for MBA students, much like the early Facebook, was in the same category. And the third, an online retailer of sports nutrition products was nurtured and launched so quickly we didn't even stop to consider stealth.

With the fourth, Coremetrics, I wish I had known then what I know now. We never really attempted to hold our cards close to the vest. The reason was that Coremetrics was competing in the early days of SaaS against the legacy leaders in the web analytics space, Accrue and NetGenesis, as a uniquely SaaS-native solution. We needed to contrast ourselves immediately and redefine the category of web analytics. But a few years after we launched, along came one of the fiercest, newest competitors in the space — a company named Visual Sciences. They made every new prospect sign a non-disclosure agreement before seeing a demo and kept the wraps on everything. They gave us fits as we and others tried everything we could to find out what they were up to, and the company disrupted us all in many ways. In retrospect, I should have found that balance between the conflicting imperatives that I'm advocating in this chapter. Frankly, I believe Visual Science did itself a disservice with its stealth strategy as they never exited out of that mode and that was among the reasons they were acquired by another competitor they might have bested, WebSideStory. At some point, you need to aggressively come out of stealth mode, market, and sell like crazy to win. But this was a time of deep lessons for all of us. And Coremetrics weathered many a storm, including the bursting dot.com bubble before we successfully exited to IBM for around $300 million. Onward.

When Brant Barton and I founded Bazaarvoice, my fifth company, we took these lessons to heart and decided to be in "stealth mode" for the first eight months. This was primarily because of the incredible response we were getting from our initial conversations with prospective retail clients. With how many customers we were signing quickly, including Golfsmith, CompUSA, and PETCO, we wanted to build up to proven case studies for the impact of our solution, so that when we launched, we launched with real force and were harder to competitively catch. The key executives we were working with at those companies, and others, were the "cool kids," which you'll be learning about in Chapter 16, *Selling to the "Cool Kids."* But there were also several other important factors.

One was that our initial solution had been built by the team at Josh Baer's Austin-based Capital Thought (a development firm off-shoot of his email marketing company), and it wasn't very hard to replicate at the beginning. We needed time to grow the solution into something that would be harder for competitive entrants to easily duplicate.

Another reason we wanted to stay out of the technology press and off of the general media radar is that a primary inspiration for Bazaarvoice was the success Amazon was having with its product reviews, first introduced in 1995, just a year after the company was founded. A decade later, in 2005, as we were diligently building Bazaarvoice to eventually launch out of stealth mode, the product review ecosystem was still very immature, with only three or so retailers in the US with product reviews. But if we were looking carefully at what Amazon was doing, it was a safe bet others were as well.

Atop of this, everyone in the eCommerce industry, including the digital retail community, was wondering what company I would found next. They expected it to be good based on the success that Coremetrics had enjoyed. At that time, clients *loved* Coremetrics. This put the spotlight on me with both potential clients and competitors. We could waste no time.

So, by being in stealth at Bazaarvoice, we got a head start in the nascent industry. But we knew we had to move quickly to lead it. Our main competitor, PowerReviews, was founded just a few months after Bazaarvoice — and funny enough, they were initially in stealth too with their first company name being Pufferfish.

If you went to the Bazaarvoice site in those initial eight months, all you would see is the image below — absent even the text. Just the image and our first logo — designed by our first intern. That was Jacob Salamon, who went on to success in Los Angeles with his launch of Wisecrack, a popular YouTube channel, but only after having a huge impact at Bazaarvoice across a number of different roles, including head of marketing in Europe.

*Bazaarvoice's logo and image used on the site, sans the text*

I didn't want to give away too much to just any viewer. At tradeshows, potential clients would ask, "Does it mean, 'Speak no evil'?" Actually, it kind of meant the opposite, as a key pillar of our ultimate success was that negative views were (and still are) posted along with the positive. Without this objectivity and authenticity, I knew our credibility and the value of the product review ecosystem we were building would crumble. This was a difficult sell to some — including one global brand that I had to walk painfully away from until it saw the light and returned. Remember this was 2005. Facebook was closed to the public. Twitter didn't exist. There was certainly no Pinterest, Snap, or TikTok. And there were no iPhones or Android phones. Digital social interactions were far from what they are today. But still, customers were talking to each other as best they could, which represented a set of conversations we were seeking to amplify. And we had to convince our customers to embrace the negative voice of their customers as well as the positive. Some people wondered if what we were building was "bizarre voice." I suppose it was to a certain degree, after all (reference Chapter 7 - *What's in a Name?* for more on naming). But it worked. The intrigue factor was high which helped us get an audience before the right people.

This is another way of underscoring my point above, that stealth should be less about secrets than really your definition of a set of concentric circles signifying those with whom you'll share details and when you'll do so. During those eight months, we showed potential clients *everything*. We showed them how our solution worked. We demonstrated how our services worked. We plotted out for them exactly how our product roadmap was unfolding. After all, they were betting on a very small company with few resources at the time. We signed and launched those big-name customers with the "cool kids" at the helm, and we ran like hell to lead the industry. Clients will give you all the credibility you need, even when in stealth, and they will serve as a reference if you've done a great job for them.

At the end of that eight months of cloistering, Bazaarvoice came out roaring, fit, and strong. Our launch was a lightning strike as our founding CMO Sam Decker blogged on the launch and my long-time friend, Emily Brady at Brady PR, riveted the media attention that we had been waiting for until the right time —

when we had strength. By strength, I mean the fact that on launch day we already had a customer base ready to be our references, and the funding that enabled us to sprint. These backers included Austin Ventures, First Round Capital, Ralph Mack and Julie Constantin (both of whom had backed me at the beginning of Coremetrics), Eric Simone, and Jamie Crouthamel (the founder of Performics). We knew we had to quickly branch out and build more solutions than customer ratings and reviews to have a real platform — and today Bazaarvoice has a very broad conversations platform.

So moving along with my own chronology, how did my co-founders and I apply these lessons at data.world? Well, we were very stealthy. For more than a year. We knew we had a lot of functionality to build. In fact, data.world was the most complex technical build of our careers. We wanted to make sure that when we launched that there was enough functionality for the very broad, global community we were trying to attract and that it would "take."

In those early months, we did something similar to the exercise at Bazaarvoice with our website's homepage. As mentioned, our website was stealthco.world. While we had the data.world domain, we felt it would be too telling. So it was to this temporary address that we redirected all visitors. You'll see on the following page the image they saw, as we started to emerge from stealthco.world to at least reveal the data.world name as we approached our launch:

*data.world's website during "stealth mode"*

When we finally launched the data.world platform on July 11, 2016, we gated initial access both for performance reasons and to make sure we studied how our initial community members were using our platform. It was only later in 2016 that we took all of the governors off and the flood of community members rushed in. Word of mouth had helped our cause. And it worked — today we are the world's largest collaborative data community and getting cited regularly for changing behavior. We are also helping enterprises with our modern catalog for data and analysis, a new category in which analysts such as Gartner and Forrester Research are helping educate the market.

We have created and are empowering the brains and nervous system of the emerging, data-driven "metaverse" that is transforming every aspect of business, commerce, education, transport, and life as we've known it. We have many enterprise customers turbocharging their businesses and we also have nearly 1.6 million-plus community members who use our platform for free to collaborate on confronting climate change, poverty, the ravages of the pandemic, and more. My reflections on this are to be found on the Digital Companion.

Stealth mode can be among your most powerful tools when launching a new company. Just keep in mind that nothing great will ultimately be created in total secrecy, and you need to bring in allies, investors, partners, and foundational customers in a thoughtful, deliberate, and open way. Success is not in the way you hide what you do. It is in the way you reveal it.

> " 'What we are doing is so mind-blowing, so unique, so incredible, I can't tell you about it...'
>     ... "Really? I doubt it."
>
> **— JOURNALIST JOHN GREATHOUSE, WRITING IN *INC.* MAGAZINE**

# CHAPTER 9
# HOW, AND WHY, TO ASK FOR HELP

*"Don't be afraid to ask questions. Don't be afraid to ask for help when you need it. I do that every day. Asking for help isn't a sign of weakness, it's a sign of strength."*

## — BARACK OBAMA

A quarter-century ago, though it feels like last week, I was a young, hungry, and earnest entrepreneur in my first semester at the Wharton School. Word circulated that Farhad Mohit, an up-and-coming entrepreneur a couple of years ahead of me, who had founded one of the first online shopping search engines, was giving a talk on campus. I was eager to go, and all-ears when I arrived.

It was a small group of perhaps 20 people in the audience. And I was rapt as I listened to his tale of living in squalor in Los Angeles, dining on cheap ramen as he struggled to get Bizrate.com — later expanding into Shopzilla — off the ground. He spoke of the pain of watching fellow Wharton classmates prosper in big corporate jobs and the constant fear of failure. And then he got to the point in his presentation when he described securing his first serious funding. His face lit up. Whatever doubts I was having about my decision to leave corporate comfort for business school suddenly disappeared. We chatted briefly afterward. I asked for his general advice. He was patient and generous. And I was hooked. I thanked him profusely. We kept in touch, and a couple of years later when we were launching Coremetrics, Farhad and Bizrate.com became one of our first partners.

These days, I ask for help weekly. As we'll discuss in Chapter 13, *How to Leverage Advisors and Investors,* I send out a comprehensive report on the company every week without fail to this entire extended team. And I always include areas, issues, and pending initiatives on which I ask their help.

No entrepreneur is without a similar story, or set of stories. No one succeeds alone. We all stand on the shoulders of someone who has gone before us. And learning how to ask for help, guidance, and advice is as critical as any technical skill you'll bring to your entrepreneurial journey. Just as important, maybe more so, is learning to "pay it forward" and help those coming up behind you to their own summit of success.

So while you don't want to be presumptuous, you do want to be systematic. This is the lesson I learned from serial entrepreneur Auren Hoffman, whom I got to know in San Francisco in the early days of Coremetrics. He was then the CEO of BridgePath, which he was to sell a few years later to cloud computing company Bullhorn, and our offices were next to one another. I was 26, and Auren was just 24. But he was the consummate networker and he had organized a very popular lunch club for the Silicon Valley elite. There was always a compelling speaker; one of the first ones I met there was the CEO of Exodus Communications, one of the world's first Internet Service Providers and a very big deal at the time, reaching a $32 billion valuation at its peak. Auren invited me to join him regularly at these, and we were usually the most junior entrepreneurs in attendance.

After joining several of these gatherings and being amazed at the networking opportunities at each, I felt compelled to ask

Auren over lunch one day, "How the heck do you do it?" He told me about how he was fearless to reach out to anyone — but he shared that he did so in a particular way. Instead of approaching them with a typical, "Hi, I'm a young guy and would like to learn from you," he was deliberate and would do his homework. He would approach them with a very informed perspective and knowledge of their business. He'd be prepared to discuss something they had said or written, an organization they were involved with, or a cause to which they were devoted. This required more research, but it was very effective. It worked because of Auren's passion and genuine desire to connect, and his ability to make it clear he was not wasting the other person's time. It wasn't just cursory research. It was an authentic interest in what he had learned about that person and their business.

Some years later, I learned that Steve Jobs had a similar philosophy. In a video I share on the Digital Companion, Jobs describes how he reached out to HP Co-founder Bill Hewlett when he was just 12 years old: "I've never found anybody who didn't want to help me if I asked them for help," Jobs explained. Not only did Hewlett give the young high school student spare parts for a device he was trying to build, but he also gave him a job the following summer working on the HP assembly line.

Wayne Baker, a professor at the University of Michigan's Ross School of Business has argued this well in an essay I include on the Digital Companion. He notes that while self-reliance is a celebrated virtue, it's also self-limiting and people frequently underestimate the willingness of others to help. That said, like Auren, Baker makes the case that you need to know what you want to ask.

"Here's something you can do to prepare…" he writes. "Focus on a current project and write down your goals for it. Take the most important goal and list the action steps and resources you need to achieve it — materials, information, data, or advice. You'll then have a series of needs that you can frame as questions…"

Baker also emphasizes that those who are open to helping others, and have a reputation for doing so, also are more likely to get help from others. Helping others also gives you a psychological edge when reaching out. You'll feel more comfortable asking for help when you have been helpful.

Personally, I've found various ways to do this. In addition to capital, advice, counsel, and mentoring is a big part of being an angel investor. I've been the Entrepreneur-in-Residence numerous times at my alma maters, the Wharton School, and the University of Texas at Austin.

In one of my early efforts to give back, I was serving at Wharton for a few days in the mid-2000s, shortly after we had launched Bazaarvoice. I was holding office hours and in walked a young undergraduate named Boris. He went on to tell me how had built the #1 sports app on Facebook and he shared with me the stats on the incredible amount of usage he was getting. But he was pained, wondering whether to jump into social media with both feet or continue toward his degree. Because of Bazaarvoice, I was really steeped in the emerging trend of social media at the time and I was very impressed with what he was doing. While most of the time I advise students to stick with their undergraduate program and earn their degree, I told Boris that he should go on a one-year sabbatical to take this to its logical conclusion. We talked about the unique time we were living in for social online. It was not obvious at that moment, but I could feel it in my bones and I shared my views about how important I believed Facebook would become. He said he would think about it and ask others as well. And that was the last I saw of Boris. For a while.

It was several years later that I was again back at Wharton, this time accepting a Wharton Entrepreneurs award at the school's annual entrepreneurial alumni gathering. I gave a speech on how others had helped me on my journey, and of course, I referenced both my Wharton professors and alumni, including Farhad. After I finished, I started to mingle with the crowd. Up walked a young man and much to my surprise he re-introduced himself as Boris. I certainly remembered him, but I was in a bit of heightened anticipation, very curious whether my advice of years before was sound. It turned out as Boris explained, he had indeed taken that sabbatical. He'd become a young millionaire after selling his sports app to another company. He also went back to finish his degree. To say I was elated is an understatement. Knowing that I had helped him in a way that changed his life forever was incredibly satisfying. And now he is paying it forward himself.

But beyond these insights, I believe there is something more at play here. I really believe that mutual help, support, and reciprocity are embedded in the DNA of our culture as Americans. Think of the 18th and 19th-century tradition of "barn raising" in rural America, when 90 percent of Americans lived on farms. Barns for storage of grains and livestock were critical to the livelihood of farmers, but also expensive and needed much more labor than a typical family could afford or provide. But people knew they could ask for help: Barn raising met the needs of the community — and the economy — by enlisting neighbors, unpaid, to assist in the building of a central feature of the rural economy. We are mostly a self-created country and a young one at that. And yet we represent about 16 percent of the world's total GDP with a little over 4 percent of the world's total population. This, I truly believe, has much to do with this spirit that is at one with our identity.

An exceptional account of this trait in our culture is to be found in the book *Founding Brothers — The Revolutionary Generation* by Joseph J. Ellis. I include a review on the Digital Companion, but the major takeaway for me was how, despite their differences, George Washington, Benjamin Franklin, John Adams, Thomas Jefferson, Alexander Hamilton, and others relied on one another, collaborated even amid rivalries, and ultimately helped one another — and the new nation — succeed.

Much the same could be said about Israel, a much younger

nation that, as I finish this book, just concluded its 74th anniversary. A decade ago, Debra and I made our first visit there, which coincided with yet another eruption of conflict. It was amazing to see how the Israeli people around us rallied. They worked around the clock to get the missile defense system, known as Iron Dome, in place to protect Tel Aviv. Israel's origin story in the wake of the Holocaust is, of course, well known and turned on amazing feats of courage and self-help, much rooted in the spirit of the kibbutz, the original communities of the Zionist pioneers that were founded on principles of mutual aid and cooperation — not unlike our tradition of barn raising. But less well known outside of Israel is its success as a nation of entrepreneurs, now the world's standout center of innovation outside of the United States. A book that explores this dimension of Israel's economy and development is *Start-Up Nation,* by Daniel Senor and Saul Singer, an excerpt from which I include on the Digital Companion. When we returned, I had an interesting conversation with my friend and fellow Austinite, David Bookspan, who founded the business incubator DreamIt Austin.

"Isn't it amazing how much Israel has prospered entrepreneurially given its surroundings?," David reflected. To which I responded: "Israel has prospered entrepreneurially *because* of its surroundings. It has a mission that is too important to fail!" David and I agreed.

Understand that you can't go it alone. Learn both how to ask thoughtfully for help, and how to graciously accept it. Always be willing to pay it forward, and help others on their journey at every opportunity. I'd be tempted to leave this chapter at that. Except for one thing.

As I was finishing this book in the spring of 2022, I was working in my hotel room in Vancouver, British Columbia, where I was attending the annual TED Conference. I picked up my phone and sent a message to Farhad via the TEDConnect app. He too was in Vancouver, attending the same conference. Soon we got together, and I connected him to two people that were interested in his latest endeavor, GoodParty.org, which I've collaborated with him a bit on before as a political centrist. Same story, 25 years later: Two entrepreneurs gathered, trying to find ways to be helpful to one another.

In short, no matter how experienced you are as an entrepreneur, you need all of the help you can get.

*"We make a living by what we get. We make a life by what we give."*

## — SIR WINSTON CHURCHILL

# CHAPTER 10
# THE STRENGTH OF NATURAL NETWORK EFFECTS

*"The richest people in the world look for and build networks, everyone else looks for work."*

## — ROBERT KIYOSAKI, ENTREPRENEUR AND AUTHOR

To effectively think about the power of natural networks, a good place to start is with a remarkable experiment by social psychologist Stanley Milgram more than half a century ago. Sometimes his study is called the "small world experiment," and it not only built on a great deal of earlier research, but it also influenced the making of a 1990 play by John Guare, *Six Degrees of Separation,* and a 1993 movie of the same name. You may have seen the latter, with Stockard Channing, Will Smith, and Donald Sutherland.

Now, I bring up this old study, a play, and a movie because I'm sure readers are already familiar with the well-known utility of the "network effect." This is often explained as "Metcalfe's Law," for my friend, the brilliant scientist, and professor at the University of

Texas at Austin, Bob Metcalfe, who articulated this years ago for purposes of understanding telecommunications networks. Simply put, the "law" states that the value of a network is asymptotically proportional to the square of the number of connected users of the system. Simply put, one phone is useless because it won't have any appliance to connect with. If there are two phones in existence, then there's a "network," but of just one connection. Increase the number of phones to five, and the value of the network is 10, meaning 10 connections. Add just two more phones, and you have 21 connections. Double the number again to 14 phones and the value of your network is 91 connections. And on from there... you can march the exponential logic out of a Harvard dorm room and on to Facebook's over 3 billion users.

And it's a prediction of that Meta scale by which Metcalfe's law, conceived in 1983, got an intellectual booster some two decades later from another computer scientist, David P. Reed at MIT. "Reed's Law" explained in a famous essay referenced on the Digital Companion, the distinction of networks that add self-reinforcing velocity. Anticipating the rise of social media in 2001, Reed argued that "the most valuable of all" networks would be the "many-to-many" —or "group-forming" — network, which allows network members to form and maintain communicating groups.

Reed certainly got it right, and the science of emergent networks is endlessly fascinating. But what I believe is less understood is that these intentional networks build on what are often natural networks, essentially grapevines or matrices that have not yet been wired. Think of the line from the Nobel-winning Irish poet Walter Butler Yeats: "There are no strangers here; only friends who haven't yet met."

This takes me back to Stanley Milgram's "Small-world" experiment. Milgram is best known for his experiments on obedience to authority in the early 1960s, prompted by the trial of Nazi Adolph Eichmann who, like others implicated in the

Holocaust, claimed he was "only following orders." But Milgram later explored the nature of human connectivity, essentially that Yeats-like experience we've all had: You know, where, for example, you get to chatting with someone in an airport lounge in Zurich while you're waiting for a flight to Miami. You bring up the fact you're from, say, Austin, Texas. Well, it turns out the person with whom you're chatting has never been to Texas but... in fact, did know a woman from his high school in Florida once upon a time who moved to Austin to get married. Lo and behold, she turns out to be your sister-in-law. Or an employee. Or next-door neighbor.

"Wow," you both exclaim simultaneously, "What a small world!" An amazing bit of serendipity? Maybe. Milgram wanted to find out if there was something more than coincidence at work in such seemingly random encounters.

In his 1967 experiment, Milgram wanted to test the connections humans share — what I call the networks of which we're not fully aware. Or, natural networks.

"Milgram was teaching at Harvard at the time, so naturally he regarded greater Boston as the center of the universe," wrote Wharton School Professor Duncan J. Watts, in his groundbreaking book on networks, *Six Degrees — The Science of a Connected Age.* "And what could be farther from it than Nebraska?"

So Milgram sent packages to 160 randomly chosen people living in Omaha. He asked this group, which he called "starters," to forward the package to a friend or acquaintance whom they judged the most likely to bring the package closer to the "target," a stockbroker in Sharon, Massachusetts. But there was a rule: The "starters" could only mail the package to someone they actually knew personally on a first-name basis. And that person, in turn, would repeat the process until at some point the mail would finally reach the intended destination. Hopefully. There were some other elements in the experiment, including "tracer postcards" that each person linked in the emerging chain would mail back to Milgram so he could map the movements of the 160 packages. Remember, this is 1967, long before anything like the FedEx or Amazon tracking that we all now take for granted.

At the outset, Milgram and his colleagues speculated it might take even hundreds of steps for the 160 packages to journey from Omaha to a stranger in greater Boston. It took an average of just six steps — as few as two, and no more than 10. And thus the meme was born: six degrees of separation.

Now there are some problems with Milgram's work, and it has been criticized. If you're inclined to math, think it through. Simplistically, if you have 10 friends and they each have 10 friends, then in one degree of separation you should be able to reach 100 people. Right? But there's the matter of "clustering." Probably five of my 10 friends are friends in common. If so, my presumed network of 100 is suddenly just 50.

But whatever the criticism, a 2008 study by Microsoft of its Microsoft Messenger service found that the average chain of contacts between users and the service was only 6.6 people. So many, including sociologist Watts, who is one of the great pioneers in network theory, conclude that Milgram's work has stood the test of time. You'll find links to some of Watts' great work on the Digital Companion.

This now brings me to my own take on networks. In the past ten years, I've seen something north of 3,000 pitches from would-be entrepreneurs. The best among them talk about their business ideas and the network effects they are striving for in a hopeful way. After all, the subject of networks is a hot topic. But most of the time the discussion is just that — hope.  And hope is not a strategy. Behind this, of course, is the fact that we often talk about building networks, as everyone is inspired by the growth of social networks and other digital endeavors like Uber or Airbnb that have scaled their networks geometrically and, in some periods, even exponentially. And that's great. However, I want to encourage you to spend more time examining and identifying the networks that already exist. Networks abound in social interaction, in the organization and evolution of cities, and in nature... to the way starlings flock, the way ants build complex structures, and to the way — as we unfortunately now know so well — that viruses mutate and spread. Watts' work, in fact, began with a study of the ways crickets coalesce into a vast ocean of synchronized chirping via natural network nodes.

This is why when we consider investing in startups at Hurt Family Investments (124 startups and counting in our portfolio as of this writing), we always look for natural network effects. It doesn't mean we won't invest when natural network effects aren't present, but it is certainly more enticing when they are. I use the word *natural* deliberately because it is far easier to build solutions that will offer network effects if your market is indeed wired that way. Not long ago I attended a discussion at the University of Texas at Austin between computing pioneer Michael Dell and author Walter Isaacson, at the time CEO of the Aspen Institute. Isaacson's many books include *Steve Jobs, Einstein,* and The *Innovators: How a Group of Hackers, Geniuses, and Geeks Created the Digital Revolution,* and he is now working on one about Elon Musk. As you might imagine, it was a broad and fascinating conversation. But the key takeaway for me was Dell's remark that the level of difficulty in changing an industry's behavior depends on how long that industry has been engaging in that behavior.

Now that might not seem a revolutionary insight when taken on its own. But it's foundational when you pair it with natural network effects, which lead you to what Harvard Business School authors Marco Iansiti and Karim R. Lakhani have called "strategic collisions." Their book on this and other topics, *Competing in the Age of AI - Strategy and Leadership When Algorithms and Networks Run the World,* is worth picking up and I've included parts of it on the Digital Companion. Its essence is all about networked companies colliding with those that are not — the confluence creating the power to accelerate change.

Think of how stodgy the hotel sector was from 1925 when Conrad Hilton innovated with on-premise retail shops and dining rooms at his first hotel in Dallas. Then Airbnb and Homeaway showed up eight decades later. The business of ferrying passengers by car didn't change much beyond the trend of painting most of them yellow beginning in 1915. Then Uber and Lyft came along almost a century later. In both cases, industries almost defined by inertia were transformed overnight by the natural networks — constellations of spare rooms in one case and unused private car capacity in the other— that had been there all along, just waiting for the technology and insight to wire them together.

In my own entrepreneurial journey, I've experienced and utilized this power of pre-existing, natural networks in virtually all of my businesses, with the exception perhaps of the first which was in consulting (although I did leverage the Wharton alumni network well to identify and win new customers). And of course, this is a big part of the ongoing story at data.world where our data community now numbers nearly 1.6 million analysts and data scientists collaborating as a natural network to confront challenges from climate change to smart policing. But the most illustrative is the case of Bazaarvoice where the market was, fortunately, wired for brands and retailers to collaborate in a kind of grand bargain.

The retailers were to provide the audience — and therefore the sales — that the brands needed. The brands were to provide the co-op advertising to support the retailer in the endeavor through what the trade calls market-development funds (MDF). This is a major part of the commercial ecosystem as co-op advertising dollars are as high as $50 billion in the US and a staggering $520 billion worldwide, according to the Altimeter Group, a researcher of disruptive technologies. Brands would get higher margins but lower revenues, while retailers would get lower margins but higher revenues (generally speaking, with Apple being a notable exception in owning both sides of the deal for much of their sales). So it was natural for Bazaarvoice to tap into this network effect and provide solutions for not only retailers, but also the brands that sold through them.

The result is that Bazaarvoice actually had — and very much has today — a working network effect that benefits all participants: retailers, brands that sell through those retailers, consumers that shop at those brands and retailers, and of course Bazaarvoice itself and some of its partners. In other words, the more participants that are on the Bazaarvoice network, the greater the effect of that network to the benefit of all. They were just waiting for an introduction. What we did was bring them together and then allow them to amplify one another and grow together in this newer and increasingly more digital aisle.

Another way to consider the case of Bazaarvoice is as the "keystone" in the network we created. When defining and studying ecosystems, which are sets of complex interlocking natural networks, biologists look for the "keystone species." These are the species that play an outsized role and sustain the overall system, even if their relative population is small. My favorite example is sea otters, which dine heavily on sea urchins. Because of the sea otters, urchins gather in protective crevices and consume smaller organisms, and leave the large kelp forests — depended on by many fish and invertebrates such as snails — untouched. Bazaarvoice became the "keystone species" in its particular corner of the retail ecosystem - again, benefiting retailers, brands, and consumers alike (the kelp forest of sorts), which is the role I encourage all entrepreneurs to seek for their startups.

Now it's important to stress again that networks and the synergies they spawn are important across all facets of life and enterprise. One of my favorite entrepreneurial examples of leveraged network dynamics is that of my fellow Austinite Mike Rypka, who started a food truck selling tacos in 2006. Austin, with its university, tech, and music scenes is big enough to have plenty of taco demand. It's also interconnected and small enough for word of tasty tacos to spread rapidly across Milgram's six degrees of linkage. Today, Rypka's pioneering of what has become known as "gourmet street food" has led to 75 brick-and-mortar outlets across Texas and four other states with revenues in 2019 of nearly $300 million. Although I'm more of a Tacodeli fan myself, Rypka's Torchy's Tacos is incredibly popular and successful (some inside baseball: this statement is like starting a war in Austin as you are either a Tacodeli or Torchy's person).

Or consider the origin of the Beatles, whose two living members, and the estates of the two members no longer with us, made almost $70 million from their music and rights in 2019. "We were four guys who lived in this city in the North of England, but we didn't know one another. Then, by chance, we did know one another," Paul McCartney wrote in an essay for *The New Yorker* that caught my attention in late 2021. "To this day, it is still a complete mystery to me that it happened at all."

A tale of a random, natural network indeed. Technology, however, is clearly where we see this "mystery" of surprising networks playing out most vividly. And in the business area with which I'm most familiar, software-as-a-service (SaaS), I see it all the time.

Most of the SaaS startups we've invested in (either as advisors or investors, or both), have natural network effects, with some inherently stronger in their industries than others. It is one of the key ingredients we look for, such as when we seed-backed ZenBusiness (Austin's latest unicorn as of this writing). I think any SaaS startup would be wise to identify if its B2B market has a natural network effect to tap into. Not long ago, for example, I engaged in brainstorming with a SaaS startup team that wasn't sure about this premise, but by the end of the session, we had all convinced ourselves (and not just hopefully, I might add) that indeed a natural network effect existed. That made all of us much more excited about the business than ever before.

A SaaS startup without a natural network effect can still be successful. For example, there are replacement-market SaaS businesses like Salesforce, which started out by disrupting a massive market (Siebel and CRM) with a better, cheaper, faster, and ultimately more function-rich solution. Salesforce succeeded because it built on a single platform versus spreading its R&D over multiple client computing platforms and armies of installation consultants. Workday is another example, running the same play as Salesforce did against Siebel, but in this case, it was Workday against PeopleSoft/Oracle. In fact, replacement-market SaaS businesses have grown much quicker than nascent-market SaaS businesses because the market already existed and can therefore be easily sized and disrupted (assuming great execution). Their success is about execution in sales, services, and feature parity ... and then eventually superiority — again, due to that single platform to rapidly evolve on advantage. But now SaaS as a superior business model as compared to on-premise enterprise software secret is mostly out of the bag. Workday enjoyed a monster IPO and Salesforce.com is the most valuable SaaS business in the world. Snowflake is a more recent example, displacing on-premise Oracle installations left and right and having the largest SaaS (or software, period) IPO in history in 2020. But these replacement SaaS startup opportunities are few and far between. This means that most new SaaS startups we see are, in fact, nascent and therefore are trying to create their own demand, which requires both a keen understanding of natural networks and a lot of evangelism and education.  Evangelizing in a nascent, or fledgling market is a topic I'll get to later, in Chapter 16, *Selling to the "Cool Kids."* I will also share ways to hire some great evangelists as full-time and part-time employees, and also as Advisory Board members, in Chapter 13, *How to Leverage Advisors and Investors.*

Back to the topic at hand, the bottom line is that when we see a SaaS startup pitch us, natural network effects in their industry (or the lack thereof) are among the first things on my mind. It doesn't mean they will be successful if their industry has the embedded advantage of a natural network effect, but it will certainly help. In investing in B2C, we also look for network effects but by comparison, they are usually those created rather than those that naturally occur. For example, Apple created a network effect by the integration of iPhones and iPads to the App Store and to iTunes. Apple then tried to extend this network effect into social with the launch of iTunes Ping, which was one of their biggest failures in recent years. Amazon created a network effect through the launch of Prime and the subsequent launches of Prime Instant Video, Prime Photos, and Kindle Owners' Lending Library. Facebook created a network effect by the launch of Facebook Login, allowing it to proliferate everywhere, and they also tapped into a natural network effect by launching at select universities (where students were naturally connected, the way it has always been) and expanding out from there. LinkedIn tapped into the natural network effect of professionals working together at companies (both as peers and as partners). These are just a few notable examples.

As a final thought, it's also worth mentioning that networks, by their nature, are emergent. That's where their mystery lies. And as such, they can be harvested to your advantage but also surprise you. Nokia, as many readers may recall, was riding on top of the world, with nearly 50 percent of the global smartphone market in 2007. That was the year that Apple launched the iPhone and we all know the rest of that story. Or consider the iconic Kodak founded in 1892. Although Kodak was successfully navigating the transition to digital photography in a plan that had begun in the 1990s, it was bankrupted in 2012. And not by a peer competitor like FujiFilm, but rather by camera-ready smartphones that became a networked and networking "black swan" that really ended the legendary firm as collateral damage.

Wherever you are on your entrepreneurial journey, think

networks. They are all around us — even on your Peloton right now if you are riding it while reading this.

*"Networks are present everywhere. All we need is an eye for them."*

**— ALBERT-LASZLO BARABASI, PHYSICIST, AND NETWORK THEORIST**

# PART TWO
## BUILDING

# CHAPTER 11
# THE MOST PROVEN WAY TO HIRE WELL

*"People are not your most important asset. The right people are."*

## — JIM COLLINS, BUSINESS AUTHOR

If there was a secret to the early success of my fifth company, Bazaarvoice, in its early days, both in building the culture and energizing performance, it was that we were obsessed with recruiting. In retrospect, some 15 years, another co-founded company, and more than 100 startup investments later, our novel approach and process back then seems blindingly obvious today. Which is why we use a version of that model at data.world. What is far less obvious is why so many enterprises continue to do this wrong.

The core issues, which I'll explore in detail, are rigor and grit. They are the force multiplier for any startup. Rigor is the difference between excellence and mediocrity in recruitment and retention. It's also rare. Grit is the measure of determination in the person you are evaluating. This was the insight Co-founder Brant Barton and I made back in those early days of Bazaarvoice, after a stumble or two at my prior company, Coremetrics.

But to back up, the playbook for recruitment is in many respects pretty much unchanged since Dwight Eisenhower's America, of a piece with the mass organization that established many of the categories of our lives, businesses, and thinking in the era following WWII. William H. Whyte's 1956 bestselling and influential management book, *The Organization Man,* is still a worthwhile read to get your bearings on the origins of today's hiring practices. Since then, the basics have been that the HR department puts together a job description, carves out the position's place on the organization chart, and assigns a pay scale. Ads and announcements go out in one manner or another, and resumes and candidates arrive similarly. There are some drills, perhaps a Myers-Briggs Type Indicator or other tests. References are checked. In recent years, security checks, citizenship, and visa compliance has been added to the ritual.

And then there's the interview. Sometimes it's an interview in a conference room with two or three managers or executives fielding the questions. Sometimes the applicant rotates through the offices of the interviewers for one-on-one conversations. I'm pretty sure readers of this book have been asked the questions: "Where do you want to be in five years?" Or, "What's your greatest strength and weakness?" Sometimes it will get a little more granular, as in "What makes you passionate about working here?" Or, "Do you see yourself as a team player?" As if anyone would answer no. And of course, there's a reciprocal search for commonalities, a bit of repartee around schools attended, hobbies pursued, sports participated in, or mutual acquaintances.

I suspect this sounds familiar. We have, of course, thankfully improved our openness, engagement, and outreach to cultural, gender, age, and physical diversity — although I believe society has a lot of work remaining. But the choreography, the *process* of recruitment, and hiring are stuck in many ways in the era of Don Draper's *Mad Men.* The only real change — and I'm not sure we should call it that — is that we've mechanized this choreography and in many ways disempowered our own HR departments with recruiters, AI scans of resume keywords, and digital tools like LinkedIn.

Now don't get me wrong. As you know from my last chapter, the virtues of identifying and using natural and created networks are central to my business philosophy. And recruiters and social media tools like LinkedIn can be network turbochargers to find and recruit talent. But they don't automatically deliver the rigor you need for a people-centric culture and motivated team.

"The recruiting and hiring function has been eviscerated," wrote Peter Cappelli, a professor at my alma mater the Wharton School, in an essay you'll find on the Digital Companion. "Many U.S. companies— about 40 percent, according to research by Korn Ferry — have outsourced much if not all of the hiring process to 'recruitment process outsourcers,' which in turn often use subcontractors, typically in India and the Philippines... To hire programmers, for example, these subcontractors can scan websites that programmers might visit, trace their 'digital exhaust' from cookies and other user-tracking measures to identify who they are, and then examine their curricula vitae."

This is crude, unnecessary, and hardly a recipe for success. And I'd like to think it's no accident that Professor Cappelli is a thought leader on this issue. Because while it was years before I fully realized why and how, it was Wharton that taught me what was to become my approach to hiring — before I'd even enrolled.

These processes that I've described, which are essentially sorting processes, really fuel the beliefs of many executives — especially experienced ones — that their gut instinct on people is what matters most. For those executives, I recommend you read the book *Egonomics* by David Marcum and Steven Smith. It too is reviewed on the Digital Companion, and it will show you why you are dead wrong.

The reality is that you *must* test those that you want to hire.

Many pristine, even perfect resumes will find you. Applicants will ace those questions I describe above. Many candidates will say that they are passionate about joining your company. They may well be sincere. But they don't know that. No one knows if they are truly passionate about joining your cause until they experience it. It is all romance in the beginning. For example, when I was a teenager I thought I was passionate about learning to play guitar like David Gilmour of Pink Floyd after I became obsessed with listening to his guitar "sing." But then I tried guitar lessons and I quickly realized it was not for me.

That experience contrasted a decade later with how badly I wanted to get into the Wharton School to earn my MBA. At the time I applied, Wharton's MBA program was ranked No. 1 in the country and had been for the prior six years. It was very intimidating to apply. It was a daunting amount of work and the fear of potential rejection was visceral. So I prepared for two months: studying for the Graduate Management Admission Test (GMAT). I wrote and rewrote my essays countless times, with my wife Debra critiquing each and every iteration, and often telling me to start over. By the time I got to the interview stage, I had searched and scoured my soul for all the reasons not only that I wanted to get an MBA, but that I wanted to get it at Wharton. This was grit. And I got in — and it changed my life.

That experience and background of running such a long testing and preparation gauntlet to get into Wharton — that rigor — framed my thinking going forward. And in the early days at Coremetrics, which I founded in 1999, I suggested to one of our vice presidents that we should test our candidates. The VP shrugged it off, spoke of trusting instincts, and used that very lazy phrase and the excuse of a competitive job market to say we shouldn't "slow the process down— it's a very competitive market for talent." I didn't know better at the time and the VP was much older and more "experienced" than I. So I let the executive run with that plan. You're probably guessing the pattern with this and several other employees in the months that followed.  A deadline would get missed. Then two. That employee hired "on instinct" would begin to complain about the work. I'd begin wondering if we'd made a mistake. And then, with little surprise, I'd be told six months later that it wasn't a great fit or that the employee was fired for lack of performance. That VP was wrong 50 percent of the time and soon we were clocking a 50 percent turnover rate overall.

What was the answer? "It's all a numbers game," I was told — and not just by that executive but by other CEOs with whom I discussed the pattern. Sad to say, this was an industry norm. More than two decades later, it hasn't changed. In fact, in 2020 the turnover rate in the U.S. workforce was 57.3 percent, according to the Bureau of Labor Statistics.  A numbers game indeed.

Meanwhile, it is embarrassing to you as the leader. It's often humiliating and painful for the person who didn't work out. It is erosive to the morale of your entire company. Most importantly, it's disruptive to your culture and your performance. Think about the opportunity cost alone. Startups are very hard. The last thing you want is constant turnover and an attitude of "it's all a numbers game." As if your creation is a soulless factory or something. These are people. It is their livelihood — and it is yours too. I struggled with this, mulling the issue with the team repeatedly at Coremetrics without ever fully producing an enduring solution. So by the time I was readying to launch Bazaarvoice in 2005 with Brant Barton, Wharton's rigor was on my mind and I wanted to make sure that we tested the grit of those that would join us, just like Wharton had tested mine. Which is how Brant and I came up with "The Test" — really a simple, but profound, insight and process.

The first person to join us at Bazaarvoice was indeed the first person to go through "The Test." This was Paul Rogers, our first VP of Engineering and a legendary CTO at several companies since. The way it worked was simple. When we got to our finalists after five to eight interviews and everyone was ready to hire them, we would call them up — typically on a Friday — and say,

"Congratulations, everyone at Bazaarvoice that you interviewed with wants to hire you." We would let that soak in. As time went on and Bazaarvoice became known for its culture, that *really* soaked in. It was a badge of honor to get to that point, as we were known to be one of the hardest companies with which to land a job, and also as one of the best performing.

And then we would drop the hammer:

"There is just one more thing we need you to do as part of this process." And this was where "The Test" would begin. We wanted them to get a small taste of what the job would be like, to make sure this wasn't a case similar to my hapless run at guitar lessons back in the day, and to really see if their expressed passion would stick. For example, for a sales director candidate, we would continue and say, "We need you to come in on Monday and present to us like we are a prospect." This was exceptionally hard for a candidate to prepare for in the early days because our company was in stealth mode. This was pretty much guaranteed to "ruin" the candidate's weekend as they needed to spend 8 to 16 hours preparing. Now I put "ruin" in quotes because it wasn't nearly as bad as either one of us making the wrong decision about their candidacy at Bazaarvoice. Everyone loses when it's a bad fit and again, we wanted to avoid the embarrassment, impact on our culture, and the loss of opportunity cost. If you step back for a moment and think about it, spending up to 16 hours is *nothing* for a job that could both transform your wealth and fulfill your soul, and even become your calling in life. During the presentation, we would interrupt the sales candidates, and push them hard on items like pricing — even though they couldn't possibly know at this point. Essentially we'd act out a tough prospect environment to see how they would react.

The Test was *much* harder for executives, and our recruiters groaned when we got to this point. It is, after all, harder to find the right executive vs. the right salesperson. For their test, I told executive candidates, "I need you to present your 100-day plan to the executive team — what you plan to accomplish at Bazaarvoice in your first 100 days." You learn a great deal with this exercise. I remember when one of our executive candidates called me from Spain, where he was on vacation at the time, and said, "You weren't specific about something — I assume it is okay if I ask my peers and potential team members what they think is most important for me to accomplish and what the company's biggest current priorities are." Bingo! "Congratulations," I replied. "You passed executive IQ test number one, which is to assume that all resources are available to you in startups and even when constraints are forced upon you, find a way!" He laughed and then spent around 50 or 60 hours preparing for his presentation — while still on vacation in Spain. It was one of the best in Bazaarvoice's history. It was not unusual for an executive candidate to spend 40 hours preparing for this.

What was unusual was when they didn't prepare at all. For example, I had some CFO candidates who didn't pass test number one and presented a very generic "here is the job of a CFO" primer. Game over. Clearly, they didn't have the passion to prepare. But even worse, they didn't have the collaborative gene, which is essential to perform in a startup environment where resources are so limited and your very existence as a company is on the line. Even worse than that, some would respond when faced with rejection, "But you didn't tell me I should prepare that way." I was very direct in my reply to that, and I hope that I helped them succeed in their career later. Life is too short to not live your passion... we spend more waking time at work than doing anything else.

What were the results? Well, at Bazaarvoice we certainly improved our success with new team members, to around 80 to 90 percent retention, which compared dramatically with the 50 percent turnover we endured at Coremetrics. And our sales defied gravity as compared to most startups in Austin. In seven years, we built a public company and had one of the top five IPOs of 2012 as named by the *Wall Street Journal*. As importantly, our process helped *keep* the best people at Bazaarvoice. Around half of our new team members came from referrals. When I asked new people why they joined Bazaarvoice, "the people" was always one of their top three answers. When I asked people why they stayed at Bazaarvoice, "the people" was always one of their top three answers, too. Bazaarvoice became an elite kind of club — a badge of honor for those getting through that "brutal" recruiting process, not unlike what I saw and felt myself, both upon arriving at Wharton with other new students and of course upon graduation.

Some years after developing "The Test," I was having lunch with the Co-founder and CEO of Whole Foods, John Mackey. I told him about how we uniquely hired at Bazaarvoice, and he shared a similar story on how they did it at Whole Foods. They would have their candidate answer questions with all of the interviewers present, surrounding them in a kind of circle. This way all objections and clarifications were clearly out there on the table for all to hear, creating a more collaborative assessment and eventual buy-in on the candidate. And then, for most of their candidates that passed, they would hire them for 30 days and determine after that whether to convert them into full-time hires. That is an extended test for sure! Does it sound intense? Well, ask yourself: does Whole Foods have one of the most respected business cultures in the world? Amazon thought so, as did *Fortune* magazine, in their 100 Companies to Work For list year after year.

Another lesson I've learned from experience is that with certain candidates, particularly executive hires, a meal is a good tactic. Think about any interaction over food, from that first sandwich with your college roommate to that initial meeting with your future in-laws. It's hard to hide over lunch or dinner, and you learn a great deal about people. If the candidate is going to be in sales, their interactions with the wait staff will be telling. Conversations become more casual, and traits like poise and self-confidence have the opportunity to be seen. You learn a lot when you interview someone over lunch or dinner, and Debra has been right there with me for some of the most important ones as she has an amazing read on people.

Needless to say, we've carried over all of this practice to data.world since the beginning. And it still surprises me how often we are wrong when we get to the test process and how thankful I am that we practice this. It is painful when we are wrong, but it would be much more painful if we were wrong for six months and had to let the person go. We have an *incredibly* strong team as a result of this practice, including an awesome leader of human resources (we call it Employee Experience) in Vice President Lisa Novak and a rock star recruiter in Stephanie Fuller. I feel very thankful to work with this gallery of heroes.

This is a subject on which I've written and spoken a great deal, through my time mentoring Austin startups, my time as Entrepreneur-in-Residence at the University of Texas at Austin, and countless interviews. I believe these lessons have been adopted by more startups in Austin than perhaps any other in my years of evangelism on the topic. We've gone from a norm of "guessing" to a norm of "proving" here, and I believe it is directly correlated with the success of startups in Austin overall.

Opportunity cost is a real cost, and time is money in a startup's life. Momentum begets momentum. This is true on the recruiting front, just like it is true in any area of business, from fundraising, to sales, to culture, to a winning spirit, and, of course, to results.

*"If you think it's expensive to hire a professional, wait until you hire an amateur."*

## — RED ADAIR, TEXAS' LEGENDARY OIL WELL FIREFIGHTER

# CHAPTER 12
# THE IMPORTANCE OF REFERENCE CHECKING

*"References get you to the truth the fastest, provided you dig deep and talk to the right people. Don't just hire slow; hire smart."*

## — MAX WINOGRAD, CEO NULABEL TECHNOLOGIES

Akin to my counsel on recruitment in Chapter 11, *The Most Proven Way to Hire Well*, the prevailing approach to the related art of reference checking is outdated, broken, and hamstrings many an entrepreneur before they even come off the starting line. But unlike my experience recounted in the last chapter, my insight into reference checking was not learned through a series of early stumbles, but rather by (perhaps) naively getting it right at my first major startup, Coremetrics, beginning in 1999.

I'll share that experience that has now served me so well from that company, through Bazaarvoice from 2005 to 2012, and now at my current firm, data.world, since 2016. That is, it has served me well when I followed my own advice, and it has sometimes gone horribly wrong when I haven't. But first, the two key lessons I've learned over hundreds of conversations with references and gleaned from the wisdom of others.

The first insight I encourage you to consider is that most companies and their HR departments devote energy to checking a candidates' reference in a fashion inverse to the importance of the position being filled. In other words, the higher the level being filled — from entry-level, to mid-level, to manager, to executive, and on to board member or investor — the greater the reluctance to check references. It's only human nature, understandably, to be most keen on validating the background of an inexperienced person newly out of school with a thin resume. You need to be sure the candidate really did graduate with honors, or did volunteer at the non-profit, or really does read and speak fluent Mandarin. But if the candidate is a senior vice president at a brand name company, supported with glowing written testimonials, or a well-known VC who might back you and join your Board... well there's certainly no need to check on their well-established bona fides.

Right? Absolutely wrong!

The second insight I hope you'll internalize is that reference checking is not — or should not be — about "checking." Widespread assumptions and practice are that candidates' applications, references, and qualifications are simply to be validated. Sure, you need to make sure they haven't fibbed about grad school or concealed a conviction for embezzlement. But the requisite ticking of boxes should be the least of it. Rather, the reference consulting process — my preferred term — should be about getting to know the candidate through the experiences of former colleagues, bosses, or subordinates. This is where you learn how they react to stress or criticism, what their work style is to get things done, and what their skills of collaboration look like. There's simply no better way to get to know how a prospective employee, partner, or Board member is likely to work out than to talk with as many people as possible who have worked with them, for them, or supervised them. Think of it as dating before you get married. As with a long courtship, a rigorous reference consultation ultimately makes for a better contract.

So to the first insight, when I started Coremetrics, Accel Partners (now Accel) wanted to invest in our first major fundraising round, our Series A, alongside Highland Capital Partners which we had already chosen as our lead. We were impressed with Highland's Keith Benjamin, a legendary investor and Wall Street visionary and he was joining our Board of Directors. (Sadly, Keith passed away in a tragic accident in 2008. He was an incredible friend, about whom I think often. I share a memorial I wrote about him on the Digital Companion).

Accel, meanwhile, put forward Arthur Patterson to join our Board alongside me, Keith, and our independent Director, technology entrepreneur Bong Suh, who remains a really terrific mentor more than two decades later. Arthur was, among other things, Accel's Co-founder, a former senior official in the U.S. Treasury Department, a venture capitalist since 1973, and the one-time Director of the National Association of Venture Capitalists. Arthur was a towering figure in the VC world and it was an honor to have him on our team. But as I had done with Keith, I insisted on checking Arthur's references.

Most people at Accel were surprised, and I think they thought I was naive at the time. After all, I was a 26-year-old CEO and they probably chalked it up to inexperience. And when I called his CEO references, some of them expressed a lot of surprise that I had the moxie to do so. But those references turned out to be extraordinarily helpful to me, especially on how to best work with Arthur as a business partner. For example, they told me to treat Arthur as a true partner, no matter how scared I may be about something happening inside or outside of Coremetrics, and share bad news as early as possible to get his advice. This guidance from Arthur's peers certainly helped us quickly match our collaborative cadence. But also, rather than be somehow offended, I believe

Arthur had more respect for me as a result of being one of the first entrepreneurs to check his references.

But to the second insight I shared above, of course I wasn't checking to see if Arthur had really gotten his MBA from Harvard, or that he indeed had a dozen or so IPOs and private exits under his belt. Of course he did. What I wanted to make sure of was that the styles, outlooks, temperaments, and values would align with our leadership team. I couldn't see any other alternative — I deeply loved Coremetrics (I still do) and I wanted to make sure that we fielded the best team possible. That included our investors and our Board of Directors.

Needless to say, I carried this practice with references on to Bazaarvoice a few years later, at least initially. As I detailed in Chapter 11, *The Most Proven Way to Hire,* we had learned to become broadly obsessive about both our hiring processes and I sought to be similarly so in our reference consulting approach. In discussion with candidate references, I would probe and probe until I got something useful to work with. Usually, I was able to get to some of the "areas for improvement" by saying something like, "Please level with me. I most likely am going to hire them but I could *really* use your advice about how to best coach them to perform at their best from day one." That type of personal plea was hard to ignore. They had been there too, with that same person. If that didn't work, I would ask them to walk me through the areas for improvement on their last performance evaluation. We all have them — no one is perfect.

Over the years, I've refined the process, and the time and diligence have certainly been justified by our high retention rates, strong corporate cultures, and commercial success at all of my companies. But as discussed in Chapter 4, *The Importance of an Always Be Learning Life*, one should always be acquiring new skills. And this was the case not long ago when I was invited to speak at the annual CEO Summit of First Round Capital, the seed-stage VC firm specializing in technology investments. First

Round was a great partner as an early Bazaarvoice investor, and co-founder Josh Kopelman was an invaluable source of guidance. A link to First Round's brilliant (and free) publication, *Review*, is on the Digital Companion and I'll have more to say about my talk at the summit in Chapter 14, *Seven Lessons Learned on the Journey from Founder to CEO*.

But the highlight of that CEO summit was, in fact, less my own presentation than the talk given by Scott Cook, the Co-founder, and CEO of the financial software giant Intuit and later its executive chairman. Both talks are also available on the Digital Companion, but I want to quote here an excerpt from an account of Scott's that was published in the *Review*, in which he underscores the importance of four qualities which he seeks insight from references: intelligence, learning ability, care for the quality of work and customer satisfaction, and the ability to get things done.

> "Keeping these four key attributes in mind, Cook gets on the phone with the reference and begins by letting them talk about working with the candidate. However, the reality is people generally want to be nice and don't have much to gain by being fully transparent and honest, so they generally start by saying how great the potential hire was and how valuable they were to the team. Cook has found that it's most effective to completely ignore this opening feedback and throw it out. Once they're done rambling on, Cook asks, "Among all of the people you've seen in this position, on a zero to ten scale, where would this person rank?" They go, "Seven." Cook says, "Why isn't this person a nine or a ten?" And then you'll finally start learning about what this person really thinks.
>
> Cook concludes the call by asking this person for other people who can give a reference on the candidate and then begins the process again. Getting as far away as possible from the

candidate's suggested references often leads to the most valuable data.

The brilliance of Scott's approach is the comparative aspect. It forces the reference to stack-rank the candidate, and the reference's integrity will most likely force them to be candid in response to such a direct and comparative question.

Now I do want to note with candor here that while I was on the right way to do reference checks early in my career, I have taken my eye off the ball to potential detriment at least once. This is why above I qualified with the word "initially" when I wrote about Bazaarvoice being diligent in checking references. One of my scariest times in the company's history was when I learned that our head of recruiting at the time had decided to stop checking references. I found out about this when one of the people we had hired had started to engage in activities that I choose not to disclose here. I started to probe how that happened when we were so diligent at checking references. "We stopped checking references," I was told to my shock. I couldn't believe it! I asked why. "Because they don't really tell you anything — they are all provided by the candidate." I then spent the next 30 minutes telling stories about how important it was to always check references, and specifically how to probe. I also talked about the importance of going off-script and finding references that they didn't provide. We reverted to our original diligent reference-checking practice immediately.

I really don't believe the dangers of failing to check references can be exaggerated. This is broadly the case, but especially so when you are interviewing Board members or raising money from new investors. And as counter-intuitive as it may seem, I'm convinced as I wrote above that the higher level you go the more important reference checking actually is, and the more like a marriage it will be.

So let me share two horror stories so that you can understand why I'm so passionate about this.

With names changed and details fudged to protect the guilty, here's horror story #1:

In this case, the leading protagonists are two CEOs and a CEO recruit. The first CEO is leading a company we'll call Acme Technologies, with great potential, a promising product, and several million dollars of funds already raised and in the bank. But, the Board of Directors has ultimate control, has tired of Acme Tech's founding CEO, and is convinced he needs to go and that they need a real professional in the job at this stage. But who to recruit?

As the fates would have it, there's another CEO of a complementary company, Balance Resources we'll call it, who is familiar to the Board of Advisors. They know this CEO because he serves on the Advisory Board of Acme Technologies. Mind you, as an Advisory Board member he has no executive authority, or decision-making shares, but he carries out the role of a sounding board. He's an advisor, after all, so they go to him for advice. Actually, they sort of go halfway when a new candidate for Acme Tech CEO — currently in a sub-C Suite management role at Balance Resources — applies for the soon-to-open position. This is someone whose boss has repeatedly lauded in various meetings. So assumptions are made without questions. The Advisory Board member has spoken highly of his employee now seeking to move up in the world. If he's from the Advisory Board member's company, he must have recommended him? He must be good? It would be offensive to the Advisory Board member if the Acme Board of Directors deigned to ask after the candidate's bonafides. Would it not?

As you might imagine, this led to precisely the scenario I've warned about. The founding Acme CEO was ousted, the new Balance Resources manager was hired as the new CEO, and things promptly went to hell in a handbasket.

Naturally, the Acme board then turned on the Advisory Board member. His response was they had never consulted him on the candidate, just made a bunch of feeble assumptions. Yes, he had spoken highly of the candidate's brilliant individual contributions. A good guy to be sure. But lots of brilliant contributors, in sales as a common example, make lousy executives. And in this, the guy who they hired as CEO had already batted out as a manager. Every one of his hires has to be let go for performance issues. Had they asked, he would have explained to them that they were making a huge mistake. But instead, they assumed.

As the truism usually credited to Steve Jobs goes: A's hire A's. And B's hire C's. This was a textbook case, just one of many in my experience. The company was eventually sold for much less than was invested and everyone lost money.

In horror story #2, I once got a reference call about a candidate for a public-company CEO position who I had worked with in the past. Their candidate had not given me a heads up that he was looking for a new job. The person on the other end was an executive recruiter and I remember thinking, "Cool, they are going off-script and I'm a very honest reference." The recruiter started to ask me their normal "reference check" questions and I quickly became disenchanted. I started to give them some of the cons (there were many pros that I had already given them), but they would quickly change the subject back to the pros. It was clear to me that the recruiter just wanted to check the boxes and get the job done. Anything they learned from me on the cons they would have to report back, and so they chose to not hear them at all. And then it hit me: I couldn't believe that a public-company Board of Directors had delegated the task of checking the references on a new CEO *to a recruiter*. Did no one on the Board have the time? What about the Chairman of the Board? What about the Governance Committee? It was a bad sign, and although the person they recruited was pretty good (at least in my opinion) — the company didn't last for very long.

The bottom line is that checking references is a critical activity and therefore it should be a cherished, celebrated practice. You are, after all, recruiting people to join your company and there is both a real financial cost as well as an opportunity cost — and a cultural cost if they don't work out — to carefully consider. Thorough reference checking isn't a foolproof practice — nothing is. But it is *a very important one*. And don't forget that as CEO it is a lot easier to let go of a team member who isn't performing than it is to dispense with one of your investors or Board members. You can get star-struck with someone's credentials and awards. The more they have accomplished, the more tempting it is to skip a check of their references. This is counterintuitive but true. An extreme example of this is the disgraced financier Bernie Madoff - how many of his prospective investors really dug into the viability of his financial results? Social signaling and intuition will bias you to spend a lot of time checking references on junior or "unknown" team members and very little time checking references on the most senior. So please follow Scott Cook's advice and truly dig in. The higher level your candidate is, especially potential investors and Board of Director members, the more you should check. Go off-script. You'll be very thankful that you did.

"It was a rather delicate and awkward situation. You should call her other past employers. I made the mistake of not doing that."

**— COMMENT MADE TO A REFERENCE CHECKER, REPORTED ON CBS NEWS BY CORRESPONDENT SUZANNE LUCAS**

# CHAPTER 13
## HOW TO LEVERAGE ADVISORS AND INVESTORS

*"Search well and be wise, nor believe that self-willed pride will ever be better than good counsel."*

## — AESCHYLUS, ANCIENT GREEK PLAYWRIGHT

There is no aspiring entrepreneur worth their salt who does not harbor an idea for the ultimate "dream team" of advisors broadly defined: engaged investors in general and trusted Advisory Board members specifically.

But as many a sage has remarked, dreams can become reality only when you wake up and roll up your sleeves. And all too often in my experience, entrepreneurs fail to convert their dreams of a robust circle of external collaborators into a consciously chosen, deliberately managed, and trusted circle that is a true force multiplier.

So I need to dwell on this dimension of your journey as I've been fortunate to have several "dream teams" of great external collaborators, particularly at both Bazaarvoice and now at data.world.

It's hard to say why building a broad support team eludes so many entrepreneurs. There are plenty of studies, books, and legal reviews on how to recruit and manage your Board of Directors. But this is a different subject than that upon which I wrote in Chapter 12, *The Importance of Reference Checking*. With corporate governance a growing issue and directors' legal responsibilities evermore complex, the attention is important. Nonetheless, there is not commensurate thought given to the ongoing ways investors and advisors are important members of your extended team once vetted and squarely in your corner. My own view on this is that investors are narrowly seen as the source of capital. And advisors, meanwhile, are too often seen as an image-building tool, the means to bolster the *perception* of a startup's competence and expertise. While raising money is obviously essential, and shaping perceptions of your company is critical, this limited outlook misses out on so much potential for your startup.

So if you're an entrepreneur at the start of your journey, I encourage you to think broadly of your "external" team, and below I'll also offer some advice on how to manage this team and vigorously communicate with it.

But first, I'll invite you to imagine three intersecting circles, a Venn diagram akin to the Olympic rings. We'll call them circles A, B, and C. In circle A, you have your investors. In circle B, you have your advisors. And in circle C, you have overlap: the investors who do function as part of your inner circle and advisors who in some cases choose to become investors.

Let's start with circle A, your investors. You need their money, to be sure. But ideally, you should be seeking a lot more, including their experience, their domain expertise, their networks, and their insight. A good (and common) example of the wrong kind of investor is physicians. Usually, they are wealthy. Often, they are looking for places to invest. But unless your startup is in the medical space, or you're a "Stage 1" entrepreneur (see Chapter 5, *Bootstrap or VC?*) with a limited remit of consulting or services, these are not the investors you want to prioritize first. As so-called "passive investors," they are not going to open doors for you or help you overcome blind spots.

That is to say, you need to be as selective as possible. You need to have empathy for those from whom you raise money. And they, in turn, need to have empathy for you, your vision, and your mission. Sure, investors are not the "man in the arena" in my often quoted phrase of Theodore Roosevelt, and they're not going to take the arrows, nor experience the thrill of victory in the same way as you. But, they can be very supportive should you choose to treat them as part of your extended team. They are putting their money (if they are angel investors), or their investors' money (in the case of venture capitalists), into your venture. And you should treat that capital as if it were your own. Part of the thrill of investing is to see the entrepreneur succeed, both changing their life and many other people's lives in the process. Investors enjoy telling their friends — other investors and family — about the success of your business. The journey is more important than any return they get (although to be clear they don't want to lose either their money or their investors' money). The more they help you, the more they live vicariously through you, and their fingerprints will be all over your business. This is called a "helper's high" by my good friend and CEO coach, Kirk Dando, about whom I'll have more to say in Chapter 14, *Seven Lessons Learned on the Journey from Founder to CEO.*

One way to think about investors is that they are on the periphery of the arena and ready to assist you. If you think of a coliseum, imagine that you and your team are the folks "in the arena" (again, a nod to Theodore Roosevelt). The spectators, meanwhile, include many people — the press, industry analysts, as well as current and potential consultants, employees, clients, partners, and investors.  Though your current clients are present, I wouldn't necessarily say they are all in the arena with you (although some of the early adopters most certainly are) — and they deserve frequent communication as well. But let's stick to investors and advisors in this chapter.

Your investors often have valuable tools for you to leverage in the coliseum, such as their contacts or lessons they've learned when they used to be the ones in the arena themselves, or from learning through one of their other investments. This is what venture capitalists call "pattern recognition." So it is not only smart to be empathetic toward your investors because you want to build a relationship with them, but also because they can really help you. To assume otherwise is either arrogant or ignorant. When I bring up this topic in speeches or when coaching an entrepreneur, I usually get a reaction of, "What a good idea." This tells me that the primary problem is ignorance — those entrepreneurs just haven't been educated on this topic, and that is why I emphasize this so strongly. As far as the arrogant, they are usually in for a hard fall.

When it comes to circle B, your Board of Advisors, most of the same lessons apply. You can just substitute investors with advisors above. Both are compensated to help you — investors through ownership of some of your equity and advisors through stock option grants that they can exercise at a later period of time. A key difference, however, is that Advisory Board members are often less familiar with you, and you're less likely to have worked together or interacted before. So many of the lessons we discussed in Chapter 11, *The Proven Way to Hire Well,* are relevant here. You should scrutinize, vet, and research the backgrounds of Advisory Board members before engaging them. Examples of the advisors I have brought in because they were the most strategic include investor and podcaster Mike Maples, Jr., VC and philanthropist Josh Kopelman, serially successful Wharton entrepreneur Steve Katz, Performics Founder Jamie Crouthamel, Fyrfly Venture Partners Co-founder and long-time angel investor Julie Maples, entrepreneur and angel investor Ralph Mack, and one-time Google executive and VC Satya Patel. Many of my advisors have been recruited with a more specific purpose, such as marketing know-how (particularly at Bazaarvoice with its marketing-oriented solutions) or experience in getting into a new industry (like financial services) or geography (like Europe).

As far as managing Advisory Boards, I tend to invite a subset of Advisors to an occasional Advisory Board meeting (usually every six months). To invite all of my advisors to a regular meeting risks it becoming unwieldy. This would mean, in my case, having something like 60 people in the room and little commonality in terms of the way they could help the company. Some companies avoid this by keeping the Advisory Board small. But limiting membership is a problem in its own right because some advisors you add for very specific purposes. Keep in mind that this should be a diverse group, really a collective of many sub-groups with different kinds of expertise that you will need to draw upon selectively.

In circle C is where the two groups overlap, as they should. The best way I can illustrate the fact that the lines in my imaginary Venn diagram are highly porous is with the story of my friend Dean Allemang, who has been a data.world advisor, investor, and is now an employee as well.

In our realm of data and digital technology, Dean is a powerhouse. Not only does he have a doctorate in artificial intelligence, but he is also the author of the seminal 2008 book, the *Semantic Web for the Working Ontologist.* The book, now in its third edition, uses the life of William Shakespeare to explore the application of the concept-connecting "semantic web." Before we even publicly launched data.world, we sought out Dean for his counsel, and particularly his validation of the ideas and concepts we were bringing together under the flag of our new company in 2015. I and my three co-founders spent almost two days with Dean, brainstorming, shaping, and refining our plans for the company. Needless to say, Dean became one of our first Advisory Board members. Later, Dean decided to become an investor and took an equity stake in data.world. Then, in the summer of 2021, he decided to join us full-time. He is now our Principal Solutions Architect and an invaluable member of data.world's executive team.

So, you say, "This is all interesting, but how do I manage such a disparate, dispersed, and loosely connected team?" The answer is an unusual communication practice with our investors and advisors. I treat them as I would want to be treated if I were in their shoes. It's the Golden Rule in action.

So ask yourself: "If this were my money, *what kind of updates would I want?*" My guess is you would want to always know how the business is doing and how you could help the business — and therefore help your investment. And this applies to all advisors as well so they get the same emails I send investors.

This is with the caveat that your communications will become constrained by insider trading regulation once you file to go public. As I did with Bazaarvoice in 2012, you should be as broad and transparent as possible with investors and advisors about the state of the business.

In the past, I've routinely written as many as three emails a week to this group. Now, I am religious about sending a detailed data.world update to all of this extended team every Monday. My updates included new client wins, major client launches, big up-sells, new executive hires, new marketing campaigns, challenges that we needed help with (such as a client contract renewal or a blocker at a client that was preventing them from properly adopting our nascent solution), new product launches, etc. For example at Bazaarvoice, I would send an update of a major client win, such as OpenTable, and get an email response from one of our investors who was friends with the CEO. Then instead of being a low-level sale, we now had high-level adoption to help drive further use of our solutions. This was especially important because our solutions needed to be evangelized to educate the client on business practices they should change as a result of having access to online word of mouth from their most valuable stakeholders — their customers — for the first time in their history. This is where the Bazaarvoice mission statement of "changing the world, one authentic conversation at a time" came from.

To reach a lot of investors simultaneously, the most efficient method is email. But then once they respond, the most efficient method is to call them, such as in the OpenTable example. When I call (or now videoconference) them, the investor and I usually get into some tangential conversations and I find other ways that they can help us. In other words, calling fosters a better relationship. Because I email updates frequently, constantly fostering the relationship, it creates a virtuous circle where I get more out of our relationship, and — importantly — they do too.

Now, to be honest, I share the advice in this chapter frequently, but few follow it. The better entrepreneurial performers usually do. As for me, I've lived this since the beginning of data.world and before that at Bazaarvoice. As a result, I have a very active and engaged data.world Advisory Board and investor base. And all of our employees receive these as well. That way everyone is on the same page, having the same information about our progress and challenges.

As I expressed in Chapter 2, *The Paralyzing Fear of Getting Started*, it is often lonely at the top. But it's a lot less so when you've surrounded yourself with competence, insight, and experience in the form of those you choose as investors and advisors. Today, at data.world our investors include Shasta Ventures, Tech Pioneers Fund, Jim Breyer, Arthur Patterson, Pat Ryan, Mike Maples Jr., and even four of our customers (Associated Press, Workday, Prologis, and Vopak). Our Advisory Board, meanwhile, includes DJ Patil, Adam Grant, Kelly Wright, Kirk Dando (my CEO coach), Bob Campbell (who wrote the Afterword for this book), and 60 other very prominent and amazing people.

Select your external team members wisely, and you'll be in and have a wise company. This is the external team that may well make a huge difference between failure and success.

> *"No man is so foolish but he may sometimes give another good counsel, and no man so wise that he may not easily err if he takes no other counsel than his own. He that is taught only by himself has a fool for a master."*

## — HUNTER S. THOMPSON, AUTHOR AND JOURNALIST

# CHAPTER 14

# SEVEN LESSONS LEARNED ON THE JOURNEY FROM FOUNDER TO CEO

*"Character cannot be developed in ease and quiet. Only through experience of trial and suffering can the soul be strengthened, ambition inspired and success achieved."*

## — HELEN KELLER

No one is born knowing how to found a company or be a CEO. And no one is born knowing how emotional the trek can be. This is a hard-earned, ever-evolving, and constantly demanding role that I hope is clear from the chapters so far. As my friend and CEO coach Kirk Dando has counseled me on more than one occasion, "The path to heaven goes through the road to hell." It certainly does, and the journey is often one of euphoric highs and gut-wrenching lows. But it's also a journey that is profound, and one I've cherished as I believe you will too.

So let's pause for a bit of reflection here, as it's worth summarizing the seven primary lessons I've learned from more than two decades as a CEO. It's been a journey through six companies, working with literally thousands of great team members, both inside the companies I've helped found and led, and as well with the CEOs in whom we've invested through our family office.

Below are my seven lessons on this transformational journey:

**Lesson #1: The CEO must be the Chief Culture Officer.**

No one else has the power to be the "CCO" but the CEO. This is because the CEO is the synthesis point for all departments and the most senior executive at the company — with the ultimate say on what a company decides to focus on, culture included. A founder-CEO especially cares about the culture because they have breathed the soul into a new being: the company. And like a parent, the CEO cares uniquely about how this new being evolves from childhood into adulthood. A company is like a person and is even legally treated as such in most countries. In their personhood, some companies have a great brain. Fewer have a great heart. And even fewer have a great soul. The CEO should care about nourishing the soul. You can tell when a company has a great soul just by walking the halls and feeling the energy. Does the company give you energy or does it siphon your energy away?

Nothing says more about your culture than who you hire, who you fire, and who you promote. The CEO has the most power to make these decisions. If the CEO promotes a brilliant jerk — one who performs very well individually but who no one wants to work with because of their attitude — then that speaks volumes about that company's culture. The CEO also has the ability to shape how the company serves its communities. I chose to establish the Bazaarvoice Foundation in our first year of our life, which ultimately decided to focus on accelerating STEM and entrepreneurial education in high schools. I was influenced by watching the documentary, *The Corporation*, and I encourage you to watch it if you haven't already. I've included a link to do so on the Digital Companion. Today, the Bazaarvoice Foundation has taken on a strong life of its own and was initially led by Executive Director Kelly Ballard with the help of a steering committee. The Foundation was led top-down only in our first year of history because I wanted to set the tone. From that year on, it was led by a steering committee of volunteers who have solicited constant feedback from the people of Bazaarvoice. After Bazaarvoice went public, Debra and I gifted a significant portion of our stock to help give the Bazaarvoice Foundation a boost. This is how much I embraced trust in our people.

At data.world, I still very much view one of my top priorities as CEO in this way. We constantly debate culture and how to make data.world a better place to work, and I often ask our people, especially our newest team members, how to improve it. And we've won Best Places to Work in Austin for six years in a row now, just like we did at Bazaarvoice before.

## Lesson #2: The CEO must constantly work on self-improvement and regularly take the time to reflect.

After graduating from Wharton, I and many of my fellow graduates felt that we had received the best business education in the world. It was, of course, quite good. But I also felt that my business education was just beginning. I had founded Coremetrics during my last semester and was now in the real, raw world of being an entrepreneur where I discovered that perhaps the most important thing I learned at Wharton was *learning how to learn*. I was determined to read hundreds of leadership and management books in my first two years after Wharton to help me in my journey and apply what I read every day. Books are read by leaders, and magazines and newspapers are read by followers. This doesn't mean I never read a magazine or newspaper, I do so voraciously. But keeping up with the 24/7 news cycle doesn't improve yourself as does a book. A book causes you to think more deeply because decades or centuries of knowledge are nicely summarized in one concise, reflective format. I discussed this mindset and practice in detail in Chapter 4, *The Importance of an Always Be Learning Life.*

Constant self-improvement means the CEO should also constantly seek out mentors. I am the product of many mentors, and I have found that if you reach out to people fearlessly they will often respond to aid you. I believe this notion to be deep in our DNA as a nation. It's worth pondering the fact that since 1776 our country has come to hold a quarter of the world's GDP and almost all of that wealth has been self-created. Yes, much of this wealth has been created amid historical injustice, a topic we'll discuss later. But that does not obviate the virtues of collaboration and mutual reliance. When you reach out to successful people in the U.S., they may see some of their previous struggles and ambition in you and remember that they too were helped by mentors to become successful. I believe the U.S. is unusual if not unique in this way. When Debra and I went to Israel for the first time, we found it to be very similar, in no small part because of the similar circumstances of how the modern-day country came into being after World War II. Like the new Americans, the new Israelis had virtually no equipment to fight for their independence, especially right after the Holocaust. As I write this in mid-2022, Israel, despite a population roughly equivalent to that of New Jersey, ranks third globally in the number of startups outside of the U.S., right behind the United Kingdom and ahead of Canada and Germany.

The CEO should also leverage a CEO coach. I have long leveraged Kirk Dando as mine, and he is now a very close friend. A podcast we did together is linked on the Digital Companion. Not long ago, my views on this point were reinforced by Scott Cook, the founder of Intuit when he said one of his biggest mistakes was not using a CEO coach for the first 23 years of his career. To prepare for our IPO at Bazaarvoice, I leveraged three additional coaches — one to help with earnings calls, one to help with investor Q&A, and one to teach me how to present to investors on the roadshow. I still work hard to build out a world-class mentor network, as evidenced by our diverse and incredible investor base and our large Advisory Board at data.world, about which I wrote in Chapter 13, *How to Leverage Advisors and Investors.*

All that said, I also believe that just as you should seek out mentors, you should also be one. I've long believed in the counsel of the French essayist Joseph Joubert, "to teach is to learn twice." This is a mantra I live by in my practice of reflection. I've served multiple times as an Entrepreneur-in-Residence, both at Wharton and at the University of Texas at Austin's McCombs School of Business. I've spoken at many events to help teach entrepreneurs, including the Capital Factory and TechStars, two of our largest startups incubators and accelerators located here in Austin. And the initial version of this book, located on Medium.com, was turned into the foundational material for the entrepreneurial leadership course at Technion, Israel's oldest university.

Taking the time to reflect on what you have learned is paramount. As author and entrepreneur, Arianna Huffington states in a podcast episode with LinkedIn Co-founder Reid Hoffman: "Knowing when to turn the lights out may be the only way to keep the lights on." At Bazaarvoice, I took five to six weeks of vacation every year and I believe this made it a better company. At data.world, I still take the same amount of vacation time with my family, to both recharge and reflect. Sometimes these vacations give me the clarity of mind to let go of an executive that I have been holding on to for too long. Sometimes these vacations have made me sharper on strategy. Sometimes these vacations helped me focus on our company more. It is easy to get defocused as a young company. So, recharge, and reflect.

## Lesson #3: The CEO should own the long-term vision of the company.

This is the torch that the CEO must carry to light the fires with everyone — investors, employees, clients, and partners. This creates tremendous energy, both for the CEO and everyone else. The CEO also decides when to sell the company or keep growing. This is aligned with the long-term vision. How bright is the future? Is it real or is it a mirage? What kind of impact do you want to make? We could have sold Bazaarvoice for $25 million after our first year in business. Instead, we chose to go long because our long-term vision was greater. Ultimately, we built the company to a valuation of more than $1 billion (our IPO was named by the *Wall Street Journal* as one of the top five of 2012), creating a much bigger impact, as a result, enriching many more people, and the community beyond ourselves as founders. For example, I'm very proud of the fact that more than 60 startups have been created by former Bazaarvoice team members following our IPO.

A very concrete way to think about the CEO's role in carrying the torch of vision is in the articulation of the firm's Point of View, or POV. More than a mission statement, the POV is the expression of the company's outlook, values, goals, and strategy. A brilliant book I highly recommend, *Play Bigger: How Pirates, Dreamers, and Innovators Create and Dominate Markets,* explores this concept. Three years ago, I took our entire data.world team through the book and I wrote our collective POV over many weekends and with much input from the executive team. It is the most important strategic document I've personally written in the history of our company. It continues to grow and evolve as our strategy does, and I make sure to take all new team members through it during their onboarding.

**Lesson #4: The CEO should always treat recruiting as a top-three priority.**

Among the many jobs of the CEO is the responsibility to serve as the Chief Resource Officer. The "CRO," if you will, is responsible for attracting the best clients, partners, investors, advisors, and, of course, employees. Beyond the critical job of creating your initial, founding team, the CEO must also be focused on constantly upgrading your team. For example, I hired three CFOs in six years at Bazaarvoice. This isn't easy, and again reflecting on vacation helped with this. As CEO, you will be defined by those that *you* choose to report to you. If there is dysfunction at the top, there will be a huge ripple effect throughout the company, causing dysfunction throughout, including at the bottom. At Bazaarvoice, we relied on a rigorous recruiting process that mostly served us well, if not always perfectly. I wrote about this in some detail in Chapter 11, *The Most Proven Way to Hire Well*, and we follow the same process at data.world. People are the raw material of your culture and ultimately of your performance as a company. Rapid growth brings out the best — or worst — in people. It causes everyone to stretch and the pace is hard to keep up with. I have found those with the wisdom that I mentioned in Lesson #2 above scale with a company's growth for the longest period of time. Recruiting your Board of Directors should especially be a focus. It is much harder to fire a Board member than any other person on your team if you have made a mistake. Don't get starstruck by pedigree. Spend the time to really get to know them and check their references. I discussed in detail how to reference Board members and executives in Chapter 12, *The Importance of Reference Checking*.

**Lesson #5: The CEO should celebrate regularly at All-Hands meetings where vision, alignment, and transparency prevail.**

At Bazaarvoice, and now at data.world, we hold our quarterly All-Hands meetings at the Alamo Drafthouse, a famous homegrown venue in Austin that is a combined cinema and pub. I've found this venue tremendous because it is counterculture. In short, the Alamo is a place with a sense of humor, mock movie posters, and an atmosphere that demands that you relax. Drinks —

including beer and cocktails — and food are available throughout the day when we have our meeting. With it being a fun movie theater, most of our presenters try to one-up each other with the funniest — but most informative — presentation. At times, we've voted on who did the best, who stoked the competition and quality even more. As we grew at Bazaarvoice, we combined the meeting with a film festival, where team members produced some of the most hilarious videos I've ever seen. We even had a company band play live. And here, all metrics are revealed. I further evolved at data.world to also use these meetings to share our quarterly presentation decks given to the Board of Directors, a practice I didn't dream up during the Bazaarvoice days. Everyone knows how we are trying to be aligned and what our goals and progress are. These events have been, and continue to be, magical. Early investors who have witnessed them have been wowed. These gatherings are my favorite days as CEO — second only to our Client Summits. We now do the data.world summit, a kind of cross between the Academy Awards and a TED conference devoted to data, each spring, and fall, and thousands attend virtually. Only the CEO can choose the means to bring the entire company to spend this time together. There are many competing priorities. I discuss the mistake I made at data.world by not having these until a few years ago in Chapter 17, *Action-Oriented Communication.*

**Lesson #6: The CEO should evolve systems to keep everyone aligned.**

In developing my own strategy to keep teams aligned, I have been very influenced by Salesforce.com founder and CEO Marc Benioff's book, *Behind the Cloud*, where he discusses what he calls his V2MOM model, for Vision, Values, Methods, Obstacles, and Measures. I include a link to an essay Benioff wrote on this on the Digital Companion and you'll find it enlightening. But I chose to make it simpler for my purposes. I called it the "declarative b," in homage to the "b:" logo that was part of Bazaarvoice's brand since a year before our IPO. The colon stages something profound that follows, and you can use it in many ways such as b: bold, b: changing the world, b: transparent, etc. The beauty of the V2MOM model as I've modified it is that everyone participates and forms their own goals to be aligned with the corporate goals. It creates an interlocking chain of goals for each unit of the company within the larger set of corporate targets and aspirations that go from the top to the bottom to keep everyone aligned — and happier. If you know how you are performing, and that you are indeed aligned with the overall strategy of the company, then your work will be more fulfilling as a result. And this allows the company to constantly measure and constantly improve. I only wish that I had discovered this model earlier. Benioff says it is the key to Salesforce.com's perpetual success, and I believe it.

At data.world, I've had the benefit of three co-founders along for the journey since the beginning. One of them is Matt Laessig, one of my best friends ever since we went to the Wharton School together as young MBA students. He serves as our COO and CFO. Matt has made practicing this lesson easier as he's established good systems from our beginning. Other members of the team have made profound contributions. Rafa Pereira, our first Director of Software Engineering, really pushed us to embrace "OKRs," for Objectives and Key Results. And I should add that Rafa went on to co-found Onebrief, which is a mission planning tool that reflects his passion for OKRs.

We are much better for using this practice to build and reinforce collective commitment. John Doerr, the famous venture capitalist once described as a "fizzing coil of energy," talked about the importance of OKRs at a TED conference that I link on the Digital Companion. I urge your attention to his talk, and also his book on the subject, *Measure What Matters: How Google, Bono, and the Gates Foundation Rock the World with OKRs.* Doerr credits the late CEO of Intel, the legendary Andy Grove, with creating OKRs as a tool to "establish the right goals for the right reasons." I'll have a lot more to say on this in Chapter 19, *The Five Critical Ingredients to Build a Big Company*. This is a very important practice indeed. Doerr cites it as the main practice that has made Google so successful since almost the beginning, as well as many of his other Kleiner Perkins portfolio companies. Our top corporate goals and the OKRs that align with them have been a very important practice over the past several years at data.world, and help keep our now 100-team-member-plus size company aligned.

### Lesson #7: The CEO should embrace vulnerability.

As the most senior executive, you are on the ultimate stage. Everyone's watching to see how you will behave — and, to a large extent, they will mimic your behavior. The CEO should have a growth mindset versus a fixed one. No book explains this better than *Egonomics,* which explores ways to achieve the right balance between ego and humility. If the CEO has closed his or her mind to learning due to their "success" (I put this in quotes because there is always someone that is more "successful" than you), then many others in the company will also choose to stop learning. Taking the time to reflect is incredibly important for learning — and a CEO is very hard to mentor if they don't practice reflection. A CEO is impossible to mentor if they cannot be vulnerable. At Bazaarvoice, we practiced vulnerability by reading books like *Fierce Conversations*, which focuses on truly meaningful communication and having training programs around them. I discuss this more in Chapter 17, *Action-Oriented Communication*.

We enable employees to regularly rate managers on whether or not we were living the core values. After all, are they just values on a piece of paper, or are we — as managers — going to truly live those values? If we don't, then the paper is not worth as much as the cost of the ink to print it. We have regularly run what we call "Climate Surveys" for everyone in the company to evaluate our overall culture and we have found ways to benchmark ourselves against other companies to see how we rank. At both Bazaarvoice and data.world we've participated in "Best Places to Work" surveys, where we were ranked against other companies in Austin. All of these are difficult practices. They require you to be open, reflective, and introspective, and sometimes what you learn is painful and the insight unveils practices that can be hard to change. Note that those with a fixed mindset will sometimes hold vulnerability against you. But choosing not to undertake these steps — and not make them a priority as CEO — is to turn your back on the voice of your people, which ultimately will affect not just your culture but your performance. The best speeches I have given have been where I have been vulnerable. Like the time I hired an executive at Bazaarvoice who didn't reflect our values and had to explain in front of the entire company how I had made a mistake. Or the time at Bazaarvoice that we faced the Great Recession and stopped hiring to protect our people. We all had to work double-time and in hindsight, we beat our goals and I wouldn't have stopped hiring had I known. But in hindsight everything is clear, and in going through the Great Recession everyone was very concerned about what the fallout might be. And it made us a much stronger company at the time to pull together like that. And I'm both very transparent with our investors and our team members about those challenging times to help set the tone for our other leaders to do the same.

A few years ago at data.world, we implemented the use of software from the team-building company RallyBright to measure individual team resiliency, which has been helpful. RallyBright's founder and CEO, John Estafanous, has become a friend. And, around that same time, our data.world Culture Club (a volunteer, diverse group of people at our company that is very passionate about culture) designed and executed an engagement survey, which was very telling and actionable. That engagement survey has become an annual event at data.world, and we are all the better for it.

To be clear, yes, I still make mistakes — lots of them. But I'm a believer in karma and you should rise above it. Your people need you to be human.

Those are the key lessons I've learned in the journey from founder to CEO, and in short, it's all about self-awareness. These are certainly not a set of magic potions, and you will undoubtedly learn your lessons on your journey. The important thing is to heed the insights that reveal themselves along the way. I hope my own will serve to help get you started and become a better, more reflective, and ultimately more successful leader.

> *"Experience is the only thing that brings knowledge, and the longer you are on Earth the more experience you are sure to get."*

> **— L. FRANK BAUM, AUTHOR OF *THE WONDERFUL WIZARD OF OZ***

# CHAPTER 15
# A CALL TO ACTION FOR CEOS ON SELLING

*"I have never worked a day in my life without selling. If I believe in something, I sell it, and I sell it hard."*

## — ESTÉE LAUDER

There is no more effective selling tool in a company's organization than the company's CEO. There are also, however, few tools less effectively utilized than this one. Sadly, this squandering of potential is because of CEOs themselves.

In one sense, this conundrum is simple, straightforward, and concrete. Sales are simply the oxygen of any business; without sales, any company will quickly suffocate. Thus, assuring the continued flow of oxygen is the chief's chief job. But in another sense, this imperative is abstract. Because, unlike the flight attendant's advice before the plane heads down the runway, "Put on your own oxygen mask first before assisting others," you have to assist others before anything else when it comes to sales. The CEO's job is to assure the oxygen is flowing to the sales team and all its supporting teams.

All too often, sales are seen as a function, one among

engineering, product, marketing, et. al. All the units in this conception are linearly connected — Henry Ford's famous assembly line with a post-industrial age twist. But sales in today's world are better thought of as a symphony orchestra, with the sales team akin to the first violin which sets the pace for all to follow — the "corporate melody" as it were. But again, as with an orchestra where the hierarchy is led by the conductor who guides the assembled musicians to align strings, brass, woodwinds, and percussion, it is the CEO who aligns the sales strategy — or corporate melody — with the corporate mission, the tactics with the strategy, and also the sales techniques with the tactics. In place of the symphony's "musical score," the CEO has metrics, "KPIs" — or key performance indicators — which form the feedback loop to keep the business thriving (or the oxygen flowing to continue with my metaphor).

To make this all happen, the CEO must be *selfless*. Particularly in today's business world, the "hero CEO" is dead. Today's CEO is the connector, who leads not through command and control but through influence. They must adopt the regular practice of serving the rest of the organization. In assuring the flow of oxygen — the choreographed feedback loop — the selfless CEO needs humility and empathy. They need to carry the bird's eye view of the company and marketplace into the sales strategy, tactics, and techniques to say "we" instead of "I," to listen, and to inspire by example. Barking commands from on high is an all too common recipe for failure.

For example, the CEO must realize that their selling megaphone is larger than any other. This is not because they are better than anyone else in the organization. Everyone in the organization is just playing their role to their best ability. It is because the CEO possesses the company's highest executive title, and the title signals several important responsibilities and distinctions:

First, the CEO is the synthesis point for the entire

organization. No matter how flat the hierarchy, the CEO is the nexus of all the workflows that lead to sales. No other role can be the fulcrum to set the priorities and direction for the entire company as effectively, because no other role is tasked with the management of the entire organization. Every other role, such as the head of engineering, is functionally focused, as it should be. By contrast, the CEO is focused on the sum of all functions.

Second, while the selfless CEO must regard all on the team as peers, peers still must be organized in a hierarchy, a lesson learned from the very beginning of business education. As a result, everyone is trained on the CEO being the most powerful person in the organization. The CEO is the only one who can hire, fire, and promote the executive team, and these responsibilities set the culture and performance for the entire organization.

And third, if the CEO is also a founder of the business, then they embody the American dream that I discussed in the previous chapter. As I suggested there, selflessness is in the American DNA, as it is in other societies founded on teamwork such as Israel. The point I made there — that there is within all of us an entrepreneur — is equally the point that within all of us is selflessness.

Selflessness is a large topic that transcends all aspects of the entrepreneur's journey. My views on this have been deeply influenced by the study of the philosophy of Vedanta, beginning with a trip my wife Debra and I took to India. A book by our teacher there, Swamiji Parthasarathy's *Governing Business and Relationships*, is another one I recommend. More on his work and the subject of selflessness is linked on the Digital Companion. But as in all areas, selflessness must be the guiding principle of the CEO when it comes to sales.

That said, it took me a while to realize the importance of selling as a CEO. Many successful CEOs, in fact, emerge from an experience in sales to rise to the top. Berkshire Hathaway's Warren Buffett, IBM's Sam Palmisano who serves on data.world's Advisory Board, Starbucks' Howard Schultz, and "Shark Tank" investor Mark Cuban all got their start in sales. Their experience tells us a lot about the importance of the sales-savvy CEO. But their route was not mine.

At the start of my founder/CEO career, it was the technical skills I had developed, thanks to my mother allowing me to focus on my life's calling from the age of seven that carried me to that initial milestone. At the outset of my career, I felt very comfortable programming and mastering the suites of technology that have been at the center of all the companies I've now founded and led. I was in the flow of the digital economy and marketplace from the beginning. But I hadn't developed presentation skills. I didn't know how to sell. However, I was lucky enough to be authentically living my calling — and that is the most effective sales tool of all.

Knowing your calling is the essence of self-actualization, which is in turn the basis of authenticity. Authenticity is required to build trust. And people only buy from those whom they trust. So know your calling. Anyone to whom you are trying to sell will feel your energy and authenticity. This is the best foundation from which to build selling skills. And you have to learn selling skills just like any other: practicing, doing, reflecting, and refining. Because developing a new skill is difficult, and some CEOs shy away from it, making an excuse for themselves not engaging in selling. Examples of these excuses include:

**Excuse #1: It's all about the product.**

The product is beautiful, some CEOs will argue. And often they are right. Some readers will remember Betamax, the video recording technology that debuted in the late 1970s and was considered superior to the rival VHS format that ultimately dominated the market. Only a few people remember the "Osborne," the first portable computer rolled out in 1981, and even fewer people remember the inventor, Adam Osborne. Or Google Glass, the wearable computer, is a more recent example of a marvelous product that fizzled. Or Apple's Ping or Google's Google+, the social networks that never were. The cell phones of Nokia and Blackberry are further heads on the pikes that warn of these perils. The history of business is littered with failures, often caused by a CEO who believed the product should just sell itself. "I just need 'coin-operated' people to sell it for me," is the attitude. If it isn't selling, then the CEO's attitude is usually some version of, "that is what I hired you for." This is hardly selfless or effective.

**Excuse #2: Selling is a "commodity skill."**

Yes, sales is a specialty but it's a basic one, something you can simply buy in the personnel marketplace. This is an attitude seen all too often. It isn't as complex as the higher function pursuits, such as managing the strategy and priorities of the overall company. Or hiring, firing, and promoting the executive team. Or managing the Board of Directors and fundraising. These and other important CEO duties become excuses. "Selling is easy" in this view. No, it's not. And it must be embraced and led from above.

**Excuse #3: I don't have time.**

This is related to the devaluation of sales as a skill. It's the excuse that a CEO's time is too valuable to be spent on such mundane tasks as sales. "I'm too busy with more important activities," a CEO might say. Or even worse: "It isn't in my job description." Sorry, but it's at the center of your job description, and you should love it.

All of these excuses are terribly wrong. The attitude prevalent in them is a *selfish* one, not a *selfless* one. Because the CEO is the synthesis point of the entire organization, if they adopt these excuses and attitudes the rest of the organization will model them. Trenches deepen. Silos rise. The oxygen of the organization grows thinner and thinner. The head of sales will be left almost solely responsible for managing selling as a result. This is why some heads of sales complain about not being supported by the CEO. And why some CEOs go through many heads of sales, all while failing to meet their sales targets.

In place of these excuses, here are the top four convictions that should frame your attitude:

### Conviction #1: The sales buck stops with me.

"It is my duty to the organization to leverage the CEO megaphone that I have been entrusted with by our investors, the Board of Directors, and all of our people, to learn how to sell. My team will teach me, or I can hire presentation and selling coaches to do the same. I will practice, do, reflect, and refine."

### Conviction #2: As CEO, I must align with my calling.

"Every human being's fundamental obligation is to find his true identity in his lifetime," wrote Parthasarathy, my Vedanta teacher whom I mentioned above. Said differently, this is your calling. And greatness will elude the CEO who is not in that job because it is a life calling. "This business is my calling in life," the CEO must believe. "Everything I've done in the past has led up to this point. And from that point onward, there cannot be any excuse to not learn how to sell. I will learn to sell or I will fail and hold the entire organization back from the great success it can achieve."

### Conviction #3: I must strive for selflessness and change the world.

"To support the team who wants to change the world for the

better through the mission of the company, it is essential that I not shy away from such an important activity," you must tell yourself regularly. "It would be selfish to neglect sales. I must be better than that. I must be selfless. As CEO, I create my own job description and it starts with generous action."

Now I realize this may seem a bit abstract. But as with the development of any skill, over time it starts to click. And with more success at doing it, it starts to become more fun. What is more important than bringing in revenue? Without it, your business doesn't survive. What is more important than bringing in clients that are attracted to your mission? Without it, your collective dream doesn't become a reality. What is more important than working as a collective and selflessly serving each other? Without it, you will not have the great culture you seek. What is more important than changing the world for the better? You will do so through sales.

**Conviction #4: I must reclaim the power of whimsy.**

"I will remember to step back in awe, engage with the team in a sense of whimsy that takes us out of our comfort zones in a spirit of adventure without fear of failure."

Think back to when you were a child, whether learning to swim, playing games with friends, or being awestruck when discovering a new skill like, in my case, discovering programming in elementary school. It's a spirit you need to rekindle in service of sales.

This isn't something you can easily plan or contrive. It must be allowed to emerge. But you'll know constructive whimsy when you see it. At Bazaarvoice, it began with our head of sales Michael Osborne, and a green soccer ball. As I recall, it was a commemorative ball from Mexico's national team when it qualified for the World Cup. It started almost inadvertently after Osborne (he always went by his last name) showed up at a meeting with the soccer ball. There was a joke about touching it for good luck or something, a round of laughter. But then Osborne brought it to the next meeting, with approval from all.

Soon, the green soccer ball became a kind of talisman, like a lucky horseshoe hung on the door of a Texas barn. Or a "lucky number," which we all have, mine being No. 7, which inspired the name of my blog. Soon, knowing that Osborne would be bringing his lucky soccer ball to sales meetings, members of the team began wearing green on those days. As the rite evolved, in the last three days each quarter, Osborne would never be without his green ball and no one on the sales team would be without some green-colored artifact or piece of clothing. Osborne's mysterious green soccer ball became a whimsical, serendipitous rallying point as we all adopted the color green as a good luck charm on the final days of each quarter. It became as a symbol of, "We are all in this together, we will achieve our goals together, we are all selling." As a result, we almost always beat our sales goals under his leadership. Osborne inspired all of us. At data.world, our team is regularly rallied by Ryan Cush, our Chief Revenue Officer, who learned from Osborne at Bazaarvoice before as one of his top performers. Ryan has also led us to consistently beat our goals, constantly reinforcing our OKRs and alignment amongst all of our teams working together to sell - and service - our customers. Most incidentally, I also need to mention here that 50 percent of our bonus at data.world is based on how well we sell together and 50 percent is based on how well we serve our customers together. I'll have more to say on this in the next chapter, *Selling to the "Cool Kids."*

Throughout my CEO journey, I have played and continue to play a part to the best of my ability when it comes to sales. I place calls, video conferences, record videos, and write emails to prospects that are on the fence. I walk the halls, or in these pandemic times walk the Slack channels, asking the sales team how I can be of service to them. I work with the executive team to ensure we can commit to delivering on a prospect's unique request, and then I communicate our commitment to that prospect. I leverage my network to help us get higher in their organization and to affect more change in their company. When I was at Bazaarvoice, I sought opportunities to present to large groups of our prospects the power of social commerce — the voice of the marketplace. Today at data.world, I'm one of the chief evangelists for the power of data to remake commerce, health care, education, and society and I am almost constantly speaking, writing, and helping our team to execute their part in this grand ballet.

In summary, *a CEO must learn how to sell*. Failing to do so is to be selfish, and to shy away from developing a critical skill that will help the entire company. To not do so is to waste the most valuable megaphone in the company (again, not because CEOs themselves are important — there are no lesser or greater than any other person working at the company — but because they are the only ones entrusted with the CEO title). Once you develop the skill of selling, you will become a more effective CEO overall. You will be better at recruiting, better at raising money from investors, better at business development, and better at passionately tapping the energy of all of the great people that are in your company and looking to you to set an example. You will be better at leading the company to beat its goals. And when your collective of amazing team members and customers win, you'll realize that the journey was the true reward, as I'll discuss in Chapter 20, *Capture the History of Your Amazing Journey*.

> *"Remember, you are not in charge; you are responsible for those in your charge."*

## — SIMON SINEK, AUTHOR

# CHAPTER 16
## SELLING TO THE "COOL KIDS"

*"Early adopters are literally the bridge to the future. Nurture them and your efforts will be rewarded."*

**— GEOFFREY MOORE, AUTHOR OF**
***CROSSING THE CHASM***

You know who they are. Or you will.

They are the "names" in your line of work. Those who the journalists call for a reaction when a new factory comes to town, or when one leaves. They're the ones on the panels when you attend a conference, describing what's to come next. In social gatherings, they draw listeners like magnets, as everyone seeks a bit of their wisdom. In Silicon Valley, they hang out at Buck's. In Austin, you'll spot them at Lola Savannah. In Boston, you'll bump into them on Newberry Street. They're the success stories and the trendsetters. The legends. The pioneers. Some are truly visionary.

They serve on the boards and committees of the trade associations. They take time off to serve as guest lecturers, or Entrepreneurs-in-Residence at the business schools. Often, they're active in philanthropy.

In a phrase, they're the "Cool Kids." And when you launch your business, you want to be in their orbit. You want to find a way to bask in their aura. Ideally, you want them to be your earliest customers. Or, you want their customers to be your customers.

To borrow and bend a phrase from George Orwell's famous novel *Animal Farm:* "All customers are equal, but some customers are more equal than others." My point is that while every potential customer deserves the utmost of your attention, the Cool Kids are the protocustomers, the influencers, and the market makers you need to court from Day 1.

Now I want to tell you more about courting this group of potential allies. But before I do, I have to ask you to take a preliminary step and look inward. An essential element of any effort to woo the Cool Kids is the aspiration to be one yourself. And a warning — it's not about hoodies, black t-shirts, TikToks, or wearing shoes without socks. Here's the test:

Do you love the industry that you are trying to sell to? Or at least, do you deeply respect it? Are you already geeking out to some degree in its ecosystem of books, newsletters, webinars, podcasts, or even trade shows and conferences? Is this industry or sector your passion? In short, and going back to the principles in Chapter 1 of this book, *The Soul of the Entrepreneur*, are you ready to step into what President Teddy Roosevelt called "The Arena" of your business stratum?

Of course, if you've journeyed with me thus far in this book, you've no doubt already answered these questions to some degree. But to put a finer point on it, the key to selling to the all-important Cool Kids is to make sure your interests and passions truly align with theirs. Until you actually begin marinating in the same industry conferences, newsletters, and magazines that the leaders among your sales prospects attend and read, you won't know if you are passionate about that industry. If you aren't, then you won't make it by faking it. In my opinion, life is too short to waste your time doing so and you should move on to something that is worthy of your energy and will fuel your entrepreneurial drive.

But if you can look in the mirror and say to yourself, "I'm going to change the world in biotech," or, "I'm going to dent the universe in nanotech..." and you are studying this field of choice like there's no tomorrow, then a beautiful thing is happening. You are ready to be among the Cool Kids that you will grow to know and need. As you spend time in their intellectual spaces and physical places, you will recognize that there are certain people in the industry that are key influencers. They are the ones who stand out and tower above the field.

The Cool Kids stand out for two broad reasons. First, they want to be seen as the key innovators in their industry. Most often, they are. This is good for their ego and, ultimately, their career. They get promoted where they work, or are recruited to their next company much faster than the average person in their industry. By ego, I don't mean anything bad — all leaders have it and it is a healthy thing. On the Digital Companion, I share a summary of a great book on the subject, *Egonomics,* that describes this animating characteristic in detail. The second quality of the Cool Kids is that they have reached a point in their careers where their energies are resonating outward — they are the student who has become the teacher. This is validated by the fact that their peers have elected them to boards and committees, that conference organizers seek them out as panelists, or that journalists quote them. And every industry has them.

There is an aphorism, variously attributed to Gautama Buddha or the Taoist philosopher Lao Szu, that counsels, "When the student is ready, the teacher will appear." This is an insight I've experienced in many ways — as both student and teacher — over the years. So I urge you to reflect upon it, understanding that the more avid a student of your chosen sector you become, the sooner the teacher will appear. This is what I mean by joining the Cool Kids.

In this vein, one of the most important entrepreneurial books I've ever read is *Crossing the Chasm* by Geoffrey Moore. If you haven't read it yet, please pick it up as soon as you've finished reading this volume; I couldn't recommend it more highly. In the book, Moore describes the key segments of virtually any industry that you will try to win: the innovators, early adopters, early majority, late majority, and laggards. I have *lived* this book — at Coremetrics, Bazaarvoice and now at data.world. In a sense, this entire book is on what I call the Cool Kids. In his terminology, they are the "innovators" and "early adopters" in the general segments of every marketplace, with the other segments being the early "majority," "late majority" and the "laggards." Simply put, the Cool Kids help activate and energize the rest.

The Cool Kids I describe are almost always in the innovator and early adopter segments. Now Moore's "chasm" concept is a large one, shared by many business sages, and I include a summary of it in the Digital Companion. But two of its key insights are critical here. First is the "chasm" itself, this gap between the two broad groupings of the market segments, down into which many an entrepreneur plummets, never to be heard from again. Moore calls this gap the "point of peril." The second key concept he elucidates is that of the "whole product," a notion that is ultimately valid for both B2C and B2B businesses. When I use the term "whole product," I mean the entirety of a solution a customer must acquire to use the specific product you are selling. To state it simply, if your product is reusable coffee pods that are compatible with Keurig coffee makers, then by definition your customer has to already own or buy a Keurig before you can sell that customer on your reusable pod.

To offer a more complex example, think of it less as selling *products* than as selling *outcomes.* Often you are selling empowerment. At Coremetrics, we were selling the ability to use online analytics. At Bazaarvoice, we were selling customers the ability to engage socially with their customers at scale. At data.world, our "whole product" is the transformation of companies to become data-driven. Stop and ponder this for a moment. Almost any product or solution you can imagine exists in this context of the "whole product" and you must keep this in mind. Cool Kids think, live, and work in the realm of "whole products."

The innovators and early adopters, on one side of the chasm, are often those intrigued with any fundamental advance or innovation. Unlike the majority and late majority, on the other side of the chasm, they are willing to experiment with the new and untried. That said, "there are not many innovators in any market segment," Moore warns. "But winning them over at the outset of a marketing campaign is essential nonetheless, because their endorsement reassures the other players in the marketplace..."

This second key notion, of "whole product" strategy, comes into play as you cross the chasm into the later market segments that are ultimately the much larger and most profitable slices of your target audience. And here the "whole product" becomes much more of an issue as the buyers become both more pragmatic and conservative, and they will again look to the Cool Kids.

"Despite the overall high-risk nature of the chasm, any company that executes a whole product strategy competently has a high probability of mainstream market success," Moore writes.

In other words, this is all about "product-market fit." As one of our largest and most helpful investors at data.world, Pat Ryan, puts it: product-market fit is "the only thing that matters." He has a video podcast series, named just that, and you can see our discussion of this topic linked on the Digital Companion.

Whether by Moore's terminology or by that of my friend Pat, the Cool Kids are your guides and mentors. Once you win them — and, *most importantly*, do a great job of servicing them and making them successful with your solution — they will work hard to help you convince the early majority, late majority, and even laggards to become your clients. It is in their best interests to do so because of the two reasons I cite above about why they want to be known as the Cool Kids in the first place.

As you think about winning your first clients, you need to frame your thinking around these strategic concepts as you ask the question: Who first? Opportunity cost — the hidden loss that is a gain forgone by the choices *not* made — is very real for any stage company, but it is critical for an early-stage endeavor. The key to success with both Coremetrics and Bazaarvoice was winning over the key industry influencers, the Cool Kids, first. Then we would write case studies about our success with them, do webinars with them, ask them to speak at our client summit, help them speak at industry events such as the National Retailers Federation's annual "BIG Show" expo, help them win industry awards, and ask them to serve as references. This was especially true when web analytics and online word of mouth were so new they were seen as the next hot things. The Cool Kids helped us cross the chasm, to be sure. But they also were critical to winning the rest of the market, which largely followed their moves.

Among those who have helped me at various times at Coremetrics was John Lazarchic, the head of e-commerce at the pet food retailer PETCO. Another was George Coll, who was the head of strategy for computer retailer CompUSA, and is now the CEO of BWW Media Group. And Matt Corey, then head of marketing at Golfsmith, now Chief Marketing Officer of PGA Tours, was a Cool Kid who helped us greatly. More recently, D.J. Patil, the nation's first Chief Data Scientist during the Obama Administration is one of the Cool Kids, now helping data.world on our Advisory Board. So is Sam Palmisano of IBM, who is both on our Advisor Board and who is an investor. Kelly Wright, who took sales from data analytics firm Tableau from $10 million to over $1 billion, also serves on our Advisory Board.

Let me pause here and explain my own background a bit because I think it will help make my points more clear. Digital retail spoke to my passion beginning when I was a child. My parents were entrepreneurs from before the time I was born, specifically in retail and direct marketing. I've programmed since I was seven years old. Most of my career has been about transforming retail into the digital age. Three of the six companies I've started have been in this vein. The first, BodyMatrix, was my online retailer selling sports nutrition products. The second, Coremetrics, was influenced by my experience at BodyMatrix as I brought the same — and ultimately much better — analytics I had developed for my own needs to retailers all over the world. The third, Bazaarvoice, was influenced by the confluence of my experiences at both BodyMatrix and Coremetrics, and brought the power of digital word of mouth to change the face of digital retailing forever. As digital retail was such a passion, I naturally studied it and became somewhat of an expert in it. This eventually earned me the recognition of my peers, resulting in me serving on the Board of Directors of what is now called NRF NXT, the digital-focused arm of the National Retail Federation, the largest trade association of retailers. I was elected by my peers — mostly retailers — to the board for three terms over six years.

In the digital retail industry, the NRF NXT is where the Cool Kids hang out. Sure, there are many other events, including eTail and Internet Retailer. But NRF NXT, — formerly known as Shop.org — is where you go to learn and network. It is a non-profit, unlike eTail or Internet Retailer, and it is where the highest level people in digital retail go as a result. Today, Shoptalk is the biggest eCommerce conference. ShopTalk is a new conference that's focused on retail tech. And of course, there's the grandfather of them all, the half-century-old Consumer Electronics Show, or CES, in Las Vegas, that draws nearly 200,000 people. And I'd of course be remiss if I didn't mention the coolest of them all, Austin's South by Southwest (SXSW) festival of the mind and senses that merges music, film, media, and technology as SXSW. The point is that in every industry, people are looking to connect with their peers, to learn, and to teach. Ultimately attendees at such gatherings seek to avoid complete bombardment by vendors while they are at their industry's events. In every industry, there is a Shop.org or NRF NXT of that industry and you need to swim in it. If you are genuinely passionate about it, that will shine through and your glow will immediately differentiate you from the many salespeople that attend these events.

So, enough on who the Cool Kids are, where they hang out and how best to meet them. Let's get to the ultimate question: Just *how* do you win them over and sell to them? For starters, you need a team. But again, as I asked of you at the beginning of this chapter, you need to look inward. To answer that question of *how,* you really need to determine *what* type of CEO and leader you are, or will be, when it comes to this all-important matter of sales.

There are four principles that can guide you to getting sales right. First is the leader of the sales team and the leader's immediate supporting cast. Second is the creation of a sale-driven culture, the oxygen generating machine that breathes life into all areas of the company. Third are the story-telling tools, the compelling "demo" that your team will use to explain the product clearly and understandably — and I'm not just talking about a PowerPoint deck. Fourth and lastly, you need a great Board of Advisors that draws from and reflects your industry, which is a point I've already alluded to but want to underscore.

Let's walk through the principles:

First as discussed in the previous chapter, I believe that the CEO must be engaged with the sales strategy and tactics for a host of reasons — led by the fact that sales is the oxygen of commercial metabolism. But not all CEOs are natural-born salespersons. It certainly makes it easier if you are that type of CEO because it is then easier to identify people that can sell like you can. But this is rare. Steve Jobs was certainly one of the best examples. IBM's Sam Palmisano is another. At the outset of my career, however, I was not, and this is the more common case in the entrepreneurial realm. You really need clarity about your own sales aptitude and temperament to determine both how you will develop your own skills and how you will shape and develop your team. As we've already discussed, your engagement with sales is a non-negotiable imperative. But at the same time, you don't want to be a loose cannon that gets in the way of your salesforce. There's a great essay from the *Harvard Business Review*, linked on the Digital Companion, on the various ways CEOs can engage with their sales team that also explores this issue in detail. The essay, *When CEOs Make Sales Calls,* dubs these kinds of CEOs as "seagulls." That's because, as HBR puts it: "They fly in, make a lot of noise, leave a mess, and fly off, maybe or maybe not returning to the same spot." And that's not the kind of CEO you want to be.

Better than being a "seagull" is becoming, or better yet hiring, a "Cassius the Closer" with whom you can work and with whom you can build a true sales culture. "Cassius" is a mythical character in another gem of a book I recommend, *Selling the Wheel*, by Howard Stevens and Jeff Cox. A Slideshare of it is linked on the Digital Companion. It's an imagined ancient parable about the invention of the wheel and about the inventor/entrepreneur who couldn't figure out how to sell his creation to the Egyptians. Cassius, as you might suspect, is the lead protagonist. He's a self-starter and is adept at demonstrating the power and practicality of this new technology called the wheel. He also can impart the vision of the wheel's potential — in this case selling it to the Egyptians who are trying to figure out how to build pyramids. Cassius, of course, resonates passion for the product and emotional energy. With his devotion to the product, he usually closes sales in just one or two meetings. At the outset, you need a Cassius, and *Selling the Wheel* also offers insight into the types of salespeople you will need to add to your team as you grow and mature. Salespeople are a very unique breed of people, and I love them for it. They will bring you revenue, and delight your clients. The best sales professionals care about the ultimate value delivered — not just the immediate deal but the "whole product" as I mentioned earlier. Ultimately it's the sales team that increases the valuation of your company and your ability to create jobs and realize your entrepreneurial dreams. Respecting them deeply is a must.

The second principle is the nurturing of the culture that will shape the mindset that channels energy toward sales. It's great that you have found a simpatico Cassius with whom you can work, and assembled a professional sales team to support them. This is a critical and very concrete set of tasks. But right behind this comes an equally important challenge for you as leader that is far more abstract. This is the creation of a "sales-driven culture" throughout the enterprise. As we discussed in the last chapter, the sales team is the first violin who sets the melody, but everyone is in the orchestra and everyone needs to keep sales top of mind. We'll discuss culture more broadly in Chapter 19, *The Five Critical Ingredients to Build a Big Company*. But here I want to emphasize that the measure of the respect you are showing to your sales team is really in the kind of general sales culture you create.

I emphasize this in part because at Coremetrics, I didn't get it right. I made the mistake of many founders early in their careers when I projected my own strengths in the wrong way. I built more of an engineering-driven culture. As the founder, that was more of my personality at the time, having grown up as a programmer. The engineer assumes that the product "will sell itself," and this mindset could not be more wrong. Our main competitor Omniture, by contrast, built a sales-driven culture. Omniture turned into the market leader and blew past Coremetrics. Coremetrics had a good outcome by most entrepreneurial standards when it was acquired for nearly $300 million. But that was certainly eclipsed by the success of Omniture, which acquired for $1.8 billion by Adobe. There is a huge difference between being No. 1 versus being No. 2 in a new category. I wasn't about to make that same mistake at Bazaarvoice. I'm proud to say that Michael Osborne, our first VP of Sales whom you met in the last chapter, and I worked hard to create a sales-driven culture. My

Co-founder, Brant Barton, also played a major role as did Sam Decker, our founding CMO. It helped that me, Michael, and Brant had all come from Coremetrics and we had learned that lesson — and it helped that Sam Decker was also a natural-born salesperson.

So, how do you create a sales-driven culture? We've talked about hiring truly passionate and convincing salespeople. We also examined the role of recruiting, and getting that right, in Chapter 11, *The Most Proven Way to Hire Well*. And we've considered earlier in several opportunities how sales is ultimately everyone's job. But all of these imperatives really converge on the principle of respect. The respect accorded to the centrality of sales is the key element in nurturing and sustaining a sales-driven culture. Sales is an incredibly difficult job, and sales professionals are constantly facing rejection and are constantly burdened with the ultimate mission of winning the revenue that allows *all* of the other functions to get funded. Simply put, sales deserves the ultimate respect. But building a sales-driven culture is much more than keeping score on revenue, as important as that is.

In the last chapter, I shared with you the story of Michael Osborne's green ball. This is a good example of a small thing that snowballed into a tradition. And you need to create traditions where you celebrate new client wins such as an ongoing "gong show" for example. At Bazaarvoice, we celebrated new client wins with our gong, where we would all gather around and discuss the win. This tradition extended to our clients where we sent them mini-gongs and they celebrated the win with us over the phone or sometimes in person. The bond this created between Bazaarvoice and our clients was truly unique. Another way to emphasize the importance of selling is to recognize the heroes — the largest quota winners — at events, such as an annual sales club or a quarterly off-site. When Bazaarvoice was smaller, we had these off-sites every quarter at the Alamo Drafthouse, a combination cinema, and pub in Austin. There, everyone could let down their hair in ways not possible in the stuffiness of a typical corporate venue. When the sales team beat a major stretch goal, they *all* dressed up as Elvis and stormed into the Alamo Drafthouse, surprising us all, to celebrate their trip to Vegas.

The third principle turns on your storytelling tools. In short, Third, you need *a really great demo*. When you start your company, you have no credibility other than your background. Some backgrounds are better than others. When I started Bazaarvoice, I had a reputation due to my success with Coremetrics and my stature as a member of the Shop.org Board. I was getting to know the Cool Kids and I was becoming one. But when I started Coremetrics, I was a bit of an outsider, relatively unknown even though I had already started three small companies. This meant that at Coremetrics it was imperative to focus on creating an amazing demo. Coremetrics invented the enterprise-scale web beacon, sometimes called a data tag, a technique used on web pages and emails to unobtrusively check that a user has accessed some content. Prior to Coremetrics, enterprise solutions like Accrue or Net.Genesis served customers with software known as log files or network packet-sniffers to monitor network and internet traffic, but these solutions were far less inaccurate. In addition, our competitors' solutions required a massive investment of implementation time, often as much as 12 to 18 months. As our approach was one of the first made by a Software as a Service, or SaaS, company back in 1999, I needed to differentiate the Coremetrics approach. To do this, I created a demo of my eCommerce site, BodyMatrix, and I would have someone mimic a customer and click around, looking at different products and putting some in the shopping cart. I was then able to show a client the real-time view of their data and essentially replay the customer actions they had just witnessed. I would then explain how I could collect this data from tens of thousands of individuals — all in real-time — and build a lifetime profile of all of their customers' interactions. That lifetime profile would allow firms using it to track the behavior of customers across many sessions and ultimately the data could be used to later personalize email campaigns and on-site campaigns, among other things. Revolutionary for the industry at that time, this demo blew people away. I've since worked with several companies that have revolutionary demos like this and you should see their prospects' reactions to it. Whatever your industry, you need to find a way to build a standardized demo that all on the sales team can use.

As time goes on, and as you move through the market segment across the proverbial chasm, the demo is of less importance as your credibility derives from your relationship with the Cool Kids you have won over in the space as they rave about the impact you are having on their business. But at the beginning, it is all about the demo. Also, the role of the demo is gaining importance in light of the pandemic that moved sales strategies, particularly in software and technology, to Zoom presentations as trade shows shut down or suffered declining participation. Invest in your demo and make it sizzle.

The last and fourth principle is one we've examined earlier, but which needs to be amplified here. This is the importance of building a great Board of Advisors of people from that industry. Think of this as your "Board of Cool Kids," or your action network to win initial clients, cross the chasm, understand and manage the "complete product" ecosystem, and help you enter new market verticals. As I discussed in Chapter 13, *How to Leverage Advisors and Investors,* you can give your advisors anywhere from 0.05 percent to 0.25 percent of equity in your company, depending on who they are and what the connectivity they bring. It is easier to do this than it may sound. The entrepreneurial spirit is very much alive in our country — our founding fathers had it in 1776 — and we are used to helping each other achieve our dreams as we are a country of mostly self-made entrepreneurs. And these advisors will not only help you with introductions to potential clients, but they can also be valuable in helping you shape your solution. With your initial clients and advisors, you need to carefully listen to their recommendations.

Remember the truism that no one succeeds alone. Embrace its corollary, that together with the right people to help and guide, anything is possible. So early in your journey, find the Cool Kids.

> *"It is not your customer's job to remember you. It is your obligation and responsibility to make sure they don't have the chance to forget you."*

> ## — PATRICIA FRIPP

# CHAPTER 17
# ACTION-ORIENTED COMMUNICATION

*"The single biggest problem in communication is the illusion that it has taken place."*

## — GEORGE BERNARD SHAW

Here's a shortcut to experience the most effective way for an entrepreneur to communicate: take a walk through midtown Manhattan, stand for a few moments in line for a ticket at Penn Station, then take a long ride in an elevator at Fifth Avenue and 34th Street. Listen carefully. No better short course exists on the conveyance of critical information. For New Yorkers, communication is "stand closer, talk louder, and leave shorter pauses between exchanges," in the phrase of Georgetown University linguistics professor Deborah Tannen, a native. "I call it 'cooperative overlap'. It's a way of showing interest and enthusiasm," she once wrote.

OK, I'm being a bit facetious here. But only a bit. New Yorkers live in an environment of constant hustle and it breeds fierce conversations. It's an environment that in many ways resembles the fast-paced, no-time-for-BS, active verb reality of a startup.

Don't get me wrong — fierce does not mean rude. It means direct, honest, and action-oriented. Quite the opposite of rude, it is actually more compassionate in that we do not want to waste each other's time. That is the goal and focus of this chapter.

Now, my intention is not to diminish the fact that communication styles come in as many forms as those communicating. But modes of imparting information essentially break down into four broad categories. "Process-oriented," is the tack generally taken by engineers or economists — bring on the data and win your case with the facts and numbers. "People-oriented" communicators, as in the way human resources executives generally look for the "who" in the subject under discussion such as "how will this affect" someone or the people in a group?" This is among the reasons we at data.world call HR "Employee Experience." There's "idea-oriented" communication, which often involves the sometimes meandering discussion of the "big picture" or the "ultimate vision." Apple's late founder Steve Jobs was a perfect example of the "idea-oriented" communicator, as is author Simon Sinek who famously advocates for finding the "why" in our conversations. I include a TED talk Sinek gave on this kind of communication on the Digital Companion.

All styles have their place and all of us have our unique styles. But in startups, you have no time to waste. Every day counts. The opportunity cost of lost time is huge. Startup life can be short and fragile. So, one way to get things done *quickly* is to communicate in an effective manner. This is why I'm such an advocate of "action-oriented" communication. Let's focus on the results. Let's hear about the steps to overcome a specific challenge. Let's be quick, direct, and pragmatic. And communicate preferably face-to-face, or at least over Zoom.

I realize, naturally, that all of these communications styles have their place in any organization. The head of IT is talking to the head of marketing about software options to improve the efficiency of prospect conversions in the marketing funnel... this is going to be a "process-oriented" conversation. We've all gathered at a brainstorming retreat to peer into the future opportunities of a radical new technology... well then, by all means, let's mimic Steve Jobs's "idea-orientation." If Lisa Novak, our head of Employee Experience, is having a difficult discussion with a team that is really stretched for capacity, then this needs to be "people-oriented," and focused on the effects and impacts on team members, and how we are helping them alleviate that. But we err when we consider these modes of communication as either/or propositions.

The point I hope to drive home here is that all modes of communication have their utility, but "action-oriented" communication is not just one among the modes. It is *foundational* to all of them. For all styles to be effective in the enterprise, action-oriented communication should be the prefix and suffix, the way to open and close the more discursive forms of conversation we all inevitably have. It makes all conversations more meaningful.

For most of us, this doesn't come naturally. With my background as a programmer — a code-focused activity classically undertaken by introverts working under dim lights —  it took more than a little effort for me to master active, action-focused communication. We all have to work at it. A life-changing book on the topic is *Fierce Conversations,* by Susan Scott. I include a great podcast with her on the Digital Companion.

Her essential point is that all "fierce" conversations need to have four objectives: One, they must interrogate reality; two, they must provoke learning; three, they must aim to tackle our toughest challenges; and four, they should enrich our relationships. I really believe her four objectives align with the styles I outlined. And the interface between them all is enabled by the action-oriented communication I advocate here.

"Staggering amounts of money are dedicated to reviewing basic business processes," Scott writes of most companies, "while employees long for one galvanizing conversation that will explain the situation and get everyone back on track." That's it, the imperative of the galvanizing conversation, which all too often never happens. I introduced *Fierce Conversations* at Bazaarvoice and it taught even the most communications-challenged people how important it was to have fierce, direct, face-to-face conversations — and *how* to have them — because as she puts it, "life changes one fierce conversation at a time." Think for a moment about how true this is within the inflection points in your own life, whether it was your conversation to decide to get married, to have children, to start a company, or to ponder some other crossroads. This is the book I wish I had read when I was a young programmer. Life is too short not to be fierce.

Another resource on the subject is the book *Crucial Conversations*, a review of which is included on the Digital Companion as well. It makes similar points and focuses particularly on managing "high-stakes" conversations: you are asking your boss for a promotion, leading your team on a change of strategy to save the company, or problem-solving when emotions are running high. Its specific utility is that it includes a training program that we used with great success at Bazaarvoice. But the bottom line in both is the same: don't waste time, and nothing beats face-to-face conversation.

This brings me to the sea change in communication we've all been through in recent years with a devastating pandemic that has forced the global rollout and adoption of communications technologies — led by Zoom videoconferencing — that will be among the most enduring features of a once-in-a-century contagion. The tricky part is that as we've moved into virtual space for so many more of our critical conversations, action-oriented communication has become even more important. And while face-to-face conversations are rarer, they are all the more useful when we can actually have them.

Remember back to the initial days of the pandemic. Zoom (or Google Meet or Microsoft Teams), telemedicine, streaming, online classes, document sharing tools like Google Docs, collaboration tools like Slack, or data.world, digital signatures, online or curbside shopping, instant message apps, and so much else were akin to floating planks in a brutal storm. Some of us were more familiar with them than others — those of us in the tech sector had a head start to be sure. So did the digital natives, who don't remember a world without the internet. But all of us grasped these relatively new creations, often in desperation, to keep lives and families together and companies afloat. But now, after more than two years as I write of on-again, off-again cloistering, cocooning, masking, and working and learning from home, these are no longer just a useful means to cope in the short term. The tools of virtual communication will be permanent fixtures in almost every company, new ways of experiencing family and community, and even the building blocks of new companies that would-be startup entrepreneurs reading this book may be now imagining.

Which makes it all the more imperative that we think seriously about action-oriented communication and the importance of face-to-face communication which will inevitably be more sparse.

At data.world, we were certainly pre-pandemic early adopters and we've used Slack since the beginning. We've integrated Google Apps with it (Docs, Sheets, Slides, Drive, etc.), which has given us what amounts to our own intranet. Of course, we've also integrated the data.world platform with Slack, and we use our own platform obsessively when it comes to accessing our data and the resulting analyses of it. We've also had regular stand-up meetings since the beginning of data.world, which was inspired by my co-founder and Chief Product Officer, Jon Loyens. This includes the executive team — we meet at least four times per week and most of us have continued the practice even with the greater use of virtuality and video to keep meetings short and focused. And we use Google Meet or Zoom constantly to communicate with our clients, prospects, and each other. So we get plenty of in-person, video-driven, and instant-messenger type communication at data.world.

However, I made a mistake in the first couple of years at data.world. We became too dependent on Slack because of just how easy it was. It is like we were *always* in a meeting and the noise-to-signal ratio was quite high. And the mistake I made was not having in-person quarterly All-Hands meetings as we did at Bazaarvoice. I thought, "Well, we are having stand-ups all of the time and we are constantly on Slack." But there is nothing like a good quarterly All-Hands meeting in person — to get outside of the office and have some more long-form communication to rally around the beginning of a quarter and reflect on achievements and lessons learned of the past quarter. Working with our Culture Club, we rectified that four years ago and started to have them at the Alamo Drafthouse, the Austin-founded combination cinema, and pub that is a favored venue of the team. At times when it has been safe to do so, we've met at different outdoor, in-person venues again (as well as the office) and I don't doubt that the Alamo Drafthouse, or something like it, will be a gathering spot in whatever hybrid form of in-person/remote work we ultimately settle into.

Reflecting on this today, we are in the age of ubiquitous Zooms. We've gone from pandemic to something closer to an endemic-with-working-vaccines world, which allows us to get together in person without fear. I've been thinking very deeply about what our new communication norms should be. On the one hand, for the knowledge economy, we've got the luxury of capturing the gains of what we learned during the pandemic and making these tools a new norm. We learned how to be efficient and effective in working from home in what has been the world's largest communications experiment in history. The entire knowledge economy, which undoubtedly is advantaged in this new reality, was boosted by that experiment as we worked remotely and strived to bend the viral curve, protecting ourselves, each other, and our medical workers from being overwhelmed. And now, in the knowledge economy, we can blend the best of a hybrid work style. This allows us to get together in person as often as we want to build up that bank of trust best achieved in person, while also enjoying the best of at-home work combined with the flexibility it offers. You can work amid and around so many tasks, from dropping off or picking up your kids at school, taking a mid-day workout break, or focusing without distractions. On the other hand, we still have our physical office space at most companies, including our own at data.world, with all of the costs that entails. Do we need a place to call home, with our core values framed and shown in the office? Do we need a place to take our customers, partners, and investors? What do we do about a place to get together for our "Weekly Hoot," what we call our regular in-person gathering each Friday at data.world to celebrate the milestones of the week?

The answer for me at data.world is a resounding yes to all these questions, even with the cost of office space. But many haven't made the same decision and are more like unencumbered nomads wandering from venue to venue around the country — or even the world — when they want to get together in person. There is no fixed sense of place in that world — only of virtual places online blended with rotating virtual spaces offline. That may work just as well. And only time will tell as we now figure this out together over the coming three to five years. Meanwhile, Google and Meta/Facebook have just finished the final touches on their largest office spaces ever in Austin's downtown. The massiveness and beauty of those buildings are breathtaking but I wonder just how many people will be physically in them, and when.

I had an incredible conversation about all of this in April 2022 with a group here in Austin deeply involved with all of these challenges. It included Robert Alvarez, the CFO of publicly-traded BigCommerce; Jonathan Coon, who founded and led 1-800-CONTACTS.com and is now leading the new Four Seasons residential development on Lake Austin; Kelley Knutson who is the President of Netspend; Bob Campbell, who founded Deloitte's Federal practice and grew it to over a $1 billion annually (and wrote the Afterword of this book); Arlo Gilbert, the Founder and CEO of Osano; Leslie Wingo, the President and CEO of Sanders\Wingo; and Emily Rollins, who was a partner at Deloitte and now serves on several public company Boards, including Xometry and Dolby Laboratories. We talked about the fact that we are still in the early innings of remote work, with collaboration tools that will be vastly improved from their current state. For example, there will surely be tools to mitigate the inevitable background noise at your Zoom location, the finicky microphones we've all experienced will get better and the fast-evolving virtual reality headsets that are no longer confined to the realm of gaming will play roles in this evolution. Microsoft Teams Together Mode has now evolved to a theater-style display and I have a video of Microsoft's vision for this on the Digital Companion.

I also spoke not long ago with Chris Hyams, CEO of Indeed, the world's largest job-search engine, who is an Advisory Board member at data.world. We spoke at Culturati, the definitive conference on company cultures founded by Eugene Sepulveda, CEO of the Entrepreneurs Foundation, and Josh Jones-Dilworth, CEO and Founder of JDI. Chris made a winning point: What you need to care about most is what your employees want. For example, perhaps for engineers, this new way of working is truly bliss because of the lack of distractions in doing highly creative and concentrated work. I remember as a young programmer when my parents would interrupt me and it would sometimes take an hour to resume the flow as I was cranking out code. But for younger people starting out in sales, and needing the constant interruption of hearing how others do it and being coached by both their peers and manager, working from home could be highly detrimental to their career. Chris is advocating the design of an optimal working environment for different types of employees with different needs.

That makes a lot of sense to me, and is the essence of the conversation we are now having right now among our executive team at data.world. Time will tell what works best, and it really is a brave new world for the knowledge economy. And I don't mean that in a dystopian sense, as Aldous Huxley's infamous book *Brave New World* suggests. Rather, I envision a utopian future quite different from Huxley's where we really lock in the lessons of the pandemic to design a more optimal future of work, a future accelerated by the massive disruption of COVID-19 which forced us to adapt and adopt at warp speed.

So, as I boil this all down, my preferred mode of action-oriented communication today really depends on what type of meeting we are having. For a highly strategic multi-day meeting, there is no doubt that in-person is best. I can't imagine spending two eight-hour days on a Zoom — well, actually I can as I did just that during the worst part of the pandemic curve. Being able to whiteboard together, rapidly iterate, and just blow off steam and enjoy each other's company is best done in-person for this type of long, usually quarterly, meeting. But for a typical workday, working from home with multiple Zooms, combined with the frequent use of Slack and data.world, could work just fine. And that can be topped off with a nice face-to-face coffee meeting to coach a team member as needs dictate. It's possible to blend the best of both worlds — in-person and virtual — in a single day. And if you need to do an impromptu video or phone call for maximum iteration in the moment, then just do it. Don't just send that Slack or message via data.world and call it a day. Speed matters — and the high fidelity of a real-time conversation, where you can hear each other's intonation or see each other's faces, can really make the difference if your goal is to move quickly. And most of the time, moving quickly should be your goal.

It took me a while to learn this, especially since I grew up as a BBS nerd. But, trust me, this is how you maintain a very efficient communication flow. But whatever the mode, the most important skill is learning when to talk, and when to listen. One of the most powerful skills to master as a team player is to know when to not share news of your dog or simply echo the thoughts of others for the sake of talking. Pay attention to the introverts, make sure their thoughts and insights are not crowded out by the ones we've all encountered trying to be the smartest in the room. Be wiser, listen carefully, and respect the time of your team members. Complement each other, don't compete for attention. Pretend you're a New Yorker, and strive for productive, kind, but *fierce* conversations.

> *'The most important thing in communication is to hear what isn't being said."*

## — PETER F. DRUCKER, AUTHOR, AND BUSINESS PHILOSOPHER

# CHAPTER 18
# FORMING YOUR COMPANY'S VALUES

*"Before you embark upon this journey of your business' vision and mission discovery, there are a few questions that you need to answer:*

*- Why are you in this business?*

*- How big do you want your business to be one day?*

*- Who is going to benefit from your product or service?*

*- What is the core purpose of the existence of your business?"*

## — POOJA AGNIHOTRI, AUTHOR, *17 REASONS WHY BUSINESSES FAIL*

In the long history of commerce, the answer to the question, "Why does a company exist?", has been reimagined many times. In our evermore disruptive, entrepreneur-driven age of deepening global challenges, it is time we do so again. Beyond the mission statement, beyond the revenue target, beyond even visions of a nine-figure exit, today's company exists — to paraphrase philosopher Viktor Frankl — to search for meaning, as discussed in Chapter 1, *The Soul of the Entrepreneur.*

I realize, of course, that few business plans include this specific quest. The journey to meaning as the basis for corporate existence, after all, has been a long one. It's still evolving and it's hardly complete. So let me back up and explain.

For classical economists, the purpose of the corporation was modeled around what was arguably the first startup, the British East India Company, founded in 1600 with 281 investors. It was created to enable profit-seeking commerce with a league of multiple partners, a novel idea some 400 years ago. As the industrial age got underway in the 19th century with railroads, steamships, and the first sprawling factories, the reason for companies was simply scale — to exploit the benefits of being big, as discussed extensively in business historian Alfred Chandler's 1978 book, *The Visible Hand: The Managerial Revolution in American Business*, that earned a Pulitzer Prize. Mass was key, as was the predictability that businesses could assume. Accordingly, firms existed to organize the *push* of mass-produced products to mass markets.

By the end of the 20th century, predictability was history. The world had moved on from brute *push* to agile *pull*, such that a duo of revolutionaries, both named Steve, could knock powerhouses like IBM and Xerox off their perches, quite literally from a workshop in a garage with a product named for a fruit.

Commerce had become leaner, meaner, faster, and driven by the cycles of microchip innovation, what we now call "Moore's Law," for the eponymous Co-founder of Intel Corp., Gordon Moore. We had moved from a world of analog *push* to a world of digital *pull*. Techniques to enable this new *pull* flourished, from just-in-time-delivery, to economic value analysis, downsizing, rightsizing, benchmarking, off-shoring, and later on-shoring. "The assumptions on which the organization has been built and is being run no longer fit reality," wrote the late, great doyen of business gurus, Peter Drucker, in a famous 1994 essay, which I include on the Digital Companion.

Now well into the 21st century, the imperatives of the firm

today are the scalability of connectivity, learning, performance, and iteration. A global pandemic, meanwhile, while tragic in scope and devastating in many lasting ways, has nonetheless accelerated the metamorphosis of the old analog economy toward the new age of the digital startup. More than 1.4 million business applications with expectations to hire employees were recorded in 2021 by the U.S. Census Bureau, a half-million more than in 2019. In the same year, more than 800 startups crossed the threshold globally to "unicorn" status, with valuations of more than $1 billion. The number of $10 billion "decacorns," meanwhile, doubled from 15 in 2020 to 30 in 2021. As of this writing, two private companies have even crossed into the "hectacorn" status, (a valuation above $100 billion): ByteDance, the parent of TikTok, in 2020; Space X in 2021.

Against this volatile backdrop, the capitalism of today's firm must be the accumulation of all the lessons learned since the founding of the British East India Company, to the launch of the MacIntosh by the two Steves nearly a half-century ago, and now beyond to so much more. Atop all of this, as the accelerating speed of technological innovation outruns the pace by which other societal institutions advance, the moral authority of the company becomes paramount. Today's firm, in addition to its commercial success, must also be the fulcrum of values, even the exponent of a kind of secular religion — if you think of one of the primary benefits of religion as a means to organize values, as I do.

As the Cameroon-born philosopher Achille Mbembe, one of Africa's leading public intellectuals, framed it in an interview in early 2022, "our core moral experience" is now the marketplace. "Both the market and technology now set the rules and procedures according to which we are obliged to live together as a connective body within new planetary limits," he argued in the interview entitled, *How To Develop A Planetary Consciousness,* which I also include on the Digital Companion.

You'll recall that at the outset, in Chapter 1, *The Soul of the*

*Entrepreneur,* I argued that at its essence, entrepreneurship is a "call to the soul." Moving from that premise, I argue here that the essential job of the entrepreneur, in turn, is to organize a community of souls into a collective — it is their shared values that make a company great. Shared values should become the North Star of the company, the guarantor that it is truly pursuing creative disruption and innovation, and not merely inhabiting the role. Examples of simple value mimicry are many, but few demonstrate this risk as dramatically as did two notable ones: the unmasking of Enron CEO Jeffrey Skilling, who resigned in 2001 and was convicted in 2004, and of Theranos CEO Elizabeth Holmes, whose fraud was revealed in 2018 leading to her 2021 conviction.

Of course, there are many ways to define, emphasize, and integrate shared core values into the DNA of your company. In one form or another, we've already discussed many of these, including Chapter 1, *The Soul of the Entrepreneur,* certainly. But also this is part of Chapter 4, *The Importance of an Alway Be Learning Life*; it's an element of Chapter 9, *How, and Why, to Ask for Help*; this is of course among the goals of Chapter 11, *The Most Proven Way to Hire Well;* and, I certainly hope it comes across in Chapter 14, *Seven Lessons Learned on the Journey from Founder to CEO.* A profound study of this, built around the insight that we focus excessively on "managing teams" as we neglect "organizing" them, can be found in the work of the late pioneer of leadership studies, Warren Bennis.

"Throughout history, groups of people, often without conscious design, have successfully blended individual and collective effort to create something new and wonderful," Bennis wrote in the classic of the leadership genre, *Organizing Genius — The Secrets of Creative Collaboration.* "The Bauhaus school, the Manhattan Project, the Guarneri Quartet, the young filmmakers who coalesced around Francis Ford Coppola and George Lucas, the youthful scientists and hackers who invented a computer that was personal as well as powerful, the creators of the Internet —

these are a few of the Great Groups that have reshaped the world in very different but enduring ways."

Bennis' effort to reveal "how their collective magic is made," is a wonderful read and I include a review to tempt you on the Digital Companion. But more immediately to the point, I'd like to share a few insights on how we've done it at data.world, where our chief organizing tool is the "Point of View," or POV. This is our Magna Carta which — just as societies do with foundational documents — we update from time to time.

It was in Chapter 14 where I introduced the concept of the POV, and the book where it all began, *Play Bigger: How Pirates, Dreamers, and Innovators Create and Dominate Markets.* As discussed there, a POV is an essential tool to shape and reinforce a company's vision. But it is equally critical as the vessel for corporate values — which is why it is required reading at data.world for all new team members. As just one example in *Play Bigger*, the authors illustrate how Salesforce.com used its POV to internally amplify values, declaring, "It would devote 1 percent of equity to charity and was intent on pushing a new kind of corporate responsibility. It would speak out on social issues. It would be the industry pirate and defy convention." As Salesforce CEO Marc Benioff himself put it, "Building the foundation from an intellectual idea to a practical reality that has served 100,000 people in need has been one of the most rewarding (experiences of my life). I have received the most remarkable opportunity to lead an organization that makes 'doing good' an integral part of doing well." On the Digital Companion, I include a review of his 2007 book on all of this, *The Business of Changing the World: Twenty Great Leaders on Strategic Corporate Philanthropy.*

Similarly at data.world we use our internal Magna Carta to strengthen our collective bonds. As a proud public benefit corporation, data.world's activities include our open data community, now the world's largest with more than 1.6 million collaborators and around 10,000 new members joining every week.

These include Johns Hopkins University, which uses it to amplify COVID-19 data, and the Associated Press, which uses the resource as a tool to enable investigative reporting. We also provide the infrastructure of the Data Foundation's "Policing in America Project," which seeks to inform the ongoing debate about reform of America's criminal justice system. More on these initiatives is on the Digital Companion. And this is only the beginning of our hopes to expand this free public resource for the betterment of humanity. I frequently remind our customers that by paying us to become world-class at the mastery of data inside of their companies, they are also helping a large multiple of others outside of their companies to collaborate for free on important issues facing humanity, from climate change to poverty.

"We proudly chose to be a Public Benefit Corporation (PBC) and Certified B Corporation to be here for the long-term and to be transparent about our sincere desire to help the world..," our POV reads in part. "... We are *passionate* believers in the power of Conscious Capitalism. We are driven by the power of data to help humanity, and initiatives like our COVID-19 Data Resource Hub and Policing in America Project come naturally to us. We are *determined* to create a data-driven world where decisions are made quickly, accurately, and collaboratively..."

One way we've used the POV at data.world to articulate our team's core values emerged during a new iteration of the document. This was in the spirit, incidentally, of a periodic review of "Operating Principles" we had learned about from the work of Netflix, and which I had the chance to discuss with the company's CEO Reed Hastings at a TED conference. I sent the following message to all of our employees:

Team, in preparation for our Lunch & Learn on Wednesday to discuss our Operating Principles, please take one minute to send me the one or two values that you personally bring into our team. Such as "integrity," "passion," "caring," "precision," etc.

— whatever you think your most important one or two values are. Please DM them to me by end of day tomorrow and I'll share the results at the L&L.

The responses I received back were beautiful. They all resonated deeply. The top five were: *Determination, Passion, Community, Integrity,* and *Curiosity*, all of which became part of the bedrock of our core values after an all-hands exercise to deliberate on them with the entire team.   At the Digital Companion, you'll find a spreadsheet with the responses from one recent exercise, and you'll see how I winnowed down the responses to move us toward a consensus on core values. When you do this yourself, don't be surprised if you get a joke or two. One of our office comedians back then, who had created bots that roamed Slack and mimicked the voice of my co-founder, our Chief Product Officer Jon Loyens, is always clever. He responded with "terseness." You can obviously discard the joker contributions, but greet them with humor too as that's part of the fun of the exercise as well.

When I presented these results at the Lunch & Learn, the feedback was overwhelmingly positive and I suggested that we adopt these as our core values because "without each of you and your incredible work, each and every day, there is no company and there are no values." Everyone agreed. And for several quarters after that, I asked new team members, as they joined us, to message me in the same way. I recompiled them every time, but when the top five core values — *Determination, Passion, Community, Integrity,* and *Curiosity* — didn't change, I eventually stopped that practice. That didn't surprise me as our people that formed these values in such a grassroots type of way were also the people doing the hiring, and I think that's a quite beautiful and self-reinforcing aspect of our culture. Get your first 50 hires right and you'll largely be set as you scale to 10x, or 500 people, and then to 100x, or 5,000 people, and beyond.

Now, you don't have to do this during your first year as a new company. I initiated our core value creation at data.world after we were a little over two years old. To be fully candid, I began doing this after attending the annual Conscious Capitalism CEO Summit where a CEO remarked on stage, "If you want to learn something amazing, just ask each of your employees to share with you the core values that they bring to work every day." He was right. That was mighty motivation. We didn't write down our core values at my previous VC-backed startups, Coremetrics and Bazaarvoice, until we had matured. You want to get some operating history and some significant team build-out going before you do this exercise, or it is just aspirational with no real resonance for how you've actually been living your day-to-day business life as a collective soul. And the most beautiful way to form your values that I've ever found is the way we've done it at data.world — it was more of a top-down exercise at Coremetrics and Bazaarvoice, which had a form of resonance, but grassroots is the way to go as it creates a very authentic buy-in from everyone, immediately.

There are other concrete means to elucidate, refine, and integrate core values into your company. A practice I strongly recommend is to incorporate this into your annual reviews for team members. As with many human resource units, our Employee Experience department organizes biannual reviews on a "360-degree" basis. This includes upward feedback from a manager's direct reports, reciprocal peer critiques from those who work closely together, and downward feedback from supervising managers to their direct reports. This is good and important, but as Albert Einstein famously advised, "Not everything that can be counted counts, and not everything that counts can be counted." So what we do differently than most companies, however, is make a discussion of our core values a part of this. Employees discuss how their personal values align with those in our POV. This helps us grow and mature as a company with a comprehensive value system that everyone shares. Not long ago I discussed all of this on a podcast with my CEO coach, Kirk Dando. You'll find that conversation on the Digital Companion.

Most broadly, we now stand at a remarkable juncture in the history of our new digital economy and the evolution of capitalism. In an essay for the online technology magazine *TechCrunch,* I argued in early 2022 that the very ideology underlying capitalism is changing, and I cited Thomas Jefferson's counsel that, "Laws and institutions must go hand in hand with the progress of the human mind," For if not, as Jefferson put it, "We might as well require a man to wear still the coat which fitted him when a boy." In that essay, I made the case for the new business ideology of Conscious Capitalism, the latest advocate for which is Larry D. Fink, the CEO of BlackRock — the world's largest asset fund managing $10 trillion — who wrote about this in his 2022 annual letter. In short, my argument was not simply that business has a responsibility to donate to PBS. But rather, that only the institutions of commerce have the scope, power, resources, and innovative spirit capable of taking on our most pressing global challenges. Both Fink's letter and my essay at *TechCrunch* are linked on the Digital Companion and I hope you'll take a look. Collective values are now at the core of capitalism.

You can and will find your own tools to nurture core values at your company. Yes, you need a business plan. Yes, you need a strategy. And, yes, you need investment. But never forget that we are at an inflection point in history, no less profound than those in 1600 with the advent of the multi-investor corporation, or the mid-1700s with the start of the industrial revolution, or in 1984 when the first Macintosh was released. In the newly emerging era of Conscious Capitalism, the core values of the collective are the most important form of capital your company will ever have.

*"Culture is a thousand things, a thousand times. It's living the core values when you hire; when you write an email; when you are working on a project; when you are walking in the hall."*

## — BRIAN CHESKY, FOUNDER OF AIRBNB

# CHAPTER 19
# THE FIVE CRITICAL INGREDIENTS TO BUILD A BIG COMPANY

"To be successful, you have to have your heart in your business, and your business in your heart."

## — THOMAS WATSON, SR., FORMER CEO OF IBM

More than a century ago, the famous architect Louis Sullivan, sometimes called the "Father of Skyscrapers," coined a phrase that has been a key tenet of building design ever since: "Form should follow function." His point was that no beautiful building could ever be constructed without a design that began with its ultimate function, the essential beauty, at the center. I feel much the same about the process of building businesses — the beautiful ones get the critical ingredients of function right from the outset.

Beyond my businesses, past and present, I've sat through countless pitches for investment, virtually all accompanied by a slide deck. I'll get to what I've learned about angel investing in Chapter 22, *Seven Critical Lessons Learned in Angel Investing*. But for now, I want to make the point that I've come to believe the culprit in bad business design is the emphasis on Sullivan's "form."

This usually comes as the "deck" of the startup idea, before thorough consideration of the critical function of the business. Readers of this book, wherever they are on their entrepreneurial journey, have no doubt spent countless hours either studying the many online business plan tutorials available, or have deep experience in the tedious task of producing one. Standard or lean? Operational or feasible? Internal and external? Don't get me wrong, you need your "deck." In fact, I include a few helpful prototype guides to assist on the Digital Companion. But please, please, please... clear your mind of any consideration of *form* until you, your partners, and early collaborators have thoroughly worked out and mapped the *function.* What will you do, and how will you do it?

The function needs to be framed around five elements: the *business model,* the *team* on opening day, the *mindset* that includes your passion and vision, the *funding* that you'll ultimately need, and the *culture* that you envision.

Not long ago, I passed on a new startup for two reasons. They had a great deck and the form of the business was duly considered. The founders had the skills to build it. They had passion and drive. They also had the skills to service the business they envisioned. But I passed because first, they hadn't thought through the market for their product, or the Total Addressable Market (or TAM in VC-speak). Second, they had no one on their initial team with the skills to sell to that yet-to-be-defined market. Alas, I quickly moved on to the next pitch though I also gave them critical, and honest, feedback to improve their team.

So let's walk through those five most critical ingredients to build a big company — one that changes the world, creates many jobs, and has a deep and lasting economic impact.

**Business model:** The most important of the five ingredients, as this is both the superstructure of the business and the ecosystem with which it will interface. To carry my metaphor of architecture, it's both the schematic diagram of the business, and the topographical map that contours the landscape in which it will operate.

Most broadly, this is your "category," so begin your work there. It's often said that great entrepreneurs don't start companies, they start categories. Visionaries from Henry Ford to Steve Jobs to Elon Musk are among the best examples of category creators, with Musk even going so far as to release his company's 200 patents in 2014; he aimed to incentivize the creation of a mass market of electric cars and battery charging infrastructure to create the EV category that Tesla could lead and dominate. Recall our work in Chapter 14, *Seven Lessons Learned on the Journey from Founder to CEO,* and our discussion of developing your "Point of View" (or POV), referenced in the great book, *Play Bigger — How Pirates, Dreamers, and Innovators Create and Dominate Markets.* For your business model, you'll need to fully identify and internalize your "category" in the marketplace and no book will help you more. In particular, read its study of the "Category Ecosystem" — the customers, competitors, developers, suppliers, analysts, media, and everyone else who would plug into the category.

Said differently, your category sets the boundaries of the sandbox in which you intend to play. And it is within this frame that you will begin to assemble your business model. There are two elements of the business model that are essential, and which I focus on most to determine a viable investment or a business that I would start myself. The first of these is the TAM. It should be large. But large in ways that you can *uniquely* address. These two imperatives — large and unique — are the core tension in your business model as they bind together two often-incompatible tasks. This is because in general, bigger means more competition. What you are seeking in your TAM is essentially the largest niche possible. The point is that the business needs the ability to scale for a significantly long period of time to become big. But it should ideally be in a niche, to avoid too much competition. However, if the niche is too small, it isn't a viable business to back.

So how do you resolve these two seemingly incompatible challenges within the larger mission of building a business centered and focused on function? Some of the best thinking on this comes from famed entrepreneur Peter Thiel. I encourage you to read his book *One to Zero,* and the notes from which he wrote the book are linked on the Digital Companion. His broad call to action is to seek niches that are monopolies, or close to it, in the category ecosystem. To illustrate, he makes the case with a comparison of restaurants in Palo Alto, California, and his first major company, PayPal. The market for food in Palo Alto is huge. It's even larger when you consider that nearby Mountain View or Menlo Park are each within reach for lunch. Within that ecosystem, British food might appear a unique niche if it's the only British restaurant in Greater Palo Alto. But in fact, people can easily migrate to other kinds of restaurant food. And pricing may be a more important determinant for customers than specific menus. "By contrast," he writes of his company in 2001, PayPal "was at that time the only email-based payments company in the world. It employed fewer people than the Mountain View restaurants did. Yet from a capital formation perspective, PayPal was much more valuable than all the equity of all those restaurants combined."

This brings me to the second element of a good business model that fits squarely into Thiel's allegory above. This is the "margin profile" of the competitors you've identified within the category you have articulated. You should be able to explain and defend anticipated net and gross margins that are equal to or better than those of your competitors. This would be very difficult, to use Thiel's example, in the restaurant space. Readers of this book surely see why. Creating a new restaurant with demonstrably higher margins on the back of a unique menu… it's easy to grasp what a challenge that would be. Yet many business plans actually push entrepreneurs toward this failure of insight.

Which is why when brainstorming Bazaarvoice, we spent a good amount of time studying the margins of SaaS companies.

The margins of public tech companies are easy to find online in the benchmarking reports of Morgan Stanley, Goldman Sachs, Deutsche Bank, and/or others. In the case of data.world, we modeled against the financials of GitHub, the internet hosting service for software developers. Our estimate that data.world would have a similarly unlimited TAM was effectively validated in 2018 when Microsoft bought GitHub for $7.5 billion, at a price close to 30x annual recurring revenue (ARR). Now we have even more examples in the data space to point to due to the massive success of Snowflake, Databricks, Tableau, Looker, and many others.

A couple of additional points on this. When modeling our TAM before launching Bazaarvoice, we realized that we would, in time, need additional business and product lines to extend into the fuller ecosystem of retailers and brands. In our case, one of the extensions we anticipated and included in our first business plan was advertising. The fact that we foresaw the need for this extension is really what enabled us to buy the vertical ad network for large retailers, Longboard Media, in 2012, shortly after our IPO. The concept here was that it allowed Bazaarvoice to turbocharge the network effect between brands and retailers, effectively placing brand ads on retail sites. Amazon reported that in 2021 brand advertising became a $31 billion business for the company, up from the $2 billion that we deduced it was earning on the same slice of the ecosystem back in 2012. Unfortunately, this part of the business never worked while I was CEO, or shortly after I left at the end of 2012, due to poor execution. But the idea was sound as Amazon's $31 billion advertising business line shows today. Keith Nealon, Bazaarvoice's current CEO and a good friend, has extended in a tighter direction with the acquisition of both Influenster and Curalate; Influenster, in particular, serves as a form of an advertising network to drive traffic.

Another nuance to keep in mind when working through the alchemy of margin profiles is the difference between financial and strategic customers. For example, our initial pricing calculator for the sales team at Bazaarvoice told us that any deal with less than a 70 percent margin would typically not be worth it. This was in line with the margins of publicly traded SaaS companies we identified. If we couldn't sell our first product, Bazaarvoice Ratings & Reviews, for that calculation then it wouldn't be worth it as we tried to build a viable SaaS company. This was our model for "financial" sales. But we also at the outset built in leeway for the sales team to go after "strategic" sales, which are those that could get us into a new vertical, geography, or product line. Having this 70 percent constraint-based model helped us effectively price what was still novel and didn't yet have any market-set price. And, again, we were smart about it so that we could lower that self-imposed threshold when it made sense to effectively buy into a new vertical market. Sadly, I've seen many businesses that have more than $10 million of revenue but with such a low margin profile that it effectively makes them unfundable when they decide to scale with investor capital.

Getting the basic business model right is complicated, and of course, it involves many elements. But the core of the model's function is first in the definition of the category, and then in these two supporting elements of articulating your TAM and then validating that you will have higher margins relative to your competition. Get these right, convince yourself of the logic and justification, and then you can script out the business plan rationally and compellingly. This will ensure that you have both a backable business and one that can turn into a large company.

**Team:** Without a great team, you cannot build a great business. My former partners at Austin Ventures, my hometown's original large VC firm, usually said that this was the first thing for which they looked. And it is true that if you have a good business model without a "complete" and great team, then you need to address this early to be successful. This process of team-building, of course, never stops because people are your biggest variable and high growth actually adds to the pressure that will bring out either the best or the worst in a team.

But what is a great team?

Again, I come back to this word *function.* In many a startup, there are often one or two founders who are rockstars in a specific function: an engineer with a black belt in software design, a top-flight marketer ready for the next challenge after his employer has a successful IPO, or a business whiz with epaulets earned at McKinsey & Company. A halo around one of the founders is good, though please mind my guidance back in Chapter 3, *Advice for the Middle- Aged Entrepreneur,* on the blinders common among those who've enjoyed success in a long-established company. Also, keep in mind that luminance often obscures deficiencies that lead to a kind of "start building and they will come" sensibility toward alignment of the team and the task. And since it's unlikely that any startup in its early days will have the resources to cover every critical task with a rockstar, the logic needs to be inverted. Instead of counting up the rockstars and their pedigrees on your starting roster, it's much better to map out the critical functions you'll need to execute from Day 1. and align them with the team you have. Maybe your software engineer, with a little help from your McKinsey alum, can wear the hat of product lead as well. Or perhaps your newly liberated marketer should roll up their sleeves and carry the sales operation until that first or second client's check clears the bank. In short, multitasking must be almost a religion to a startup's founders and you need to figure out this functional choreography before you begin crafting that pitch deck.

For example, Brant Barton and I had worked together at Coremetrics and we decided to partner in the founding of Bazaarvoice largely on the realization that we are both utility players with highly complementary skills. At Bazaarvoice, he initially played the lead roles in client services, content moderation, marketing, and product management. He also assisted greatly in sales. After all, we were selling a Software as a *Service* platform and his composite role combined both the software and the services we were coupling on the platform. The clients *wanted* to talk with him. I initially played the role of CEO and VP of Sales. I was responsible for hiring the team, fundraising, establishing our Board of Directors and Board of Advisors, and selling our initial clients. I greatly leveraged my eCommerce and broad Shop.org network to do so. I intentionally waited until we were 12 months old and had our first million in annual client bookings to hire our first VP of Sales, Michael Osborne, who left Coremetrics to join us. This was because I wanted to run with my network first and get the business model right before we added too much fuel to the fire. Momentum, both positive and negative, has a way of building. Winning becomes a pattern, and unfortunately so does losing.

A few years later, the exercise was similar when I found myself brainstorming my next startup with my soon-to-be Co-founders of data.world: Matt Laessig and Jon Loyens, both alumni of Bazaarvoice. One of Jon's best friends from his Trilogy and HomeAway (now Vrbo) days, Bryon Jacob, soon got involved as our fourth. Bryon and Jon could build almost anything. Matt and I could sell and service almost anything. And we could recruit the teams to report to us as resources allowed and buildout required. From the beginning, our dream team of multitaskers was the most experienced founding cast I'd ever been part of. And we've gone on to attract other dream-teamers and build data.world into a successful company.

**Mindset:** Before you proceed in this chapter, here's an exercise to check your mindset. Go to the Digital Companion. Click on the icon for "Peter O'Toole - *Man from La Mancha.*" Listen to O'Toole describe the "mission of each true knight" and then sing "*To Dream the Impossible Dream*" in the 1972 film, the song composed for the original Broadway Play by Mitch Leigh. If you are moved, then this is the spirit that must animate the design of your business model and plan. Do your hopes for your business include changing the world? Will your startup dent the universe? And most importantly, are you and your founding team in it for the long haul? Sprinters do well on Wall Street, or as stars who rise quickly in large corporations. And you will find plenty of sprinters in the startup realm. But their companies are usually the first to be taken over by acquirers. So if you want to go big, then you need to be prepared to go long and this demands the stamina and endurance of marathon runners. Back in Chapter 4, *The Importance of an Always Be Learning Life*, we discussed having a "growth" mindset in contrast with a "fixed" mindset. There, I introduced the book by Carol Dweck, *Mindset: The New Psychology of Success,* which I again recommend here. People with a growth mindset enjoy challenges, they strive to learn, and they consistently strive to develop new skills. And this is the mindset of the successful entrepreneur. If you can establish a growth mindset in your organization at the outset, this sets the stage for trust, empowerment, a culture of innovation, and your ability to commit to the perhaps most important test, the long haul of the marathon run.

As just one example, Brant and I could have sold Bazaarvoice for $25 million when the company was a year old and a public company offered to buy us. That discussion between us didn't last more than five minutes. Instead, we doubled down. We wanted to go for a much bigger outcome, which creates larger ripple effects. If we had sold for $25 million, it would have enriched us personally. But, it wouldn't have created so many jobs and financial outcomes for so many later. Capitalism can be the greatest force for good, a subject on which I touch in Chapter 1, *The Soul of the Entrepreneur.* The Conscious Capitalism movement is one about which I've extensively written elsewhere and one inseparable from the ethos of entrepreneurship in the 21st century. If we had not adhered to that ethos, and if we had sold early to enrich only ourselves, the company we created wouldn't have served over 2,000 clients around the world, including over one-third of the Fortune 100 (I'm sure this number is multiples higher today). We wouldn't have the potential today that the company does. Bazaarvoice wouldn't be worth over $1.5 billion today and rapidly growing still. We wouldn't have created over 1,100 jobs. We wouldn't have offices all around the world. Today, I find myself most proud of all of the jobs we created around the world, as well as the impact we had on commerce overall. It was soul-nourishing work, to say the least.

You also must have the mindset of increasing the pie for all. Today, we are running data.world with this same mindset. We've grown very quickly, serving many Fortune 500 and other large companies and helping so many others globally with our free and open data community. As I write this, we just closed our Q4 for the fiscal year 2021-2022 at 135 percent of our goal and beat our sales goals for all four quarters. Broadly, karma is at work here — the belief that deeds and intentions influence the future. So embrace this mindset today for the company you want to have in the future.

As Swamiji Parthasarathy writes in *Governing Business and Relationships:* "Everything in the cosmos works on the principle of service and sacrifice," concepts we discussed in Chapter 4, *The Importance of an Always Be Learning Life*. "The Sun gives us vitality. The clouds provide rain. Earth yields vegetation. Nightingale sings. Rose gives fragrance. With no ax to grind. A leader must emulate this magnificent magnificence of nature. And learn to serve his organization dispassionately for overall growth." Parthasarathy, under whom I studied at the Vedanta Academy in Malavli, Maharashtra, India some years ago, adds to this: "Give rather than take. Few realize the grandeur and power of serving, giving. The more you give the more you gain is the inexorable law of life..."

This brings me to my next and the fourth of my five elements of functionality, because your mindset should lead you to raise money sufficiently enough to become a very important player in your industry.

**Funding:** At some point, if you want to build a large company, you are almost certainly going to need to take outside funding. Companies like Apple, Facebook, Google, and Microsoft all had to do so. And even if somehow you avoid it until your IPO, remember that an IPO is a fundraising event itself. If you have the mindset of "I need to own it all and I can never give up control," as explored in Chapter 5, *Bootstrap or VC?*, it will limit your options when it comes to building a large company. You need capital to hire salespeople to capture your market quickly, or someone else more aggressive will likely take the lead. The expense of salespeople takes a while to recoup, even in the best of business models. And when you think big, you think global, as we did at Bazaarvoice and as we are now doing at data.world. As we also discussed in Chapter 5, it's akin to that scene out of the movie *The Matrix*, where Neo takes the red rather than the blue pill from Morpheus on his promise to, "show you how deep the rabbit hole goes."

Remember that whomever you take money from, whether it is an angel investor, a VC, or private equity (PE) firm, the red pill partnership is like a marriage. You better "marry" the right person. Just like you better partner with the right people for your team. But it is easier to part ways with members of your team than it is to move on from your investors. Also, you must maintain a bootstrap mentality to the greatest extent possible after you take funding. I suggest you internalize Seth Godin's brilliant read, *The Bootstrapper's Bible*, which is available for free and linked on the Digital Companion. Brant and I read this book at the beginning of Bazaarvoice, and we really took it to heart. I wish I had done the same at Coremetrics, and it was ironic that I didn't because I bootstrapped my first three businesses and they all had great cash flow. But it was the dot-com craze and all of the metrics (eyeballs, page views, etc.) that counted back then were squishy at best. Treat your money like it could be your company's last, because it may be.

**Culture**: In one sense, culture is the sum of much of what we've been talking about in this chapter, even in this book. It's the mores, the values, the individual and collective pursuit of meaning upon which I've repeatedly touched. Culture, in this initial sense, is an abstraction, even an aspiration. As important as this dimension of culture is, because it's abstract, we too often take it for granted, and regard it as a kind of self-evolving and self-reinforcing. But in another sense, one frankly less discussed in business circles, culture is very concrete because it is foundational. It's the operating system or "OS" of the company. It's the set of rules, guideposts, and invisible algorithms that shape and animate virtually the entire business. In this sense, culture is the most profound toolset at the entrepreneur's disposal. Culture, I often argue, needs to be intentional. This abstract side of company culture can be compared to sound waves. The most profound music in the world cannot travel through a vacuum, Beethoven's 5th would be just futile vibrations in outer space. Sound needs a medium of air, water, or steel. The medium, in this case, is the foundational side of culture, the intentionality. Intentionality is what brings together the systems for expressing culture that I will come to. But first, let's examine this abstract side of culture, the belief system.

"Every entrepreneur needs to wake up and hear the message that they need to think about what are their highest values that they are really going to anchor their company to," argued Salesforce.com founder and CEO, Marc Benioff, in a 2019 interview with *TechCrunch* magazine that I include on the Digital Companion. Benioff's passion for the importance of culture is further examined in his marvelous book that explores the emerging cultures of dynamic, 21st-century businesses in *The Business of Changing the World*. While a bit dated now after its first publication in 2007, it is nonetheless a priceless exploration of the ways companies can make the world a better place while enhancing their own company culture. It is an expansive compendium of the principles and moral codes of business leaders from Benioff to Michael Dell of the eponymous computer maker, from the late CEO of Japan's NEC Corporation's Akinobu Kanasugi to Laura Scher, who founded Working Assets, the credit card, and internet services company that donates millions to progressive causes. Klaus Schwab, the founder, and CEO of the Davos-based World Economic Forum has a chapter, as does the singer, songwriter, and activist Peter Gabriel. It's a book I encourage every entrepreneur to have for periodic reference. Pick it up, thumb through with your eyes closed to a page, and just read the insights where you land; every time you will find something new and thought-provoking.

"Consider what would happen if a top-tier venture capital firm required the companies in which it invested to place 1 percent of the equity into a foundation serving the communities in which they do business," ponders Benioff. "If we find ways to help the environment, to help workers, to help raise the standard of living in Third World countries, we will all do better," declares my fellow Austinite Dell. "When we founded the company we thought we would acquire 10,000 customers in our first three years," writes Scher, of the company she co-founded in 1985. "In fact, we had that many applications after just eight months." NEC Corporation's Kanasugi argues expanding the firm's remit beyond strict business concerns to education, disaster relief, and other activities transformed his corporation. "My work is still of the same importance to me," he reflects. "I have found, however, that by branching out beyond the basic fundamental principles of business, my career has become more rewarding." Schwab, who founded the famous World Economic Forum more than half a century ago, notes in the book the rise in anti-business sentiment fueled by headline-making greed, scandal, and fraud. "The only way to stop this wave of antibusiness sentiment is for business to take the lead and to reposition itself clearly and convincingly as part of society."

Now, of course, I'm sure you're musing: "Fair enough,

admirable convictions, but how to build such virtues into the 'OS' of a company?" There are many ways, of course, most of which we've discussed throughout this book, including in the previous Chapter 18, *Forming Your Company's Values,* where we touched upon the corporate "Magna Carta" — the evolving "Point of View," or "POV," document as a repository of values. But even these tools are inadequate without the *medium* that I described above. Without a systematic way of marrying the abstract elements of culture to the concrete and onto action, your culture is at risk of becoming Beethoven's 5th broadcasting into the vacuum of space.

One *medium* to transmit culture is Objectives/Key Results, otherwise known as OKRs. First developed by iconic Andy Grove, the CEO of Intel, OKRs are far more than just another acronym or magic potion. While simple, OKRs are not simplistic and implementation is difficult. But when properly understood and used, like the rock climber's carabiners, they are the best means ever to anchor lofty goals and aspirations with the face of your culture as you scale toward any commercial mountaintop.

In brief, OKRs are stated goals that are then in turn supported by the key results that, if and when delivered, can propel you toward that goal. Here's a simple example of just one of data.world's actual Q1, 2022 OKRs to illustrate:

| **Objective:** |
| --- |
| Increase volume of Qualified deals |
| **Key Result 1.1** |
| Generate 68 net new Qualified deals from ALL SOURCES |
| **Key Result 1.2** |
| Roll out messaging and positioning for key verticals, data mesh governance, and KG-powered automation — Kickoff 3/2/22 |
| **Key Result 1.3** |
| Amplify "Voice of the Customer" in our Marketing – Kick-off 3/2/22 |

I hope you'll notice a few things about this table. First is the difference between *objectives* and *key results*. Objectives are broad and aspirational, but they still must be definitive and quantifiable. It's not just, "let's increase our revenue" it's, "let's increase volume of *Qualified* deals." Key results, by contrast, are focused, specific, and binary, meaning you can easily see whether the key result was achieved or not. Did we or did we not generate 68 *Qualified* deals? And third, this sets the stage for key results to be quantified — as with the objective — but also measured in detail so that the process is of true utility, enables decision-making, and can be refined. It must provide useful metrics. How many deals? How many messages and what positioning in two key verticals? And on and on. This particular example comes from four pages of OKRs, devised for planning in just a single quarter. There are different ways to set up your scoring for OKRs, and I include an essay on the Digital Companion on how Google does this with a 0-1 scale with 10 gradations. You can find your own. The cadence and use of OKRs is also a decision that depends on context. But at data.world we set and report on OKRs quarterly and also have a mid-quarter check-in on how we are progressing.

Without question, the best resource on OKRs is *Measure What Matters — How Google, Bono, and the Gates Foundation Rock the World with OKRs*. The author is John Doerr, the chair of the famous venture capital firm Kleiner Perkins and a legend who has backed some of the most well-known entrepreneurs, including Larry Page, Sergey Brin, and Eric Schmidt of Google; Jeff Bezos of Amazon; and Mark Zuckerberg of Facebook. I include some links on OKRs on the Digital Companion, including Doerr's TED talk on the subject. But I truly hope you'll read his book as well, as it captures the many uses of OKRs and how they can be aligned with one another while aligning teams as well. I think of OKRs as "carabiners" for their utility as you reach for the summit. Doerr calls them "Swiss Army knives, suited for any environment."

"Objectives and key results are the yin and yang of goal setting — principle and practice, vision and execution," Doerr writes. "Objectives are the stuff of inspiration and far horizons. Key results are more earthbound and metric-driven. They typically include hard numbers for one or more gauges: revenue, growth, active users, quality, safety, market share, customer engagement."

If you carefully craft your business model, team, and culture, then the funding will follow if you let it. Then you will create a truly special, big company and change the world in the process.

"Ideas are commodity. Execution of them is not."

## — MICHAEL DELL, DELL CHAIRMAN AND CEO

# CHAPTER 20
# CAPTURE THE HISTORY OF YOUR AMAZING JOURNEY

*"Never measure the height of a mountain until you have reached the top. Then you will see how low it was."*

**— UN SECRETARY-GENERAL DAG HAMMERSKJÖLD, IN *MARKINGS***

As we near the end of our word journey together among the final chapters of this book, I include the quotation above from the late, great Swedish diplomat Dag Hammerskjöld for three reasons: First, it's an inspiring message, one that all entrepreneurs should reflect upon in the inevitable somber moments of their own journeys. Two, it's an opportunity to make the larger case for reflection itself that comes from Hammerskjöld's personal journal *Markings*, discovered and published in a half dozen languages after his death in a 1963 plane crash. The journal is a remarkable testament to the importance of reflection by leaders, and I include links to the original and several commentaries that illuminate the work of this global peacemaker.

But the third reason I open the chapter with that quote is that I'd like to add a line to its message: *And when you get to that summit, take a picture.* As my colleague at Bazaarvoice Nishant Pithia did when he got to the top of Mt. Kilimanjaro in 2010, and which you'll see below.

*From the summit of Mt. Kilimanjaro in 2010. Photo: Nishant Pithia*

Which takes me to the broad point I hope to make: that along with all the important lessons we've discussed here — from animating the *soul* of your company to bootstrapping vs. VC, from the role of network effects to the extension of your team through advisors, or from category creation to the essential role of values — the essence of leadership is *insight.* The founding of your company begins with an *insight*, your spotting of something that others have not seen. Your ability to compete turns on the *insights* you have into the marketplace, being the first or best with a product or innovation. Your leadership depends on your *insights* into your team, their strengths, their weaknesses, and most importantly their needs. Where do *insights* come from? They come largely from reflection, from listening to ourselves both as individuals and as organizations. And in turn, we need the means to record these reflections for them to become tools for decision-making and success. This is why you need to capture your amazing journey.

An important way to capture this is through writing. Many leaders in business and government keep journals. Not just the late Hammerskjöld mentioned above, but Barack Obama, Sir Richard Branson, and many others. After the allegorical Bible, the most widely read nonfiction book in history is the journal of a teenage victim of the Nazi Holocaust, who authored *Anne Frank — The Diary of a Young Girl*, which chronicled the oppression of Jews in the Netherlands and her two years in hiding before her discovery and death in a concentration camp at age 15.

"Asking questions that bring us back to what is most meaningful to us personally, as well as to what we believe is most important for society and the planet, deepens our sense of purpose..," writes business philosopher Nancy J. Adler, in an essay I include on the Digital Companion. "Reflecting in your journal on inspirational words from world leaders or wisdom traditions can act as an antidote to superficiality and parochialism," she further states.

Writing in other ways is equally a means of reflection. In addition to reading as many as 500 pages a day, Warren Buffett writes regularly, most notably in his letters to shareholders; he even personally writes his company's annual reports. Many leaders now blog, including Bill Gates, Reid Hoffman, Mark Cuban, and Brené Brown. I have been blogging my thoughts and reflections since 2012 at *Lucky7*, named in honor of my mother for helping me discover my passion at age 7 and nourishing it.

This book, in fact, grew out of this process of reflection. A thought on a Post-it, a remnant of a conversation, a note penciled in the margins of a book, an inspiration on a walk among the challenging hills that surround my home in Austin... These are the base elements of *Lucky7*. The blog, in turn, became the foundation for the first edition of this book, published on Medium.com for free. And that ebook evolved to become this set of reflections and learnings that you've been reading.

But what I want to advocate for here is a new way of reflecting as a team, or rather a way that was not always practical until now. This is, in our age of ubiquitous cell phone cameras, to capture your journey in pictures. For when you take photos along the way, something *magical* happens.

At data.world, we've had powerful camera phones since our beginning in 2015 — about the point these devices became truly ubiquitous worldwide. So, taking photos has never been easier. To help the process, I created our #history channel in Slack, and I've made sure to set the tone as CEO by sharing these in that ever-growing album. It was one of the first channels I created in our Slack, and it is really amazing to go back to the beginning of our journey and see the historical journal that has been captured since. And it's not just photos. Among the gems is a screen capture of the texts I sent to data.world Co-founders Matt Laessig and Jon Loyens asking them if they would like to brainstorm new business ideas with me. Thankfully they said yes, and then Bryon Jacob, our fourth Co-founder, got involved pretty quickly after that and has been an amazing addition to our founding team, including coming up with the kernel of the idea we eventually ran with to start data.world. Some of these photos I've shared publicly, some you'll find in the album in the center of this book, and our gallery was extremely helpful to mark the occasion when we came out of stealth and went live on July 11, 2016.

I emphasize chronicling with photographs because if you want to build a strong company culture, then you should care about the people in your company almost as much as you do about family. We discussed this and the importance of reflection back in Chapter 14, *Seven Lessons Learned on the Journey from Founder to CEO*, and I've thought deeply about how our work family has shown, and continues to show, how much we care about each other. I suspect most readers of this book, including you, are good in their personal lives at taking photos while they are on vacation. My wife, Debra, is particularly good at this and meticulously puts together photo albums after each vacation, which we only cherish more as time goes on. We want to document the very important time we spend together, and we know that our children will only be this age once. This is a natural practice for most families, especially those with young kids, as their appearance changes so much from year to year.

So why should it be different for companies? After all, you are on a very important journey together. Your company journey is your livelihood — it gives you the means of having other journeys, such as that vacation time with your family. I've often thought of Benjamin Franklin's maxim that "time is money." True enough, but the reverse can equally be true. Your livelihood enables time. Not just your life and special times with your family, it enables as well the pursuit of your passions, your journey to the top of Abraham Maslow's famous "hierarchy of needs," where self-actualization and esteem are to be found. The utility of money enables us to take more time to think about our purpose in life and to reflect upon the mark that we want to leave on the world. As entrepreneurs, you are doing something that many others may tell you is "impossible." The entrepreneur's journey is fundamentally no different than my colleague Nishant's journey, which he undertook with a few brave souls from Bazaarvoice to raise money for an important cause. Of course, they took a lot of photos — it was the journey of a lifetime and they wanted to remember all of it. Shouldn't it be the same for companies? Isn't that a journey worth remembering? Brant Barton and I thought so, and we took *a lot* of photos along the way. So did great people like Oliver Wong, Tung Huynh, and Nishant of course. Brant and I owe a lot to those three for selflessly spending so much of their time at company events to take photos. And, as our CEO, I encouraged them to take more every chance I got, especially when we reached new milestones on the climb up that company-building mountain.

As I noted above, when you take these photos along the way, something *magical* happens. And it isn't all that different from what happens when you come back from your family vacation and put together that all-important photo album. I'm sure you've had the same experience when you look back at your vacation and you remember it being even better than you thought it was when you were there. The magic is that you start to care about the journey more than you ever have. So carry this magic to your company and the entire team will model you in this regard. You will get a real sense of creating a legacy together. And as you achieve new milestones — as your "baby" (in this case the infant company) grows up into a "child" (the young company) and finally a "young adult" (the public company that Bazaarvoice became) — you have so many photos to look back on and remember "the way it was." A note of caution, though. As the CEO, you cannot just reminisce — you also always need to be celebrating the best of the present and looking toward the future. The *whole* journey matters, not just the journey as an infant and child. You are *always* creating memories and for those that just joined your company, their journey is just beginning.

After we grew to around 500 people and eventually to 850 and beyond, the most popular *optional* presentation in Bazaarvoice's history became the history presentation that Brant gave. It was a humble display, showing how we bought our first computers at Costco, worked in free office space with borrowed desks, and struggled to find our initial product-market fit — meaning the building of a product that people would love while avoiding the risk of taking down a customer website if our product failed to load. The room was always packed, standing-room only. The slideshow was full of photos, and many stories of the Bazaarvoice infant and child journey along the way. Why was it so packed? Because people that are on the journey with you want to have a sense of its origins. Where you start often leads to where you end up. And I believe there is an entrepreneur in all of us here in

America, as I wrote about in Chapter 9, *How, and Why, to Ask for Help*.

So treat your company like you would your family. You don't have to love it like you love your spouse or your children — that, frankly, isn't the right way to look at it. Family is forever. But you should love it immensely and you should model the same practices you have as a family to nourish the soul of your company. A good best practice as the founder is to try to remember to take your camera — now easier than ever with high-quality cameras a standard feature of all mobile phones — out every day and take a few photos. And be explicit with everyone in your company about why you are doing so. Tell them that you want to remember this time in the company's history forever. That you will cherish these memories, and you hope they do too. Let them know that the journey is what counts the most, and you will not take it for granted. That everything in life — money, fame, or whatever — is not in the same league as the journey. When you are much older and looking back at the life you lived and the people you worked with and helped, you'll remember the journey the most.

Founders: Cherish the journey, respect it, and *document it*. Capture your insights, your essential intellectual capital, and use them to reflect as both leader and team. With journals, with diaries, with blogs, and most importantly with photographs. A picture is worth a thousand words.

*"A good photograph is knowing where to stand."*

## — ANSEL ADAMS, ENVIRONMENTALIST, AND PHOTOGRAPHER

# CHAPTER 21
# ON FAILURE AND RESILIENCE

*"And once the storm is over, you won't remember how you made it through, how you managed to survive. You won't even be sure whether the storm is really over. But one thing is certain. When you come out of the storm, you won't be the same person who walked in. That's what this storm's all about."*

## — HARUKI MURAKAMI, NOVELIST

Of all the bromides in and around the world of business and entrepreneurship, none seem to get the attention quite the same way as this chapter's subject — success and failure. Entrepreneurs are told to fail early and fail fast. It's often said in business circles that the line between success and failure is wafer-thin. Failure is not just about error messages, it also yields valuable data. Failure on the road to success builds character, reinforces grit, and demonstrates the willingness to take risks.

If that sounds familiar, it's because it's all true. But if inspiring, is it ultimately helpful? For Americans, perseverance is a virtue central to our identity. We celebrate the come-from-behind, underdog stories of persistence: Thomas Edison's thousands of non-functioning lightbulbs before he got one that worked, Michael Jordan's rejection by his high school basketball coach who didn't let him on the team, or Steve Jobs' banishment and return from the wilderness to lead Apple to greatness. It's no wonder that how-to-succeed themes always dominate the books on offer at the airport kiosk.

I embrace all the sentiments. I'm endlessly inspired by Edison, Jordan, Jobs, and so many others. And I've read more business books than I can count — my library at home is full of them and it's only a sample of what I've digested.

But my summary of it all is fairly simple: While there are a million ways to fail, there is really just one way to succeed. This is resilience, sometimes called grit. But resilience too needs to be unpacked as a concept. Vince Lombardi is credited with saying, "Hope is not a strategy." Similarly, resilience is not just hanging on, burning more cash, or lighting an incense stick to appease the gods of commerce. In other words, it's not Albert Einstein's parable of quantum insanity: "Doing the same thing over and over and expecting a different result."

Above all, resilience is all about mastering the art of the pivot. Because just as generals advise that no battle plan survives contact with the enemy, no business plan survives contact with the marketplace without an entrepreneur capable of the pivot.

I've done my share of pivoting and witnessed many others, and it's often akin to a walk across hot coals. I'll share more on that later. But I also want to share the experience and counsel of two good friends who I believe to be the true grandmasters of the art of the pivot. One you have already met in Chapter 3, *Advice for the Middle-Aged Entrepreneur*. This is Austin's Cotter Cunningham, the founding CEO of RetailMeNot, a company that has gone through a series of transformations since it launched in 2010. It had a successful IPO in 2013 and was acquired in 2017 for $630 million. He's now an Entrepreneur-in-Residence at the Austin-based VC firm, Next Coast Ventures, in which we are proud investors. The other pivot virtuoso I want you to meet, if you don't already know him, is Co-founder and partner at Floodgate, Mike Maples Jr. Floodgate, one of the nation's top VC firms, is based in Palo Alto but active in Austin. Before that, Mike was the founder of serial startups and an early investor in not only Bazaarvoice but also Twitter, Chegg, Okta, Lyft, and many others. On the Digital Companion, you'll find an interview I did a few years ago with Cotter when I was Entrepreneur-in-Residence at the McCombs School of Business at the University of Texas at Austin. I also include a lecture Mike gave some time back at a forum of the Founder Institute sponsored by *TechCrunch* magazine.

In Cotter's case, it was the hard lessons of failure that I think really laid the foundations for his later success. As you'll recall from the earlier chapter, Cotter was a successful executive but didn't become an entrepreneur until his 40s. The opportunity he saw was in information services for people going through a divorce, who need advice, support, and guidance on the inevitably painful process — an event that Cotter, thankfully, has not had to endure. The company he founded was called Divorce360, and while he was backed with $1 million in funding from the VC firm Austin Ventures, he also wrote a check personally for the same amount to launch. In the first year, Cotter spent $400,000 and earned just $19. In the second year, the company spent $1.5 million and made $300,000. Ultimately, it was time for that hardest pivot of all, and Cotter sold the company.

"I felt like we failed because of the business model," Cotter told me. "I didn't feel that it was something I'd personally done wrong. We judged the market poorly." His takeaway lesson is that divorce is an intense distraction, and those experiencing it simply want to get beyond the trauma and begin building post-divorce lives. Their attention for the kind of services he was offering, actually comes later. And so he moved on. But it's certainly a credit to Cotter that Austin Ventures realized that while the business may have failed, he had the spark and drive to pick up and try again. So Austin Ventures backed him in his next venture, which became RetailMeNot, and which has been wildly successful. So I hope you'll listen to the full story of Cotter's journey on the Digital Companion.

Mike's experiences, however, are of a very different dimension. Although he was an entrepreneur himself in the early days, he's since become a national powerhouse as a VC and he's backed firms, as mentioned, from Twitter to Lyft to, of course, Bazaarvoice. What you'll learn if you listen to his talk on the Digital Companion is that most startups do a great job of building the *business plan,* which is really an operational document. But few, he argues, build an effective *business model,* which is all about defining the ways that you will convert innovation into economic value: "It describes how your company creates, delivers and captures value." As Mike explains it, 95 percent of startups don't even have a defined *business model.* And this is what gets them into trouble. When your *business plan* is failing, the entrepreneur's reflex and response is to iterate, accelerate, and make changes on the margin. But when it's clear that your *business model i*s failing, that's when you *pivot.* Or as Mike puts it, you iterate tactically, but you pivot strategically. Please, take time to hear Mike out on this on the Digital Companion, where I also include an essay from the Founder Institute that is specifically about the art of the pivot.

Which is an art I have been slowly but steadily learning throughout my career. Now with the six companies I've founded, I've thankfully not failed yet. But I sure have come close. My most dramatic near-death experience came with Coremetrics, when we hit the dot-com bust barely a year into our existence. As detailed in Chapter 6, *The Fallacy of Risk in Entrepreneurship,* I had allowed extraneous projects to overshadow our core product, and we only saved the company with a painful pivot.

We pivoted away from pure dot-coms to sell to traditional retailers, which had only begun to sell online, after letting go of two-thirds of our people, many of whom I considered close friends. It was one of the most gut-wrenching experiences of my life. Walmart was an early win after that pivot, and then we took off. If it wasn't for a fierce conversation that I had with Arthur Patterson, the Co-founder of Accel Partners, Coremetrics would have gone out of business in early 2001. Arthur stepped up and made a big statement to the market by leading a huge round of funding in our company at that time. Trust me, I *know* all too well how thin the line can be between success and failure.

We even had a difficult time getting data.world off of the ground. I estimate that it took us at least $40 million of funding to get to our first significant amount of revenue. One of our investors, Workday Ventures, liked to joke with me — or lift me up depending on your perspective — that it took them $100 million of funding to get to their first dollar of revenue. That is because the "surface area," or in other words the amount of functionality required, in the Workday product had to be so large to effectively compete with PeopleSoft, which Oracle had bought in a hostile takeover. One strategy we tried at data.world that failed spectacularly was the launch of our paywall to convert from a free account to private use-cases. We falsely assumed that many would automatically convert. We made bets on how much revenue we would get from this strategy, and we were *all* wrong in the *wrong* way. It was anemic, and there was a lot of consternation about it. In hindsight, it made sense — data.world's enterprise data catalog is a pretty complex sale. It requires a lot of integration with customers' internal data tools, such as Snowflake, Databricks, Tableau, and Microsoft Power BI. As a matter of fact, we already have over 90 of these integrations. And our enterprise customers really want to make sure our solution is secure and compliant. We are talking about cataloging their most valuable private data, after all. We always knew we would have an enterprise salesforce, even mythical "automatic-paywall-conversion" companies like Slack and GitHub have them. We still have the paywall, and we still get customers that way, but it is a fraction of our enterprise revenue today. We built out a world-class enterprise sales team, and if we hadn't done this there is no way that Goldman Sachs would have proudly led our $50 million growth round, which we announced on April 5, 2022.

Another moment of terror was the early days of the pandemic, a time chronicled in my series *Leadership in the Time of COVID-19 — A CEO's Journey*, which you'll find on the Digital Companion. As you can imagine in those early days of the pandemic, amid worries about our health and those of loved ones and employees, the markets had shed some $20 trillion in value by the end of March 2020. Overnight, we moved to a "distributed workforce." We doubled down on Slack to get random eyeballs on problems and keep everyone apprised. We raised the synchronous sharing of Google Docs and Sheets to an art form. We became more expert internal users of our own data.world platform, adopting more of what we evangelized to our customers. We invited customers, partners, investors, and board members to join us more regularly on Google Meet or Zoom, to help lift the wind in our sails by telling us how much they believed in us.

At the time I thought of this moment as "Dead Reckoning," a phrase of mariners. I'm not a sailor, but I think the term is a good way of thinking about resilience. It's the final tool of the captain when the GPS fails, the radar's broken, the records of distance traveled disappear, and there's little information on the distance to your destination. In other words, a pivot. And we made it through. You can too. Like that famous ad for Johnnie Walker, the point is to keep on walking — strategically.

We all know the famous story of Apple, which at one point kicked out its Co-founder and CEO, Steve Jobs. After his walk in his wilderness, both literally and figuratively, he returned with a vengeance. In early 2022, Apple hit a net worth of $3 trillion. It is now the world's most valuable company, leaving Exxon Mobil — the world's most valuable company in 2013 — trailing with roughly 12 percent of that value. What if Steve Jobs had *not* shrugged off failure and gotten his mojo back?

One of my friends is going through a "failure" right now. The market for the product simply wasn't a good one. It is an emotional time for him, but you simply can't *know* this until you try.

So think of that Johnnie Walker ad, but think of it in a new way. Keep on walking. And be ready to keep on pivoting.

> "*Do not judge me by my success. Judge me by how many times I fell down and got back up again.*"

> **— NELSON MANDELA**

# PART THREE
## HELPING

# CHAPTER 22
# SEVEN CRITICAL LESSONS LEARNED IN ANGEL INVESTING

*"Your job as an angel investor is to block out the haters, doubters, and small thinkers, because if you think small you'll be small. I'd rather see my founders fail at a big goal than succeed at a small one."*

## — JASON CALACANIS, AUTHOR, *ANGEL: HOW TO INVEST IN TECHNOLOGY STARTUPS*

As I transition into the Helping section of this book, I hope it's been a short but effective overview of both my passion for the entrepreneurial life and of the reasons I encourage the intrepid, the daring, and the world-changing to roll up their sleeves and create the Next Big Thing. But beyond all that we've discussed, beyond the fear, beyond the mastery of network effects, beyond the ingredients of growing big and rich, there is something even larger than that Next Big Thing. This is The Next Big Frontier, the 21st-century economy itself, a sustainable economy of innovation, community, inclusion, and fairness.

This is a change on the scale of the Industrial Revolution itself.

Venture-backed entrepreneurs will create this revolution. Angel investors, the foundation of this new venture ecosystem, will enable it. I realize that's a bold statement, but I'm hardly alone.

"We are witnessing profound shifts across all industries, marked by the emergence of new business models, the disruption of incumbents, and the reshaping of production, consumption, transportation, and delivery systems," wrote Klaus Schwab, founder of the World Economic Forum, in his 2016 book *The Fourth Industrial Revolution.* That book is one important window into our economic future.

My friend and fellow Austinite, polymath author, serial technology entrepreneur, and all-around genius Byron Reese sees the future in even bolder terms. Beyond just being a shift in economics, his 2018 book *The Fourth Age - Smart Robots, Conscious Computers and the Future of Humanity,* argues that we are at the frontier of societal transformation as profound as those wrought by the discoveries of fire, agriculture, and the written word. "A world without disease, poverty, hunger, or war is an old dream of humanity, one we are close to achieving," Byron argues.

Now of course you'll find more on both of these books on the Digital Companion, and I encourage you to read them. Ideally, before Byron's next book, *Stories, Dice, and Rocks That Think — How Humans Learned to See the Future and Shape It,* comes out in August 2022. But both of these books build toward a third, just published as I was concluding my own. This is Sebastian Mallaby's *The Power Law — Venture Capital and the Making of the New Future*, which I've referred to earlier. Of sweeping scope, *The Power Law* really explores how this new system of business finance has already changed the world and will transform it.

To summarize and combine Schwab's new revolution, Byron's new age, and Mallaby's new future, the leitmotif running through all of their insightful studies of new modes of a capitalist organization is that the world generally, and the economy specifically, is increasingly built on intangibles. "In the past, most corporate investments were tangible: capital was used to purchase physical goods, machines, buildings, tools, and so forth," Mallaby writes. "Now much corporate investment is intangible: capital goes into R&D, design, market research, business processes, and software."

Now, for our purposes here we don't need to go into how our farms will become high-rise laboratories, our universities' life-long learning modules, our transportation systems entirely robotic, and our medicine genetically engineered. But let me give the example of my current company, data.world. Founded in 2016, we're on track to grow this year to more than 200 employees across 21 states. We've raised more than $132 million and we're constantly branching into new markets for our primary data catalog products — the newest being our new product feature suite named Eureka. But what we produce are systems to manage something that you cannot see, cannot hold, and that intrinsically has no value until combined with other intangible assets. People say that data is the new oil but in this case, it truly is invisible in the sense that it's virtual and it doesn't stain your hands.

In addition to the creation of an economy based on intangibles, we've also inverted the conceptualization of risk. In the "old" capitalist economy that really emerged in Europe in the first half of the 19th century, commerce was all about avoiding long shots; investors were inherently conservative. Venture capital — which assumes that just 10 percent of investments will provide the bulk of returns — is by definition all about long shots and the power law of returns. And this is the prime accelerant of the innovation defining our new age.

We are part of the new means of economic value creation that traditional banking, financing, and even hedge funds are at best poorly designed for. Only a mere 60-odd years since its invention in Boston and migration to California, venture capitalism is the animator of this new world order. Interestingly, it's a phenomenon that so far has all but bypassed Europe where the most rigid laws still punish failure and innovation is slow to appear — although that's changing with such success stories as Early Venture Capital, active throughout Eastern Europe and led by Cem Sertoglu, an alum of the University of Texas at Austin. And venture capital — much of it originating in the Silicon Valley — is also a major driver of China's rise to technological prowess, although China's most recent moves at limiting their best entrepreneurs for political purposes could potentially kill their entrepreneurial golden goose. It may not be a system of production well understood by central banks or governmental regulators, but venture capitalism's dramatically successful embrace by Israel is the main reason behind the 2020 Abraham Accords peace deal between Israel and a now-growing number of Arab states that need and desire the know-how. Clusters of VC activity are also emerging in Southeast Asia, India, and in 2021 there was a big first as three big venture investments in Latin America appeared on Forbes' Midas list. And needless to say, this new order of business has long since broken out of the Silicon Valley to Austin, Miami, and even once-rusty industrial cities such as Cleveland, Detroit, and Pittsburgh.

I realize that's a pretty long preamble to an explanation of why I now, in addition to being an entrepreneur, have become active as an angel investor as well. This is not just the logical progression of the successful entrepreneur, it is the emerging center of planetary transformation. If you acquire the means to do so, it makes sense to help in this way, as many have helped you before. You can both honor them and pay it forward. Angel investors are critical first because they are investing their own money, not as with conventional VC firms who raise a fund to invest the money of others. Secondly, the role of angels is expanding in importance as the broader VC system matures and most early-stage VC funds move upstream of Series A or "Seed" investment. Angels are now the "keystone species," the organism that defines the entire ecosystem. This is the further role I first embraced in 2010, and now, 3,000 pitches later, my wife Debra and I are investors in more than 124 startups and 40 VC funds.

So without further delay, these are the seven lessons I've learned:

## Lesson #1: New angels' most common mistake is too much capital in too few startups.

I've limited our net worth in startup investing, cumulatively, to around five percent of our wealth. Very few angel investors I've met are that disciplined as greed can get the best of you. The beta risk is high as many startups go bankrupt and what you are looking for is the few that will generate a large enough return to make your efforts worthwhile. Others have made this observation, including author and book publisher Tucker Max of Austin. Mike Maples, Jr. of Floodgate, whom you met in the last Chapter 21, *On Failure and Resilience,* has written about the power-law dynamic in VC startup investing which is referenced on the Digital Companion. To put this in practice directly, if you have a million to invest, you are much better off putting $25,000 to $50,000 into each startup than $100,000 to $200,000. You need to stay in the game, where you will see, as Debra and I have, that this can be a profitable endeavor. A great resource on this is the work of Jason Calacanis. In addition to his podcasting on the subject, he's the author of *Angel: How to Invest in Technology Startups.* Too many angel investors try it with just a few startups, don't get good returns, and conclude that they are awful angel investors. The reality is that they didn't give themselves a real opportunity to learn the craft. On the Digital Companion, there's a blog on the topic by VC Jerry Neumann; it's priceless.

## Lesson #2: Invest in what you know.

For me, this is Software as a Service (SaaS). Half of our startups are SaaS. You'll be able to help these companies better as a mentor. It doesn't mean you won't be able to help other companies, and we are in many B2C startups, for example. Often your mentoring will be focused on topics like how to raise money (and make connections for the startup CEO), how to recruit, how to manage your Board and investor relationships, how to sell, etc. Those apply to all sectors of startups. But you'll have better pattern recognition (and therefore likely better outcomes) in the sector you know best. Billionaire investor Mark Cuban is among the many who has made this point repeatedly, but it should be obvious to you overall.

**Lesson #3: Serial entrepreneurs, on average, generate better returns than first-timers.**

Michael Dell, Mark Zuckerberg, and Bill Gates were first-time entrepreneurs. Or close to it, if we don't count Michael's early entrepreneurialism before Dell, or Gates' first business in high school. So you may question this logic by thinking, "I'll miss out on the best if I don't take that risk on that first-time entrepreneur kid genius." Maybe that is right in rare circumstances, but there are many, many more examples of successful serial entrepreneurs. Among them are Reid Hoffman at LinkedIn, Reed Hastings at Netflix, Aneel Bhusri with Workday, and John Mackey who launched and leads Whole Foods here in Austin. I could go on and on and on. Some very rare, young entrepreneurs indeed have otherworldly wisdom but most of us, including myself, build that entrepreneurial wisdom over time. I'm on my sixth startup at data.world. With my fifth startup, Bazaarvoice, our initial investors generated a 70—110x return! Imagine that — if they invested $100,000 they generated up to $11 million if they held onto the peak of Bazaarvoice's stock price. Some of our most exciting angel investments in Austin are led by serial entrepreneurs and include startups like AlertMedia, Dosh, Dropoff, ClearBlade, Convey,

Rollick, Pingboard, ZenBusiness, Rocket Dollar, and others. In 2021, both AlertMedia and Convey had very exciting exits, which generated a large investment return for us (and much more for them, in a very well-deserved way as they are the ones in the arena). This is certainly not a comprehensive list. And it's not a hard and fast rule, either. We've indeed helped some first-time entrepreneurs that are really exciting. One great example of the exception making the rule is Julia Taylor Cheek who we backed when she founded the digital health services company EverlyWell in 2015. As of this writing, her company has a valuation of $2.9 billion and we haven't sold a share.

**Lesson #4: If an investment is performing well, make sure you join in the next round.**

Momentum begets momentum. So you should be ready to join the next round, at least at your pro-rata amount. VC funds always reserve 30—50 percent of their fund's capital for follow-on rounds. In general, we invest in seed, Series A, and sometimes Series B rounds — and sometimes in all three for a single company when things are going well. Investing early means taking on more of what VCs call "beta risk," meaning relatively high volatility. On the other hand, if the investment really hits, there is much more so-called "alpha" benefit, meaning returns higher than standard markets or benchmarks. You'll find a good tutorial on this on the Digital Companion.

**Lesson #5: Invest in proven VC funds when it serves to diversify your portfolio.**

We are investors in the VC funds of CAVU Venture Partners, which focuses on startups producing healthy foods and sustainable food systems. In part, this is because we believe in what they are doing, very much in sync with the transformation I described above. But it's also a way to diversify our startup portfolio beyond our areas of expertise and with the safe hands of proven experts. We are not experts in consumer packaged goods (CPG), but were fortunate enough to become angel investors in Austin's Deep Eddy Vodka. Deep Eddy is headed by our good friend Clayton Christopher, who per Lesson #3 above was a serial investor and had founded Sweet Leaf Tea. And when Clayton sold Deep Eddy Vodka and started a venture fund, we knew we had to be investors. We already believed in the macro trends of niche brands, and retail differentiation (and disruption) in the age of eCommerce. Consumer tastes and diets shift faster than big CPG companies can keep up, so it's a sector ripe for the new age of capitalism. In all things being equal — capital being capital — we thought that entrepreneurs would want to work with CAVU to get experienced guides for their journey — proven CPG experts, who understood shelf placement, branding, and market research. Likewise, we invested in Multicoin Capital's first fund because we personally don't specialize in cryptocurrency and blockchain. And we invested in Forerunner Ventures because they understand B2C and serve a different geography. We've invested in many other funds as well. In general, this means we are primarily in SaaS and in Austin startups as direct investors and leave expert VCs for the rest, including diverse industries and geographies. As of this writing, around 57 percent of the capital we've invested in startups is directly invested and around 43 percent is through VC funds.

**Lesson #6: If you can really help, consider serving on an investment's Advisory Board.**

If you have insight or expertise to offer a startup in which you are investing, consider serving on the Advisory Board in exchange for common equity above and beyond your preferred equity investment. Entrepreneurs are very interested in protecting their common equity and maximizing its value, which you can help them accomplish when aligned as an Advisory Board member.

This has worked out very well for us and allows us to help the company even more directly. For the hit companies in your portfolio, you'll make money on both the preferred and common equity this way. If the company is early enough in its history and the stock value is very low (such as it is at a company's founding, before it raises any money), then you should see if the founders are doing what's known as an "83(b) election" and whether you can participate as an Advisory Board member. This IRS rule can allow you to pay taxes on the value of the grant when it is made, rather than on the value at the time of stock vesting, and the difference can be substantial. Note that you have an advantage as compared to venture capitalists in that they cannot earn equity in this way — it is unique to the angel model (i.e., VCs don't get additional equity for serving on your Board of Directors or being an advisor to your company as it is expected from their limited partners and they need to share in the standard 80/20 model). As an entrepreneur, I practice what I preach here — we have over 65 Advisory Board members at data.world.

If the company becomes a fight for preferred over common, in almost all cases no one is going to make a lot of money and it is not a great outcome overall for anyone. Entrepreneurs have to do well for investors to do well, generally speaking. This is as it should be — they are doing the real work every day. This is why I seldom invest in a company that is early-stage and already has a big Board of Directors of angel investors that already control the majority of the equity (with little to no VC involvement) — that is a clear sign of an entrepreneur being micro-managed and not very incentivized. This is also usually a sign that those investors are playing for a conservative base hit instead of swinging for a home-run outcome. Again, to make a lot of money — for both entrepreneurs and investors — the power law return has to be a possibility. A bad setup kills your power-law potential.

**Lesson #7: Don't just trust your own instincts, make introductions.**

Building a network is a very valuable activity for you as both an entrepreneur and investor. When I meet a new entrepreneur I like, I make a lot of introductions to potential investors and advisors. This is not just easy to do, it is really valuable for the entrepreneur as well as us as the potential investors. I get market intelligence from people I know can help, and they get to see the deals that I'm looking at. Plus it incentivizes them to do the same — show me their deals. This activity also bonds you to the entrepreneur — they genuinely appreciate it and know the value of a warm vs. cold introduction. When you are just beginning as an angel investor, go out there and start selflessly serving the community. Karma will inevitably kick in. Becoming a mentor is a great way to build your global brand and expand your expertise. In Austin, Capital Factory, TechStars, and SKU are just some of the places known for helping entrepreneurs who could use your shoulder to their wheel. In the Bay Area, these opportunities abound at places like Y Combinator. Business schools are often looking for mentors and I've served numerous times as Entrepreneur-in-Residence at the McCombs School of Business at the University of Texas at Austin and my MBA alma mater, the Wharton School. This will ultimately help you build a network rapidly.

So in conclusion, these are my main lessons learned from angel investing, to cap my broad thoughts on the future of the economy, society, and innovation. As we've explored, it is entrepreneurs who are leading the world on this journey. It is a journey of risk and reward, of innovation, of public benefit corporations, of Conscious Capitalism, of exhilarating highs and subterranean lows, and of restorative commerce in a fast-changing world in desperate need of leaders who can keep up. Let me leave you with the thought of one of the most profound thinkers of challenging times. Roll up your sleeves, and let's get to work.

*'There has never been a better day in the whole history of the world to invent something. There has never been a better time with more opportunities, more opening, lower barriers, higher benefit/risk ratios, better returns, greater upside than now. Right now, this minute. This is the moment that folks in the future will look back at and say, 'Oh, to have been alive and well back then!''*

**— KEVIN KELLY, AUTHOR AND FOUNDING EDITOR OF *WIRED***

# CHAPTER 23

# CONCLUSION: ENTREPRENEURS MUST LEAD OUR NATION'S HEALING

*"Many conversations about diversity and inclusion do not happen in the boardroom because people are embarrassed at using unfamiliar words or afraid of saying the wrong thing — yet this is the very place we need to be talking about it."*

## — DAME INGA BEALE, FORMER CEO, LLOYDS OF LONDON

Throughout the course of writing this updated and more comprehensive second edition of *The Entrepreneur's Essentials,* dramatic and historical events have been unfolding at a breathtaking pace. The Black Lives Matter protests that followed the on-camera murder of George Floyd riveted attention worldwide, as do continued and tortured debates about policing. The pandemic that was still new when I began this project has accelerated the use of technologies as we've discussed. But it has also revealed stark disparities in American life, including the much higher mortality rates of Black, Brown, and Native Americans. Gun violence and hate crimes, including anti-semitism, are on the rise. As our political divides widen, race and identity are always scarcely below the surface of our discourse, if not front and center. In my home state of Texas, it needs to be said, voter suppression and thinly veiled political attacks on LGBTQ+ people are a near-daily occurrence.

Concluding this book with a polemic is not my intent. I'm a political independent, I've voted for as many Republicans as Democrats over the years. And I'm a proud American, loving this country with all of its beautiful pros and unfortunate cons as a patriot. If your blood pressure is going up as you read, trust me I'm with you on the "Defund the Police" branding, and probably a lot of other things. My allergy toward the binary thinking that we've explored together extends to characterizations of states, cities, and communities in red vs. blue simplicity. The country is much more purple than the inflammatory characters who dominate a lot of our 24/7-media attention in an attempt to stand out suggests. Simplistic formulas try to divide us, and "Defund the Police" branding is a good example of the growing "us vs. them" dynamics when public safety requires a racially just and equitable commitment to *both* law enforcement and the community. That said, a book on entrepreneurialism simply can't end without acknowledgment of both business' role in our current state of affairs, and the inescapable reality that business — and very specifically the innovative entrepreneurs who are creating a new economy — must drive the deep change that is urgent. It is not just that entrepreneurs *should* lead the healing of our society and civic culture, it is the fact that only entrepreneurs *can* lead — because you are the true architects of the future.

As with the iterative evolution of this book, these views have been building within me for a long time. I've arrived at the belief that the more success you earn, both by grit and luck, and the more educated you become on the very real history of racial injustice and inequity in our country, the greater moral imperative you have to strive for a much more diverse, equitable, and inclusive workforce — in all areas of business, of course, but particularly in technology which has frankly been slow to shed its White-male domination.

I want to share some of the learning experiences I've had, and acknowledge the many friends and institutions who have helped me realize the importance of diversity in the innovation economy. I also want to share the resources that have helped me and be very practical and prescriptive about what can and should be done. But there is some background I need to share.

We all know the story — or at least some version of the story — of chattel slavery in America, the displacement of Native Americans, the lynchings of both Blacks and Hispanics, and the discrimination against Asians, including the internment of Japanese-Americans in camps during World War II. We know about segregation, "colored only" drinking fountains, and the heroism of the Civil Rights Movement.

So, let me address the elephant in the room before some readers tune me out. Before the racial and political reckoning amplified in 2020, some and maybe even many White Americans believed that the Civil Rights Movement successfully eradicated the problems related to America's original sin of chattel slavery and the racial injustices that this system produced. "It's time to move on," is the sentiment of many. After all, how could a nation that annually celebrates Dr. Martin Luther King Jr.'s holiday be racist? Most White people do not want to discuss race, and it is also true that many White people are financially hurting in our country and are scared about their futures. White working-class incomes have been stagnant for a generation. Opioid addiction has run rampant in many White communities. Poverty and pain aren't limited to people of color. So, before I discuss how these learnings and endeavors have moved me to create a much more diverse company at data.world, I understand that for many this is not a comfortable subject. And I realize that the debate over the stirring *1619 Project*, or the remarkable book *1776* by David McCollough, will never end. Nonetheless, there are some hard truths about the history of business in this country that are less discussed, but immediately relevant to our task as entrepreneurs. The story we tell ourselves about American history deeply impacts entrepreneurs. Confronting the most difficult chapters of our history will not only contribute to the healing of the wounds of racial injustice, but also allow for the unleashing of human potential that will benefit businesses, entrepreneurs, and leaders everywhere.

For starters, I often remind friends who bristle at the phrase "White privilege" that as historians have documented, some 46 million White Americans today — a quarter of the adult population — can trace their family wealth to the 1862 Homestead Act, celebrated in films and on postage stamps. Virtually for free, some 10 percent of the land in America — an area larger than California and Texas combined — was distributed to 1.5 million White families. Until it was repealed in 1976, the act was the longest-running, race-based affirmative action program in America and the largest transfer of public wealth into private hands to date. Much of the land was seized from Native American peoples, and Black Americans were excluded from the Homestead Act.

White access to land through this legislation paralleled the Reconstruction era, a period where dreams of Black citizenship and dignity — one intimately tied to not just education but land and wealth and entrepreneurship — faltered under withering assaults that included racial violence, land dispossession, and segregation. Public policies that were designed to injure Black America, from convict leasing that offered a prelude to our contemporary system of mass incarceration to restrictions expressly designed to suppress the Black vote.

But it's not just about barriers to creating wealth. We also need to consider its destruction. From mortgage redlining to bans on credit to Black farmers, examples are many. But it is only in the past few years that details have come to light of the destruction of America's "Black Wall Street," the financial center of Black

American life in Tulsa, Oklahoma until June 1, 1921. Details of this are among the many items I include for this conclusion on the Digital Companion. But the top-line takeaway is that violence that began with a threatened lynching led to the obliteration of 34 city blocks, the destruction of more than 1,200 homes, more than $200 million in damage in today's dollars, and as many as 300 deaths. Home to some 10,000 Black Americans, Tulsa's Greenwood District never recovered and the trauma to Black American entrepreneurialism resonated throughout the country.

Bringing this sad portrait forward to our day, and expanding its frame around my own sector, let's explore just a few numbers compiled by Sebastian Mallaby in *The Power Law*, a new book on venture capital that I've cited earlier. As of February 2020, women were just 16 percent of investment partners at VC firms. That same year, just 6.5 percent of venture deals involved female founders. To be fair, 15 percent of VC partners are of Asian origin. But Black Americans, who are 13 percent of the population, make up just 3 percent of venture partners. Even more disturbingly, Black American entrepreneurs raise less than 1 percent of venture dollars, Mallaby found. The situation for Hispanics is comparable. Hispanics make up 19 percent of the U.S. population, and headed half the new small businesses created between 2007 and 2017, but in 2021 garnered only 2 percent of all VC investments.

We can do better. We must. And at data.world we are committed to doing our part. I believe that the pursuit of equity, diversity, and inclusion in our work sphere is not just good for business, but is a moral imperative. America, at its very best, is a place where all things are possible. Turning this vision into a reality is the work of this generation.

One study concluded U.S. GDP would grow by 2 percent if we were to address these failures. That and a compendium of research on this subject by *Crunchbase News,* an ongoing series titled, *Something Ventured - How entrepreneurs access opportunity in America,* are on the Digital Companion.

This background is a preface to my own engagement with these issues that began in 2014 when my good friend Josh Baer nominated me for the Henry Crown Fellowship at the Aspen Institute. The Fellowship looks for successful leaders at inflection points in their lives. I was "retired" when Josh told me he had nominated me. I had achieved my dream of founding and taking a company public with Bazaarvoice around my 40th birthday, a goal I had set for myself at age 25 while I was at the Wharton School earning my MBA. I was primarily backing startups and actively helping entrepreneurs through our family office, Hurt Family Investments, and I honestly wasn't sure if I would start another company myself. But the Fellowship really motivated me to do so and that led to the founding of data.world alongside my three incredible Co-founders, Bryon Jacob, Jon Loyens, and Matt Laessig, about whom you've heard much.

In the Fellowship I was first introduced to the writings of Ta-Nehisi Coates. We read *Letter to My Son*, which quite literally moved me to tears multiple times while reading. Along with other work cited here, it is on the Digital Companion. We had a very intense discussion about it, along with two of my Fellow colleagues, both very successful Black American leaders. If you haven't read it, I really encourage you to open up your heart and do so. I was in denial while I read this — I just couldn't believe this was still America. I frankly didn't want to believe it, it was just too painful to accept. Our Fellowship discussions are confidential, so I can't tell you what happened as we discussed it, but I can say that tears were shed there too. Our willingness to be vulnerable around the issue of racial inequality opened my eyes to the harsh reality of contemporary injustice. How could this be in the country that I love so much?

We also read and discussed Frederick Douglass's speech, *What to the Slave Is the Fourth of July?* Mr. Douglass gave this speech nine years before the Civil War. He was just 34 years old. I can't even begin to tell you how many times I've sent this speech to friends. I truly consider it the best speech I've ever read. If you haven't read it, do yourself a favor — now is the time. As you read it, think about the moment in history in which it occurred and how he was the only Black man — a former slave — at the crowded July 5th, 1852 event, surrounded by American flags waving in the wind as a large crowd looked on.

We also wrestled with Rev. Martin Luther King Jr.'s *Letter from a Birmingham Jail*. Written almost two years before the 1965 March from Selma to Montgomery, Dr. King's letter is a powerful reminder of the relationship between race and democracy. Like Frederick Douglass's speech, I have sent this to a countless number of friends. Yes, I studied it in school at some point as a much younger man, but it just didn't have the resonance then that it does now after being a leader and entrepreneur for so long. Again, do yourself a favor and read it — it's a masterpiece.

The Fellowship also took me to South Africa, where we delved into the origins of apartheid and the incredible leadership of Nelson Mandela. How Mandela pursued racial justice and dignity after apartheid remains fresh in the South African political and cultural imagination. I'll never forget standing in the former prison cell of President Mandela on Robben Island — imagining how a man of his stature managed to live in such a tiny cell. How cramped it must have been and yet how it didn't break him after *27 years of captivity*. And how gracefully he dealt with his oppressors after becoming South Africa's first Black President.

Fast-forwarding to another period in my life, and thanks to the encouragement of Austin tech business leaders Stephen Straus, Christopher Kennedy, and Heather Brunner, in 2019 I joined the Beyond Diversity™ Courageous Conversations, a two-day seminar on systemic racism and ways to discuss race. After becoming more educated on how race shows up in everyday life in America, the course gave me the tools to discuss race with a diverse spectrum of non-White people. I've had my haircut from the same friend for 18 years now, even before either of us had children. And we had never really discussed his experience as a Hispanic American. What I learned from our frank discussion about race truly moved me, and it led to a much stronger bond as friends. Lisa Novak, our VP of Employee Experience (our better term for HR) at data.world, attended the course with me. She had an equally profound experience. Given how much it moved us, we wanted the rest of the executive team involved. They subsequently took it and were equally moved. Then we decided together to fund *everyone* at data.world to take the course, starting with the rest of our leadership team. It is taught all over the nation, and you can find it in your local area.

Shortly after Floyd's murder, I got an email from a close friend, also a Henry Crown Fellow and fellow CEO. He asked me if I wanted to get involved in his group, *White Men for Racial Justice*. He recalled my referencing of our nation's original sin of slavery during a 2018 talk at Austin's SXSW festival and he thought I would be interested in further study and investment. He was right and it's been a really soul-stirring and challenging endeavor. We met every other Tuesday night for six months and discussed many readings and listenings, including the very moving podcast series *Seeing White* and the documentary *Suppressed,* which will help you understand voter suppression in Georgia and the incredible leadership of Stacey Abrams. We are a support group for each other and I've gotten a lot of value out of being involved. To be candid, it has been very uncomfortable sometimes as ignorance is bliss when it comes to our history. This callowness, of course, has translated into our current reality.

I realize of course that many reading this will simply write me off as "woke" and perhaps a far-leftist. "Woke," after all, is the new "virtue signaling" insult — it is a way to nullify someone's message because they aren't part of your "tribe" or "beliefs." But let me set a few things straight. First of all, as mentioned, I'm an independent voter. Not only do I vote across the spectrum, but I also make political contributions to Republicans, Democrats, and independents. I didn't inherit my wealth. When I got married, I had $1,000 and my wife had $2,000. It took *a lot* of both grit and luck for us to become successful. And I certainly believe in meritocracy, which we discussed in Chapter 11, *The Most Proven Way to Hire Well.* But I don't believe in *mirror-tocracy,* which is the malady we have to conquer. And it's a malady that is easy to ignore, as we have done, in a country that is roughly 73 percent White. If you were born White, there are inherent advantages you have. When you are in the majority, that majority shows up in leadership positions more often and the majority of wealth is concentrated there. When you were born, you weren't aware of this. I certainly was not. This also doesn't mean if you are White that you don't have to work your ass off to become a successful entrepreneur, especially a self-made one. I'm not advocating casual hand-outs and I'm hardly a socialist. I believe fundamentally in the power of capitalism — Conscious Capitalism as we've discussed — to lift people up and make all of our lives better. I'm not saying that you don't deserve the success you've earned because you are White. I am saying that the odds were far more in your favor and this should not dissuade you from learning about the way our country has been set up — quite literally, starting with the original sin of chattel slavery. As you do learn — as I have — the more you will realize the institutional, structural, and personal privileges that come with being born White.

Recognizing this reality is the first step toward an inclusive future. And frankly at data.world we are now sprinting. In no small part due to Lisa's leadership, our workforce is now 59 percent female or minority. While we have been doing this there have been *zero* tradeoffs on performance. Quite the contrary, it has made our company much more fun and higher performing. There has been no "lowering of the bar" or whatever you may be thinking right now. If this is what you are thinking then you *really* need to stick with me to the end of this last chapter. Stephen DeBerry, a close friend, and Black American venture capitalist, put it best when he said that we all just need to chill out and really think about what is on the other side of racial equity. It's beauty, it's holding hands, it's dancing in the street, it's celebrating the best of being *American*.

That is my goal at data.world — to make it not just a standard-bearer for diversity in venture-backed technology, but also to make it a more *American* company. When I hear my fellow White CEOs and other leaders tell me they just can't find enough _____ (fill in the blank race or gender) candidates for a role, a big part of that is that they just aren't in the places where those people hang out. I'm White but also Jewish, and therefore I'm going to get invited to more Jewish events than a non-Jew. I've been invited to just one Black Chamber of Commerce event and that was for me to see a friend get an award. If you are female, you get invited to more female events. And so on. To hire diverse people, you need to figure out a way to show up at diverse *places*. If you aren't seeing diverse candidates in your pipeline, you need to think hard about whether you are part of the problem or if this is important to you. This is why it is so important that you do the internal work. How hard have you tried, really?

I'm not sure any of us are qualified to suggest the right "steps" to change society. But it was with such a plan that started at our own company, and as a thought process, I believe it can help any company. Here are the five steps on which Lisa and I collaborated to bring transformation to data.world:

**Recognize:** Recognize and accept that there is a problem that needs to be solved. That's the essential beginning, followed by the recognition that both our companies and our society must be actively involved in the solution.

**Learn:** Educate yourself. In our case, our task was to get all of data.world educated — leaders and team members. As mentioned above, after George Floyd's murder our commitment to learning galvanized us to send all of our people to Beyond Diversity™ Courageous Conversations." It's why we have book clubs with books on racial injustice or being better allies. It's why we invite expert speakers on diversity to come and talk with us at data.world. Another resource you'll find on the Digital Companion is the Center for the Study of Race and Democracy at the University of Texas at Austin. Since its founding, I've proudly supported Dr. Peniel Joseph and his team's work there, including serving on his Advisory Board (and he is on ours at data.world as well).

**Develop your philosophy and goals:** Make recognition and education part of the fabric of your company. At ours, it's an ongoing part of who we are. We include "community" as one of our values, and diversity is among specific company goals. In fact, diversity is among the "OKRs" that we discussed in Chapter 14, *Seven Lessons Learned on the Journey from Founder to CEO.* It's easier to build your philosophy and goals from the outset rather than to correct down the road.

**Communicate:** Create tools and an internal *voice* to ensure there's a place for even the most challenging and difficult conversations. In our case, it's #parliament-pod in our internal Slack channel. It's a forum and opportunity for new ideas and ways to constantly improve.

**Share:** As a company that may be doing things well, it's our responsibility to share approaches and ideas that work. All companies on similar journeys should be doing the same and spreading the positive results. It's why we speak on panels about building and sustaining diversity. It's why we're part of groups in Austin to help guide other startups through their diversity journey.

So in conclusion, recall what I wrote in Chapter 1, *The Soul of the Entrepreneur,* that at no time in history has the world faced the challenge to adapt that it does today. And entrepreneurs, broadly defined, are the people to lead this adaptation. As I noted in the preceding Chapter 22, *Seven Critical Lessons Learned in Angel Investing*, our fast-changing world is in desperate need of leaders who can keep up. So my parting message is a call for entrepreneurs to embrace all of that, *and* to recognize that your company can have a workforce that reflects the best of what America truly offers. What a boring place America would be if we were all of one race, with one type of food and drink, one type of architecture, one type of entertainment, one type of literature, one type of political party, and so on. We have a moral obligation to lift each other up and embrace our uniqueness and the beautiful melting pot that our country is. It is the source of our strength as Americans, and it can be a huge source of strength in your company.

*"Diversity is America's most valuable resource. It is what makes us the most innovative nation on Earth."*

## — NICK HANAUER, VENTURE CAPITALIST

# AFTERWORD

BY BOB CAMPBELL, CEO OF CAMPBELL
GLOBAL SERVICES

I first met Brett Hurt over 25 years ago. He was completing his undergraduate studies with a major in Management Information Systems at the University of Texas and was aspiring to a management consulting position. I was one of his interviewers. He tells me that it was his toughest interview and that he had no idea where he stood in my eyes. He jokes today that he is still not sure! In fact, I found a bright, personable, and high-performing student, and Brett came away with a consulting job offer.

Brett started his career in technology development at a large global management and was a very strong performer. However, as with many young consultants, Brett became interested in going back to graduate school to secure an MBA. He was accepted by the highly regarded Wharton School.

At Wharton, Brett caught the entrepreneurial bug and never looked back. He spent the next two decades starting and building companies. I spent the next fifteen years overseeing and leading a practice at the consulting organization. Over that period, Brett was an entrepreneur immersed in the startup world. I, in turn, was focused on large clients and projects as an *intrapreneur* and rather oblivious to the startup world.

Brett built a successful track record of building advanced technology companies including the Web analytics firm Coremetrics and the social commerce firm Bazaarvoice. His success allowed Brett and his family the resources both to give back to society, as well as the ability, through their family office, to further stimulate entrepreneurship through angel investing in other intriguing startups and venture capital funds.

Seven years ago, I retired after almost 40 years of service. I headed out to build a second career and found an emerging interest in advising young, bright entrepreneurs with big market disruptive game-changing ideas, and selectively making angel investments in such ventures. That is the arena in which Brett's world and mine reconnected.

I have always believed in the constructive role which business can play in our society. In fact, my college honors thesis authored almost 50 years ago was on the subject of emerging trends in corporate social responsibility. I also believe strongly in the responsibility that business leaders have to lead with the highest standard of personal and professional ethics. That is where the Public Benefit Corporation, also known as B Corporations, movement came to my attention. One of the early technology companies in that emerging space is data.world.

data.world was Brett's sixth startup, and was first structured as a C corporation but then converted to a B Corporation on the day of its public launch on July 11, 2016. Its mission is to be the global place where those who analyzed and shared data collaborate. It is a very bold vision, and one which captured my attention as a market disruptive technology with global market potential.

Over a several-month period, Brett and I renewed our relationship that had initially been kindled 25 years prior. I found Brett to be the same bright, energetic, hardworking, and personable young person who I had first interviewed on campus many years prior. And for my selfish interests, I found a source of experienced-based learning and insights in Brett as I allocated more of my time to the startup world.

I had the good fortune of being asked by Brett to serve as an advisor to data.world and readily accepted. Over the past two years, I have worked with Brett to help with business strategy, relationship building, and opportunity pursuit. That also provided me with the opportunity to see Brett in action as a CEO.

I have found a leader who is passionate about ideas and innovation. I have found a CEO committed to building and developing talent, along with his cofounders. I have also found a leader who demonstrates a collaborative style, sharing responsibilities readily with his cofounders and other members of the management team. And I have found a leader committed to transparency and frequency of substantive communication to his Board, investors, staff, and other stakeholders. His regular and detailed weekly communications are, in my opinion, a best practice for the industry, as he details so clearly in this book's Chapter 13, *How to Leverage Advisors and Investors*. It is so interesting to me that these attributes of an effective startup leader are similar to the attributes of an effective consultant — the world in which we first met!

Business aside, Brett shares my passion for social justice and advancing women and others of diverse backgrounds professionally. Brett has been a strong supporter of several impactful groups. Those values are also quite evident in the workings of the non-profit Austin100, which Brett co-founded and pioneered to bring Austin's business and community leaders together. Today Austin100 is led by Lawton Cummings, an incredible female leader that Brett and his cofounder, Josh Baer, recruited to the cause.

This book represents the culmination of Brett's 20 years to date as a successful entrepreneur. I believe the insights and suggestions are relevant for any young person considering this career path as well as accomplished entrepreneurs striving for continued professional growth.

# ACKNOWLEDGMENTS

First, I want to thank my wife Debra for always believing in me. We've been married for almost 26 years now, and I became an entrepreneur shortly after we got married. We both had entrepreneurial parents from our childhood, so that helped us relate to the massive ups and downs that entrepreneurship inevitably leads to — but we simply wouldn't have had the success we've enjoyed without her support. While I was at Wharton earning my MBA, she worked very hard as an interior designer to support us so that I could give living my entrepreneurial dream a real try while in school. When I graduated, we had no income from Coremetrics for a long time. She never faltered in supporting me and through a lot of grit and luck, we've made it to this point in our lives. We've come a long way from the $1,000 and $2,000 in net worth that we brought to the table at the beginning of our marriage (I always joked that I married the wealthier woman.)

Second, I want to thank my mom and dad, who unfortunately are no longer with us and who I miss every day. *Lucky7* is named after my mom, and my dad was also a very supportive entrepreneur and extremely generous to his family, friends, and neighbors. When I first read the book *Outliers*, I gave a copy of it to my mom and said, "See what you created?!" I had calculated that I had programmed around 22,000 hours from age 7 on. She believed in me from the very beginning — she knew I had found my passion early, and many around her thought I was "wasting my life" on that "computer thing over there".

Third, I want to thank our children. Our daughter, Rachel, inspires me and it was her writing *Guardians of the Forest* at the age of 13 while making terrific grades in middle school and doing a superb job on her Bat Mitzvah, that made me think, "Well, why not now?" when I began writing the first edition of this book. Our son, Levi, is quite the chip off the old block and is constantly creating on his computer. Parenting is the most challenging, but also rewarding experience of my life. It's the ultimate entrepreneurial endeavor!

Fourth, I want to thank my writing team for the second edition of this book. David Judson is like no other writer that I've worked alongside — he is truly a savant and such a good friend. He and I worked for many months and weekends to bring this second edition to life. Clarissa "Clo" Fuselier is an amazing editor and was terrific at Bazaarvoice too, where she created *The Annual Coozie*, a collective of writing that brought out the best in all of us there. She also designed the cover, which I love, and we had my Facebook friends vote on it to make our final cover selection. Finally, Amy Liang skillfully created TheEntrepreneursEssentials.com, where the Digital Companion of this book lives. She is a student at the University of Waterloo, where we frequently recruit co-ops from for data.world, and she has a bright future ahead.

Fifth, I would like to thank Josh Baer for all he does for the entrepreneurial scene in Austin and for nominating me for the Henry Crown Fellowship. The Fellowship has been one of the most inspirational experiences I've had as an adult, and it had a lot to do with me getting back into the arena to found data.world.

Sixth, I would like to thank Jay Coen Gilbert and the B Lab team for all they do. We were brought together by the Henry Crown Fellowship, and I'm proud to be alongside them pioneering a new way of *being* as a business. I have felt equally inspired over the years by the many CEO speakers and the team at Conscious Capitalism.

Seventh, I would like to thank the hundreds of people that I've worked with at Coremetrics, Bazaarvoice, and now data.world who believe in me. So many of the lessons in this book are their lessons too. We learned together. We cried together. We laughed together. We worked so hard together. We created the future together. We changed industries forever.

Eighth, I would like to thank many people who have inspired me along the way and also serve as role models for inspiring others. As Kirk Dando, my long-time CEO coach, would say, they are the definition of for-you leaders:

- Of course, Kirk, who is one of my closest friends and the author of *Predictive Leadership* (he's seen me make every mistake listed in his book and supported me all the way through, serving as my CEO coach since 2007)

- Dan Eggleston, my middle-school computer teacher, who stoked my passion for programming

- Rick Byars, my favorite Management Information Systems professor at U.T. Austin, who showed me that the path of life can take many twists and turns as you live your passion

- Stew Friedman, Peter Fader, Eric Clemons, Il-Horn Hann, Len Lodish, and many other professors at Wharton who taught me valuable entrepreneurial and leadership skills

- Eugene Sepulveda, CEO of the Entrepreneurs Foundation, who helped me learn how to apply philanthropy to entrepreneurship and that eventually led to the creation of the Bazaarvoice Foundation (and will one day lead to the creation of the data.world Foundation)

- Bong Suh, my first Board Director at Coremetrics,

who mentored me as a first-time VC-backed entrepreneur

- Arthur Patterson, co-founder of Accel Partners and my first Series A investor at Coremetrics, and now a personal investor in data.world

- Keith Benjamin, General Partner at Highland Capital Partners at the time and also my first Series A investor at Coremetrics (I wrote a tribute to honor Keith when he passed)

- Julie and Mike Maples — Julie has invested in me since the beginning of Coremetrics, Bazaarvoice, and data.world; and Mike since the beginning of Bazaarvoice and data.world; Julie created the V Foundation's Wine Celebration, which raises millions each year to fight cancer (my mother passed from lung cancer and never smoked)

- Ralph Mack and Steve Katz, who have believed in me since my Wharton years; Ralph has backed me since the beginning of Coremetrics, Bazaarvoice, and data.world, and Steve since the beginning of Bazaarvoice and data.world

- Chris Pacitti, Tom Ball, Neeraj Agrawal, Brian O'Malley, Satya Patel, Mitchell Green, Scott Booth, Jamie Crouthamel, Suneet Paul, Eric Simone, Dwight Foster, Emily Brady, Richard Marcus, and Josh Kopelman — who made a real difference in helping Brant Barton and me grow Bazaarvoice from the early years on as very supportive and creative investors and advisors

- Jason Pressman, Managing Director at Shasta Ventures, whom I've known since the beginning of Coremetrics (he was our initial breakout customer as the head of operations of Walmart.com) and has backed Bryon Jacob, Jon Loyens, Matt Laessig, and me since our Series A at data.world

- Pat Ryan, Stuart Larkins, Peter Christman, Lindsay Knight, Jon Medved, Laly David, Josh Wolff, Ron Stern, Leighanne Levensaler, Mark Peek, Brittany Skoda, Sarah Ospina, John Mackey, Walter Robb, Gary Hoover, DJ Patil, Steve Katz, Paul Hurdlow, John Gilluly, Venu Shamapant, Adam Zeplain, Ravi Mohan, Nitin Chopra, Adam Ifshin, Doug Ulman, Christian Frey, Patrick Chang, Frank Quatro, Jim Kennedy, Dean Allemang, Andy Sernovitz, Seth Greenberg, Sarah Laessig, Devi Ramanan-Stauffer, Bob Campbell, Jono Bacon, Craig Fryar, Theresa Kushner, John Morkes, Kelly Wright, Adam Grant, Paul Miller, Scott Kokka, Ken Backus, Kate McLeland, Scott Booth, Bob Chicoski, Matt Schneider, Mike Reilly, Paul Albright, Bob Kelly, Kelly Wallace, Wes Garrett, Rob Adams, Brook Stroud, Jonathan Meltzer, Will O'Donnell, Brett Jenks, Adam Lyons, Jim Breyer, Ted Breyer, Daniel Breyer, Lincoln Brown, Leo Brand, Sam Palmisano, Rick Braddock, Steve Pagliuca, Bernie Brenner, David Reuter, Brandon Allen, Chris Zock, Gretchen Hayes, Scott Stephenson, Zachary Wahl, Joseph Hilger, Bart Swanson, Chris Geczy, Zachary Karabell, Sally Jenkins, Rishad Tobaccowala, Stephanie McReynolds, Anoop Lalla, John Lucker, Ajay Bhargava, Mike Boyle, Tony Capasso, Dr. Peniel Joseph, Michael Murray, Mike Milburn, Dave Liu, Mohammed Aaser, and the many other investors and advisors that help us fight the good fight every week at data.world

- All of the entrepreneurs that give us the opportunity at Hurt Family Investments to be a part of their journey — we've learned a lot from seeing you in action, and you inspire us

- My YPO Forum, both current and past — and a big thank you to Steve Katz for introducing me to YPO in the first place

- Many TED speakers that I've seen over the years — you have to be really brave to step in the middle of that red circle, realizing your passionate talk will be archived for the world to judge, and I've learned so much from them (TED is the world's best classroom with the world's best teachers and students)

- Dara Harmon, who I'm lucky to work alongside as she is the fearless CEO of Austin100, the non-profit that Josh Baer and I created, and our amazing Board of Directors there, including our prior Austin100 CEOs Lawton Cummings and Marjorie Clifton

- And too many others to list...

I can honestly say that I'm the product of *so many* that have believed in me. I'm lifted up on the shoulders of giants. I feel very blessed, I feel very lucky, and I feel very loved. I do my best to honor them.

# ABOUT THE AUTHOR

 Brett A. Hurt is the CEO and Co-founder of data.world, the enterprise data catalog for the modern data stack. data.world's cloud-native SaaS (software-as-a-service) platform combines a consumer-grade user experience with a powerful knowledge graph to deliver enhanced data discovery, agile data governance, and actionable insights. data.world is a Certified B Corporation® and public benefit corporation and home to the world's largest collaborative open data community with more than 1.6 million members, including 90 percent of the Fortune 500. The company has 48+ patents and has been named one of Austin's Best Places to Work six years in a row. Brett is also the co-owner of Hurt Family Investments (HFI), alongside his wife, Debra. HFI is involved in 124 startups, 40 VC funds, and multiple philanthropic endeavors.

Brett co-founded and led Bazaarvoice as CEO, through its IPO, follow-on offering, and two acquisitions. Bazaarvoice became the largest public SaaS business in social commerce and was named by the *WSJ* as one of the top IPOs of 2012 after becoming a unicorn. Brett also founded and led Coremetrics, which was rated the #1 Web analytics solution by Forrester Research and, like Bazaarvoice, expanded into a global company and leader. Coremetrics was acquired by IBM in 2010 for around $300 million.

In 2017, Brett was given the Best CEO Legacy Award by the

*Austin Business Journal*. He is a Henry Crown Fellow and Braddock Scholar at the Aspen Institute. Brett began programming at age seven and doing so on the internet at age eighteen. He finished his first online edition of *The Entrepreneur's Essentials* in August 2019.

# ACCESS THE DIGITAL COMPANION

Looking for more resources and references from *The Entrepreneur's Essentials*? Scan below to access the additional materials referenced in this book by chapter online! There, you'll find videos, blog posts, podcast episodes, etc. within the Digital Companion to pair with your reading.

Made in United States
North Haven, CT
09 May 2022